MELBOURNE

AFTER THE GOLD RUSH

The Land Boomers (1966)
Who's Master, Who's Man? (1971)
Land Boom and Bust (1972)
An Australian Camera (1973)
Lola Montes (1973)
Life in the Country (1973)
Life in the Cities (1975)
That Damned Democrat (1981)
Historical Records of Victoria (1981-91)
The Victorian Gold Fields (1982)
Australia: a History in Photographs (1983)
The Long Last Summer (1985)
Australia: Spirit of a Nation (1985)
The Exploration of Australia (1987)
Who Killed the Koories? (1990)
Old Melbourne Town: Before the Gold Rush (1991)

MELBOURNE AFTER THE GOLD RUSH

Michael Cannon

First published in 1993 by
Loch Haven Books
Arthur's Seat Road
Main Ridge
Victoria 3928

National Library of Australia Cataloguing-in-Publication Data

Cannon, Michael Montague, 1929-
   Melbourne after the gold rush

   Bibliography
   Includes index
   ISBN 1 875308 12 1

Jacket designed by Tom Kurema
Text pages designed by Michael Cannon
Produced by Island Graphics Pty Ltd, Melbourne
Typeset by Solo Typesetting, Adelaide
Printed in Singapore

CONTENTS

Introduction

A city transformed

The world had never seen anything like it. Here was a remote colonial seaport, founded by a few adventurers in search of new pastures, and best known in 1850 as a straggling town of 20,000 people exporting wool worth less than £1 million a year. Suddenly, as though by a miracle, huge quantities of gold were discovered nearby. The eyes of a restless world turned immediately to this new El Dorado. Almost overnight, sleepy Melbourne became transformed into a hectic, over-crowded transit camp. Hundreds of thousands of ambitious immigrants tramped its muddy unlit streets, on their way to the fabulous wealth of the Victorian diggings.

Many would-be gold-seekers got no further than Melbourne. Others returned from the diggings to spend their wealth—sometimes on wild living, sometimes more sensibly on buying blocks of land and 'settling down'. To their own surprise, many developed a fierce love for their adopted city. They abandoned plans to return to their homelands, deciding instead to raise their families and help build a better Britain on these faraway shores.

Victoria's population expanded with extraordinary rapidity during the 1850s—'unprecedented in the annals of British colonies', according to immigrant statistician William Archer. At the census of 1851, taken just before the first major gold rush, Victoria held 77,000 inhabitants. By the census of 1854, the total had climbed to 237,000, apart from Chinese and Aborigines whom nobody thought it worth while to include. The figures kept on growing wildly: to 410,000 in 1857; and to 540,000 in 1861—nearly half the total population of Australia at that time. Of this vast increase, about one-quarter dwelt in Melbourne, with most of the remainder at goldfields centres.

This swirling mixture of people and wealth created an urban land boom during 1852-3. The traveller William Howitt, visiting Melbourne at the time, wrote that 'the land mania rages here increasingly'. People

Melbourne's main
features in 1858 are
included in this map
drawn by Blackburn,
engraved by Frederick
Gosse, and published by
William Fairfax. The
southern portion is
shown on pages 182-3.
Key to numbers:

1 Presbyterian Church
2 Benevolent Asylum
3 St Mary's Church of
England
4 Cattle Yards
5 St Mary's R. C. Church
6 Old Cemetery
7 Flagstaff
8 Military Barracks
9 Officers' Mess
10 Spencer Street Station
11 St Augustine's R. C.
Church
12 Immigration Barracks
13 Western Gaol
20 St James Cathedral
21 St James School
22 Gold Escort Office
23 Crown Lands Office
24 Exhibition Building
25 Police Station
26 Government Offices
27 Electric Telegraph
29 Bank of NSW
30 Bank of Australasia
31 Wesleyan Chapel
32 Western Market
33 Merchants' Exchange
34 Custom House
35 Oriental Bank
36 Union Bank
37 E. S. & A. Bank
38 Melbourne &
Hobson's Bay Station
39 London Chartered
Bank
40 Colonial Bank
41 Post Office
42 St Francis Church
43 St John's Church
44 John Knox Church
45 Melbourne Gaol
46 Court Houses
47 Police Station
48 Public Library
49 Melbourne Hospital
50 Primitive Methodist
Chapel
51 United Presbyterian
Church
52 Baptist Chapel
53 Olympic Theatre
54 Theatre Royal
55 Eastern Market
56 Female Gaol
57 Independent Church
58 Scots Church
59 Mechanics' Institute
60 Police Office
61 Town Hall
62 United Presbyterian
Church
63 Bank of Victoria
64 St Paul's Church

65 Registrar of Births
66 Melbourne &
Suburban Railway
67 Water Works
68 La Trobe's 'Jolimont'

69 MCG
70 Richmond Cricket
Club
71 Police Barracks
72 'Bishopscourt'

73 Chalmers Church
74 Scotch College
75 Unitarian Church
76 Lutheran Church
77 St Patrick's College

78 St Patrick's Cathedral
79 St Peter's Church
80 Parliament
81 Police Station
82 National School

83 Wesleyan Minister
84 Gaelic Church
85 St George's R. C. School
86 St Mark's Parsonage

87 Police Station
88 United Presbyterian Chapel
89 Wesleyan Chapel
90 St Mark's Church

91-2 Independent Chapels
93 Free Church
94 Wesleyan Chapel
95 St Stephen's Church

Victoria began 1851 with one of the worst natural disasters in its history. On 'Black Thursday', 6 February, much of the new colony was burned to ashes in a series of huge bushfires. William Strutt immortalised the day in this painting. Terrified settlers tried to

escape the conflagration, but many were injured or burned to death. Strutt, who was etching a design for the Anti-Transportation League at Ham Bros. in Collins Street, wrote that he had to brush layer after layer of soot from the lithographic stone. (VPL).

were paying preposterous prices for suburban houses: 'A short time since, a house and garden were bought for £4,000, and would have been dear at that price in London, and today they were resold for £12,000'.

So many workers vanished to the diggings during 1852-3 that wage rates also rose to remarkable heights. Howitt reported late in 1852 that the few artisans left in Melbourne were earning up to £10 a week, while even labourers could earn £1 a day, four to five times the normal rate.

Yet somehow the number of buildings in and around Melbourne multiplied by the end of 1852 from 1,000 to 5,000. By early 1854, no fewer than 9,000 habitations were counted. Many of these were mere slab or weatherboard constructions, but they contained a huge and restless immigrant population.

As always in Melbourne's tortured history, the boom was followed by depression. The immediate problem was that ambitious merchants had ordered far too many consignments from overseas. In 1854 they panicked and threw out the goods at distress prices. Land speculation immediately came to a halt, and the banks began calling in their debts. Hundreds of property gamblers were forced into insolvency, leading to further loss of confidence.

Fortunately the recovery was just as rapid. Large amounts of wool, hides and other goods were still being produced to add to the rich flow of gold. During the second half of the 1850s, Melbourne won back its confidence and embarked on a huge permanent rebuilding programme. Even at the beginning of 1855, rate collectors could count 11,500 occupied dwellings throughout the metropolis.

Many solid stone buildings and extensive public works were now under way. Everywhere the visitor looked, contractors were busy on permanent wharves, roads, streets, drains and bridges. Foundations were being dug for impressive parliamentary and government buildings, schools, public library, university, banks, churches, theatres, hotels, hospitals and asylums. Piped water supply—but alas no sewerage—was being installed. The merchant William Westgarth, returning to Melbourne in 1857, marvelled that 'Business is on a great scale, with great works of all kinds going on, and high wages to the labouring classes, who occupy a very dominant position under the new political order'.

Melbourne, with surplus wealth to invest, was also being transformed by new technology. Fast, reliable steamships thronged the bay. Steam cranes appeared on wharves and warehouse ramps, speeding up imports and exports. The first trains began running between city and suburbs. Mains reached out from the first gasworks, lighting the streets and reducing the need for other fuel. The amazing electric telegraph relayed government and private messages instantly between populated centres. Portents of the coming age could be seen everywhere.

Retail trade recovered with the rest of the economy. In 1859 the merchant Patrick Just wrote of his pleasure in seeing large city establishments being faced in white freestone or stuccoed and painted. Many now boasted plate-glass windows. The visitor could view 'elegant buildings on either side of streets of a width seldom seen in the older cities of the leading nations of the world, and well macadamised, while handsome flagged foot-pavements line the sides'.

Suburbs by the end of the gold decade astonished even their builders. Collingwood remained an overcrowded slum, but the southern and eastern suburbs were already being covered with substantial middle-class villas and mansions. The sardonic 44-year-old visiting Irish barrister William Kelly described the scene in Melbourne each afternoon, when 'the thoroughfares in these various directions seemed lined as if by processions, from the unbroken lines of omnibuses, private gigs, and carriages carrying the crowds of Mammon-hunters to their little rural paradises'.

The exports which underpinned most of this expansion reached £13 million a year by 1860. Gold was still by far the most important product, at nearly £9 million for the year—about a third of the world's total output—while wool exports remained steady at £2 million.

At the time of the 1861 census, 80,000 Victorians were employed in gold-mining, and 40,000 in pastoral and agricultural work. Building engaged the attention of another 22,000 workers, while cartage employed 14,000 more. About 14,500 people spent their time in trading of all kinds—wholesale, retail and finance. There were 10,000 engaged in food and drink dealing, with a further 3,000 working in hotels and lodging-houses. The professional classes—doctors, lawyers, teachers, clergy, etc.—numbered only 5,000 throughout the colony. Some 6,000 prisoners and paupers were maintained at public cost, or lived as vagrants. Only 1,000 people defined themselves as being of 'independent means', living off their investments. Of the 1,530 Aborigines who survived the European takeover of Victoria, only 160 had jobs, mostly as farm hands. Few were ever now seen in Melbourne.

The preponderance of male immigrants during the gold rushes temporarily upset the balance of the sexes. In 1861 the colony contained 330,000 males but only 210,000 females. About 20,000 women found employment as cooks and housemaids, while another 4,000 said they

1	BATSON'S HILL.	7	THE QUEEN'S WHARF.	13	BARRACKS FOR MOUNTED POLICE.	19	THE GOVERNOR'S HOUSE.
2	GUNPOWDER MAGAZINE.	8	CUSTOM HOUSE.	14	ST JAMES' CHURCH.	20	THE JEWS' SYNAGOGUE.
3	GOVERNMENT DOCK.	9	PUMPS FOR WATER CARTS.	15	THE EXHIBITION.	21	LEGISLATIVE ASSEMBLY HOUSE.
4	P. & O. COMPANY'S WHARF.	10	ST PAUL'S CHURCH.	16	THE TREASURY.	22	WESLEYAN CHAPEL.
5	RALEIGH'S WHARF.	11	THE THEATRE.	17	THE SURVEY OFFICE.	23	UNION BANK.
6	COLES' WHARF.	12	THE CITY GOAL.	18	ROAD TO MOUNT ALEXANDER.	24	BANK OF AUSTRALIA.

This elevated view of Melbourne in 1854 shows most of the city's features, especially the first train service which ran from the end of Elizabeth Street across the Yarra River to Port Melbourne. The scene was sketched by Goodman Teale and completed in England by

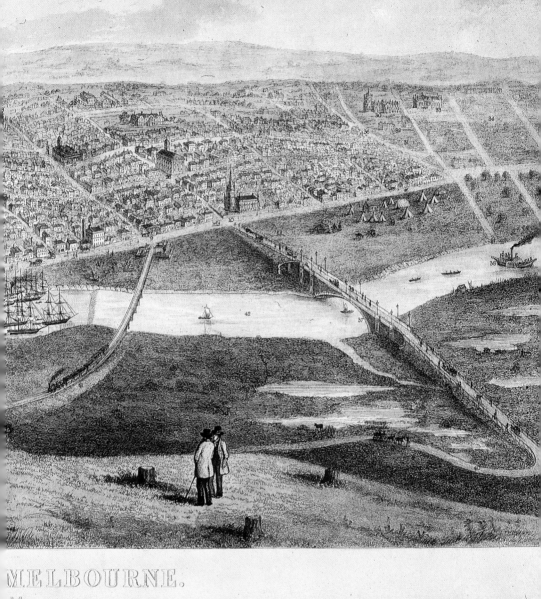

MELBOURNE.

..IA.

KETCHES TAKEN IN 1854, BY G. TEALE, ESQ^R MELBOURNE.

POST OFFICE.	31 UNIVERSITY GREEN.	37 PRINCE'S BRIDGE.	43 THE FLAG STAFF.
THE TOWN HALL.	32 PUBLIC SCHOOLS.	38 THE CREMORNE GARDEN STEAM BOAT.	44 THE OLD CEMETERY.
THE HOSPITAL.	33 ROMAN CATHOLIC CHURCH.	39 ROAD TO ST KILDA.	45 THE ELECTRIC TELEGRAPH FROM WIL-
ST FRANCISS' CATHOLIC CHURCH.	34 PROPOSED SQUARE.	40 THE SANDRIDGE ROAD.	— LIAMS TOWN TO THE CUSTOM HOUSE.
SUPREME COURT & GOAL.	35 BISHOP'S PALACE.	41 RAILWAY TO HOBSON'S BAY.	46 TELEGRAPH OFFICE & TIME BALL.
ST PETER'S CHURCH.	36 THE AMPHITHEATRE.	42 THE RIVER YARRA YARRA.	47 BENEVOLENT ASYLUM.

Nathaniel Whittock. Its main errors were to show St Francis Church on the wrong side
of Elizabeth Street, and a spire never added to St Paul's Church. (La Trobe Collection).

[9]

worked as dressmakers, milliners and needlewomen. Most women over fifteen soon married and began producing large families, leading to enormous pressure on educational resources during following decades.

To supervise this entire population, there existed in 1861 a tiny bureaucracy consisting of 1,000 civil servants, judges and salaried magistrates; assisted by 700 minor functionaries such as messengers and clerks (including eight women). The whole police, army, navy and penal force numbered 3,000. Municipal government depended on only 300 full-time officers scattered through the colony.

The new people who took over Victoria were largely concerned with urgent practical matters. But they also found the time and ability to make astonishing political advances. The strength of democratic opinion among the immigrants was shown early in the decade when jury after jury refused to convict gold-miners involved in the Eureka rebellion. That was swiftly followed by the winning of political freedoms unknown in the old world, and the beginning of better treatment for the 'lower classes'. The *Age*, itself a creation of the gold rush, chortled in 1858: 'We have the ballot; we have manhood suffrage; we have abolished the property qualification for the Assembly . . . in liberality of public opinion and feeling we have made wonderful advances. We may safely say that the social tyranny of sectarianism is non-existent in the free breezes that blow over Victoria'.

All this was true. The gold rush injected remarkable new vitality into the somnolent pastoral giant that had been Port Phillip, enabling it to rise to its feet and begin life anew.

This book does not attempt to give a general political and economic history of the whole colony during that marvellous decade, already extensively analysed in Geoffrey Serle's master-work *The Golden Age* (Melbourne, 1963). Instead, I have continued the approach of my two earlier books, *Old Melbourne Town* and *The Land Boomers*, zooming in on finer details of what happened in Melbourne during critical decades in its history. I hope the reader will find the result emotionally satisfying as well as informative. Above all, I wanted to show how Melburnians, emerging from conditions far more primitive than we can comprehend today, were enabled to face the future with courage and hope.

M. C.

Melbourne,
1993

I

The revolutionary
impact of gold

Gold! It was nothing better than a 'cursed lust', according to Virgil, poet laureate of ancient Rome. But to nineteenth-century Melbourne, gold was the explosive force which transmuted an insignificant seaport into one of the world's major cities.

Traces of gold had been found in the Port Phillip District during the 1840s. The most convincing discovery was made in 1849 by a 22-year-old transported 'Pentonvillain' named Thomas Chapman, employed as a shepherd on 'Glenmona', the squatting run of Charles Hall and Edmund McNeill, near Amherst, in the Pyrenee Range west of today's Avoca. Chapman absconded to Melbourne with about two pounds of almost pure gold, sold it to a Collins Street jeweller named Charles Brentani, and disappeared from view.

Another Pyrenees settler named R. J. Halloran reported to the government on 26 January 1849 that the jeweller had brought an assayist named Alexander Duchêne to the area and commenced searching for more gold. Superintendent C. J. La Trobe immediately sent Crown Commissioner F. A. Powlett to investigate. Powlett confirmed the discovery, reporting on 5 February that 'indeed I have seen a piece of considerable value'. La Trobe ordered Powlett to prevent any 'un-authorised occupation of the Crown Lands on any pretence'. He also instructed William Dana to ride from Melbourne with his Native Police and evict anyone not in possession of a squatting or mining licence.

But it was too late to prevent rumours from spreading. 'Gold is the only subject just now of men's talk in Melbourne', reported the *Port Phillip Gazette* on 5 February 1849. In Australia's first gold rush, dozens of men set off with picks, spades, food and rum to experience the thrills of digging and drinking in the bush. When Commissioner Powlett

Most able-bodied men—and even a few families—flocked from Melbourne along the arduous, boggy trail to the gold diggings. Soon, wrote Mrs Charles Clacy, the country was 'cut up into innumerable tracks'. John Gilfillan, who emigrated from New Zealand after Maoris massacred most of his family, painted this scene outside Melbourne about 1853. (La Trobe Collection).

arrived, he found that 'thirty or forty people had congregated at an outstation called "Daisy Hill", 10 miles west of the Deep Creek (one of the branches of the River Loddon)'. The Native Police cleared them away, but could find no sign of gold. The local story was that the shepherd Chapman had 'told different stories to various people', then was 'generally supposed to have gone to Sydney', where police sought him in vain.

La Trobe was congratulated by Governor Sir Charles FitzRoy on 20 February 1849 for preventing an unauthorised gold rush. La Trobe wrote to a friend a few days later that he had personally examined a nugget 'about 14 oz in weight'*, but that 'the discovery of a good vein of coal would give me more satisfaction'. With that thought, the excitement died away, and Melbourne returned to the humdrum business of buying and exporting wool and tallow — at least for the time being.

Within a year, the lust for gold flared again. In March 1850, a 40-year-old Scottish-born squatter named William Campbell, riding across 'Clunes' station with his friend Donald Cameron, found pieces of gold embedded in quartz rocks. They kept their discovery secret, for fear that diggers would invade the run and ruin it. But the news would not be suppressed. Renewed rumours led Melbourne's ambitious citizens, including 34-year-old mayor William Nicholson, to summon a public meeting at the Mechanics Institute on 9 June 1850, and offer a substantial reward for discovery of the first profitable gold mine. Several small finds were made along the Plenty River north-east of Melbourne, and King Parrot Creek west of Yea.

Louis John Michel, 25-year-old licensee of the Britannia Hotel in Swanston Street, formed a search party. In June and July 1851 they discovered traces of gold in Anderson's Creek near today's Warrandyte. Three hundred diggers rushed to the spot, and mining continued there intermittently for the remainder of the century. According to a Legislative Council report in 1854, Michel and his party 'clearly established their claim to be held as first publishers of the discovery of a gold field in the Colony of Victoria'.

At almost the same time, however, more significant finds were being made north-west of Melbourne. A German geologist named Dr George Bruhn, exploring alone on horseback, went through squatters'

* Worth about $5,000 today.

Early discoverers of gold in Victoria.
Left: Melbourne publican L. J. Michel, first man to publicise gold found near Warrandyte.
Right: Thomas Hiscock, who discovered gold near Buninyong.

runs at Mount Mitchell (Burn Bank) near Clunes and found quartz rocks 'in which gold was plainly visible'. He sent these to Mayor Nicholson's gold committee late in June 1851.

A 29-year-old Irish-born bush carpenter named James Esmond now entered the scene. Esmond had returned from the Californian gold rush to continue contracting work on stations around Buninyong. He met Dr Bruhn, who told him of the deposits near Clunes. Esmond and his partner James Pugh rushed north to the area, recovered a few ounces of gold from Creswick Creek, and showed them to the *Geelong Advertiser*. The newspaper trumpeted on 22 July 1851 that 'The long sought treasure is at length found!' A rush from Geelong and Melbourne began immediately. Within a few weeks hundreds of men—and two women—were encamped on the Clunes diggings, supervised by fourteen black troopers under a white sergeant.

The next discovery was made by a resident of the tiny hamlet of Buninyong named Thomas Hiscock. Exploring a ravine still known as Hiscock's Gully, near Buninyong Cemetery, he found several rich specimens and sent them to Geelong for assay. The *Geelong Advertiser* promptly announced the discovery, leading to another rush. Hiscock's Gully was soon exhausted, but eager gold-seekers continued searching in all directions. About seven miles further north, prospectors soon uncovered the huge riches of Golden Point, near which today's city of Ballarat began to develop.

As gold fever spread throughout the colony, Melbourne dissolved into chaos. Would-be diggers who saw the chance for instant wealth left their jobs in hundreds, then in thousands. Those who were used to hard physical work, such as labourers, artisans and quarrymen, were among

Melburnians who arrived first at Golden Point, Ballarat, quickly learned how to pan and dolly for gold. The artist William Strutt described the scene in 1851 as 'a huge ant hill',

with hundreds of diggers rocking cradles and producing a noise 'like low rumbling thunder' which could be heard miles away. (Victorian Parliamentary Library).

the first to go, and survived best in the arduous conditions of goldfields life.

They were followed by a multitude of office clerks, printers, shop assistants, and male domestic servants. More than half of Melbourne's police and prison warders walked away from their posts. Although Port Phillip had just achieved independence from New South Wales, and was now known as the Colony of Victoria, there was not sufficient loyalty in the junior ranks of the new civil service to keep many employees in their secure billets: they too joined the rush. 'All government works are at a standstill', La Trobe reported sadly to Earl Grey on 10 October 1851.

Seamen could be punished by up to five years' hard labour for deserting their ships, but this did not stop them from absconding. According to official statistics, of the 825 seamen on overseas vessels anchored in Port Phillip in December 1851, 417 deserted. In vain, masters threatened them with pistols, or offered £100 bonus to make the return trip to Britain. Cleverly, the captain of the *Statesman* gave his men an outfit for the diggings, and remained at anchor. Within a month, most had returned empty-handed, declaring that a miserable life before the mast was preferable to the hardships of the diggings.

City and suburbs lost much of their adult male population. Wives left behind often moved in together for mutual support. They could not be sure of water deliveries: some women took their turn to operate heavy pumps on the Yarra to fill buckets and carry them home. They dug holes to dispose of nightsoil, because collection had ceased. Even their children sometimes joined the exodus to the diggings. Edmund Finn ('Garryowen'), who remained in his reporting job on the *Herald*, observed that 'striplings ten or eleven years old, some of them barefooted and many in rags, darted off like so many wild animals'.

Hardware stores were soon stripped of all picks, spades and other tools which might assist in the search for gold. Until fresh shipments arrived, some shopkeepers simply closed down and joined the rush. Almost every horse and dray vanished from Melbourne to join the long lines proceeding northwards. One group even harnessed four bulldogs to a cart to haul their belongings along the rough trail.

Some gold-seekers shipped to Geelong, but most followed the usual route out of Melbourne along Elizabeth Street and Flemington Road. Crossing Moonee Ponds Creek, they entered the boggy trail later called Mount Alexander Road and (if they were lucky) were able to rest at one of many inns which sprang up on the route to Ballarat. 'The scene on the road almost baffled description', wrote one traveller. All were bowed down with goods, or were whipping animals into renewed effort. Even a few women trudged along, carrying babies in their arms. When heavy rain fell, some mud-spattered individuals gave up and returned meekly to work in Melbourne, but most pressed on to endure life on the diggings. By October 1851, government officers estimated that 7,000 people were camped at Golden Point, and the whole countryside around was being dug up.

Before long the riches of Ballarat were surpassed by extraordinary new finds near Mount Alexander, in the Castlemaine district. Christopher Peters, a hut-keeper employed by Dr William Barker on 'Mount Alexander No. 1' station, accidentally found gold in a waterhole. During November 1851 the area was 'rushed': in that month the new Gold Escort took to Melbourne more than 11,000 ounces of metal, about six times the amount being won at Ballarat.

A renewed exodus from Melbourne followed this news. Edmund Finn claimed that fewer than fifty adult males remained in the city in December 1851. 'The finger of scorn was often pointed after me in the streets', he wrote, 'and I was put down as a poor, spiritless, unplucky sort of creature'. The government doubled the wages of its few remaining employees, in order to keep a skeleton staff on the job.

A few weeks later came further massive discoveries near Sandhurst (Bendigo), and away rushed many of the gold-seekers to that area. William Westgarth recalled that 'Bendigo was indeed a wonder of its day'. By mid-1852 there were said to be 50,000 diggers along Bendigo Creek.

Many prospectors who survived the rigours of goldfields life but made little profit crept back quietly to add to the increasing number of slum dwellers on the Collingwood flats and elsewhere.

Other diggers who had 'struck it lucky' liked to cause a sensation by parading Melbourne in flamboyant outfits, lighting their pipes with banknotes, and 'shouting drinks' all round. 'The wildest revelry reigned', wrote educationist James Bonwick, who had tried his luck at Forest Creek before returning to Melbourne. Wealthy diggers called for 'another pail of champagne', and 'all passers-by were bidden to the draught'. One man was supposed to have shod his horses in gold; another made nuggets into a set of golden stirrups. The housemaid at one city hotel was alleged to have collected £1,000 in gold dust by

Heavily-armed private and government escorts brought millions of pounds worth of gold to Melbourne. William Strutt painted this scene outside the Treasury in William Street in

August 1852, where a consignment was being unloaded for safe-keeping under military guard. (Victorian Parliamentary Library).

shaking out the mats in rooms where diggers slept. Even if these stories have been exaggerated over the years, they still show the frenetic spirit which possessed Melbourne.

Dozens of new inns and brothels sprang up in the city to meet the demand for grog and women, on whom the gold was spent freely. According to merchant Patrick Just, 'the streets were daily perambulated by figures in silks, satins, and jewellery, looking very ill at ease in their new acquirements'. Some miners even 'married' their temporary girl-friends in colorful ceremonies. One enterprising firm provided bridal carriages with hearts painted on the doors, and drove its drunken customers wildly through the streets to 'cut a flash'. Scottish immigrant Alexander Finlay wrote in May 1852 of cabs 'flying in all directions', with 'returned diggers hallooing and calling from one cab to another'. William Fairfax, a Melbourne printer and publisher, said that 'Life became a riot, and its courtesies were in a great measure disregarded'. Another observer, Daniel Puseley, complained that Melbourne 'is a kind of modern Babel—a little hell upon earth'. That period of extravagant dissipation lasted only a few months. Soon enough, Melbourne had to face up to the changes necessary to create a tolerable life for the majority of its new residents.

Fortunately, lack of capital was rarely a problem. By the end of the gold decade, the astonishing total of twenty-five million ounces of gold had been won from Victorian diggings. Even at the time, when gold sold for about £4 an ounce, the product was worth £100 million, roughly seven times the value of Victorian wool exported during the same decade. Today, when gold sells for about $400 an ounce, the production of the 1850s would be worth some ten billion dollars.

The injection of this kind of wealth into a comparatively primitive pastoral economy, where people had been content to lead simple lives, gave Victorians the feeling that they had been specially blessed by Providence. Their confidence soared: anything seemed possible. 'There was something wonderfully infectious in the atmosphere of hope and cheerfulness, of buoyancy and joyful expectation, which enveloped us', recalled noted journalist James Smith. Melbourne was able to set about the creation of a city which would stand as a monument to human endeavour, material well-being, and spiritual self-satisfaction.

2

Shipping in the new
population

In tens of thousands they came—the raw material for a new nation. Dredged from the slums of Britain's overcrowded cities, swept from the servants' quarters of London homes, plucked from farms and villages, filtered from professional chambers and noble mansions, came a flood of human beings ambitious to make a new start in the fabled land of gold. During the decade up to 1860, no fewer than 386,000 males and 160,000 females ventured on to crazy little ships which fought their way through ocean perils and tipped them out on Melbourne's strange shores.

In the absence of international telegraphs, news of the first major gold strikes had taken several months to reach Britain. Confirmation of the rich Mount Alexander discovery was not received in London until April 1852. Almost immediately, 'the Australian madness' began to infect every corner of the British Isles. Novelist Charles Dickens saw crowds of would-be emigrants 'struggling and elbowing' at shipping offices for places on any kind of ship headed for the promised land. By the end of 1852, more than 80,000 hopefuls had embarked. With new gold discoveries being reported every month, shipowners placed orders for streamlined 'clipper ships', carrying enormous spreads of sail, which could cut the voyage to less than three months. The slim-hulled clippers looked beautiful, but mortality below decks, especially among children, was sometimes horrific, and only partly ameliorated by a revised Passenger Act hastily brought into force on 1 October 1852.

Rugged Liverpool shipowner James Baines made a fortune during the gold rush with his Black Ball Line of clippers. The first was the *Marco Polo*, captained by James 'Bully' Forbes, which reached Melbourne in October 1852 after a record passage of only seventy-eight days. Two years later the clipper *James Baines* cut the record to only sixty-five days, much faster than steamships of the time. By the end of the 1850s, seven Black Ball clippers had established a regular service from Liverpool to Melbourne, leaving on the 5th of each month. Seven competing clippers of the White Star line sailed the same route, leaving Liverpool on the 20th and 27th of each month.

The first primitive steamships did not provide much competition for sailing vessels over long distances. However, arrival of the P. & O. Company's 80 h.p. mail steamer *Chusan* in Melbourne on 28 July 1852 after a fast trip from Suez showed the shape of things to come.

Gibbs, Bright & Company's huge iron-hulled screw steamer *Great Britain* was taken off the American run, to leave Liverpool on 21 August 1852 with 630 gold immigrants. It arrived safely in Melbourne eighty-three days later. This remarkable vessel carried 35,000 gallons of fresh water, and condensers to produce more from sea water. During the next twenty years it brought thousands of immigrants to Australia without serious incident. William Westgarth, who returned to Melbourne by P. & O. steamer in 1853, asked, 'What has caused those magnates of the steam world to stretch their arms to the very outside of the Empire, and to invade these remote waters of Port Phillip? It is gold . . .'. The *Great Britain*'s success encouraged Gibbs, Bright & Co. to build in 1855 a companion vessel, the *Royal Charter*. This giant reached Melbourne on 16 April 1856 on the first of several successful voyages, but was wrecked off Wales in 1859 with heavy loss of life.

Better navigational aids were needed to assist gold-rush fleets into Port Phillip. By the 1840s, masters of all large vessels were using accurate instruments to calculate their latitude and longitude, and establish where they were on the trackless ocean. But even the best chronometers could lose precise timing on the long voyage to Australia, giving navigators false readings. Sudden storms could sweep vessels on to notorious death traps like the rocks of King Island.

The first lighthouse on Victoria's south-western coast, which began operation at Cape Otway in 1848, gave mariners a fixed point on which to base their reckoning. From there it was a comparatively straightforward matter to steer towards the lighthouse built five years earlier at Queenscliff, and enter Port Phillip Bay through the Rip.

Some vessels still managed to run aground on the long peninsula of Point Nepean, opposite Queenscliff. Gangs of 'wreckers', thought to be from Sullivan Bay near Sorrento, were suspected of hoisting false lights

George Gilbert's painting of Shortland's Bluff (Queenscliff) shows the new lighthouse built to supplement the original small structure of 1843, which can be seen slightly to the right on a lower level. The more powerful light was a boon to immigrant vessels searching the coast for the entrance to Port Phillip Bay. (La Trobe Collection).

A. Cooke's engraving of Williamstown in 1858 shows a paddle-steamer being pulled off the patent slipway on which large vessels were once repaired. (Newsletter of Australasia, *October 1858).*

to mislead unwary seamen. When ships were disabled, the wreckers swarmed aboard. 'The sails, rigging, and every other movable article soon disappear', said the Melbourne *Herald* in November 1853. 'Nor is the cargo any more secure; as fast as a case or cask is landed on the beach from the shattered vessel, it is pounced on by ready hands, and immediately secreted under the sand'.

The government's solution was to erect a fixed red light tower on Point Nepean, and install a flagstaff to show the state of the tide. In addition, a floating lightship was anchored at the end of West Channel leading into Port Phillip Bay. By using these facilities in conjunction with the main lighthouse at Queenscliff, mariners of the gold-rush era were able to proceed more safely.

As a further guide to masters approaching the coast for the first time, five more lighthouses were opened by the end of the 1850s, at Portland, Griffiths Island near Port Fairy, Warrnambool, Cape Schanck, and Wilson's Promontory.

Ships which followed sailing directions carefully, usually reached Melbourne without mishap. However, so many minor groundings and collisions took place that in April 1854 the Victorian Legislative Council passed an Act putting pilots under the control of a new Pilot Board, and making it compulsory for all overseas vessels to take on a pilot outside the Heads. To finance the new procedures, steamships were charged 10d a ton and sailing ships 1s 3d. By the end of 1854, seventy-six pilots were registered: their brightly-lit schooners flying red and white horizontally-striped flags sailed back and forth outside the Rip to meet incoming vessels.

The first essential for pilot and health officer boarding a ship was to establish whether any infectious disease had broken out. So quickly had gold-rush emigration developed that many of the first ships sailed without proper inspection or clearance by British port authorities. Poor sanitation and ventilation on board, especially for steerage passengers below the waterline, meant that disease could spread rapidly. More than 1,000 assisted emigrants in 1852 died before they even sighted Melbourne. Four clippers alone reported a total of 500 deaths among their 3,250 paying passengers. Hundreds more perished as the vessels lay in Hobson's Bay or at a temporary quarantine station set up at Point Ormond. Most of the bodies were dumped in a rough cemetery not far from the time-ball tower in Williamstown.

A new quarantine station was hastily established in October 1852 near today's Portsea, between Observatory Point and Point King. Two limeburners, William Cannon and Patrick Sullivan, were evicted and their huts taken over to accommodate dying immigrants. Pilots were instructed to guide all fever ships to that locality, so that patients could be transferred to the convict hulk *Lysander*, converted to an emergency hospital ship.

These facilities were established just in time for the arrival of the worst of all fever ships, the 1,500-ton clipper *Ticonderoga*. Captain Thomas Boyle drove this beautiful new ship with its 795 passengers mercilessly through the high seas to reach Port Phillip on 3 November 1852. On arrival, health officers found that the ship was in 'a most filthy state'. Its lockers were 'full of dirt, mouldy bread, and suet full of maggots'. Underneath the bunks were 'receptacles full of putrid ordure [faeces] and stale urine'. Nearly 100 passengers had already died of various diseases during the voyage: another 300 were ill enough to be put ashore at Portsea. Some had to shelter miserably beneath blankets draped over tree branches. The *Ticonderoga* was not allowed to proceed to Hobson's Bay until 22 December, when the remaining passengers were able to land.

The disasters of 1852-3 led to much stronger government intervention, and better facilities for treating the ill. The first timber hospital was built at Portsea in 1854. During the decade it was replaced by a series of

The extremely crowded state of the anchorage in Hobson's Bay during the gold rush is shown in this damaged contemporary painting by W. F. E. Liardet. (La Trobe Collection).

two-storey sandstone isolation wards (including one for lepers), a police station, washrooms, boiler house, and administrative block.

Health Officer Dr J. Reed, appointed in 1855 to what was now called Point Nepean Sanitary Station, reported four years later that only eight ships had to be quarantined during 1858. The worst cases were the *Bermondsey*, on which five assisted immigrants died of typhus; and the *Merchant Prince*, where two immigrants died of scarlet fever. Constant cleansing of ships and boiling of infected clothing 'succeeded in every instance in stopping and extinguishing the disease', said Dr Reed.

Yet constant vigilance was necessary. After Dr J. B. Callan took over as Resident Surgeon, he was forced to report in 1862 that the *Phoenix* from Liverpool had suffered nine deaths from typhus. On board

the *Donald McKay*, also from Liverpool that year, eight passengers and two crew died of typhus. Dozens of other passengers had to be kept in the hospital until the fever abated.

Some of the old quarantine buildings still stand, and are occasionally opened to the public as a grim reminder of the days when ocean travel could be deadly.

The trials of gold immigrants did not end when they were released from quarantine. Vessels drawing more than nine feet of water were forbidden to enter the shallow lower reaches of the Yarra River. This meant that the masters of most overseas ships were forced to anchor in the deeper water of Hobson's Bay, between Williamstown and Port Melbourne.

Wilbraham Liardet's painting 'View of the north shore port of Melbourne' on this page gives an excellent idea of the overcrowded state of the bay at the height of the gold rush. On one day in October 1853, no less than 340 ships were using Hobson's Bay and the river. This total included 106 barques, 92 schooners, 76 brigs, 62 fully-rigged three-masters, and several steamships. Since all the sailing ships needed considerable room to manouevre, confusion reigned. Further chaos was caused as each ship lowered boats to fill casks with fresh water 'under the spout at the Port Melbourne watering-place'.

In the midst of this excitement, incoming migrants were at the mercy of hardbitten boatmen who for the first time in their lives could see the chance of making large profits. Where they had previously been content with a shilling or two to land a passenger and his luggage, the minimum price soon rose to a guinea. Eureka rebel Raffaello Carboni had to pay £5. Even when the government made it compulsory for shipowners to bear the cost of landing, matters did not improve much. Seweryn Korzelinski, who arrived on the s.s. *Great Britain*, recalled how the captain hired lighters and tried to remove all 650 passengers in one day to save costs. As luggage was hoisted out of the hold, it was 'roughly thrown to the side and occasionally breaks open, strewing the contents on the deck . . . This provokes screaming, cursing and more confusion'.

As night fell, some masters continued to unload passengers at the nearest wharf. Richard Horne, disembarking from the *Kent* late in 1852, wrote that 'There was not a single lamp on the wharf': goods of all kinds were trampled into the mud. 'Men, women, large families, with the children all crying, now a dog running between your legs, now you running up against a horse who had also lost his master, and all this in a strange place, in the rain and dark . . .'. James Armour, arriving the same month on the *Lady Head*, described docks 'littered with the wet chests and softer baggage of the houseless . . . to the evident distress of the wives', who watched helplessly as their valued possessions were ruined or stolen.

An old naval captain named George Ward Cole owned more than thirty of the lighters which profited hugely from the immigration boom. In 1851 he built Australia's first screw steamer, naming it *City of Melbourne*: this too joined in the game. Some retribution came in 1852 when the government compulsorily acquired Cole's Wharf near King Street, and kept him waiting sixteen years for compensation. The embittered Cole sold his lighters as soon as the gold rush passed its zenith, and survived the slump which followed.

In the confusion of 1852-3, other Melbourne merchants trying to clear goods for resale suffered severely. William Kelly, sailing up the

Yarra in May 1853, saw the crews of a dozen lighters 'sampling for their own satisfaction the cases and packages with which they were entrusted'. John Shillinglaw, Acting Superintendent of Water Police, caught several crews 'breaking the packages to pieces'. The timber wharves built during the 1840s collapsed under the weight of activity: the north bank of the Yarra, wrote Kelly, became 'a slough of dark mud', alongside which was 'a line of lighters and intercolonial vessels, four deep, discharging promiscuously into the mire bales of soft goods . . . piled up in mountains in the muck'.

British exporters consigned all kinds of goods to Melbourne, some useful, some ridiculous. One exporter sent twenty dozen ice skates. Consignees had to pull their bales out of the mud within twenty-four hours, or see them seized and auctioned by Customs officers, sometimes for a few pence. 'Ridges of merchandise may be seen in perfect pyramids opposite the shops of the great traders', reported Thomas McCombie.

After several heated deputations from importers, La Trobe and his Legislative Council agreed to rebuild Queen's Wharf, under direction of David Lennox, Superintendent of Bridges. A tender of £42,000 was accepted, but the final amount paid increased to £80,000. The contractors laid massive bluestone foundations, built new wharves with heavy vertical timber supports, and carted 1,000 loads of filling every day from Flagstaff Hill and Batman's Hill. By August 1853, the Melbourne-based American merchant George Train was able to write: 'Now we have a nice McAdamised thoroughfare the whole length of the quay, and a raised footpath for pedestrians'. The height of the new quay helped to make this busy mercantile section of the city comparatively floodproof.

The Legislative Council next attempted to enforce better safety regulations on incoming steamships. Under the Victorian Steam Navigation Act of 1853 (16 Vic. No. 25), a Steam Navigation Board of five experts was set up. One of their functions was to appoint 'fit and proper' persons to be ship surveyors. These men set to work inspecting twice a year all steam vessels trading in Victorian ports, ensuring that they were not overloaded; were fitted with watertight compartments, lifeboats and distress flares; and possessed accurate navigation instruments. This pioneering Act gave people more confidence in the safety of steam transport.

The first Victorian Passenger Act, passed in November 1854, greatly strengthened the provisions of the British Act of 1852. Henceforth, ships arriving in Melbourne and Geelong were permitted to carry only one passenger for every seventy cubic feet of air space. Passenger ships were prohibited from carrying gunpowder, vitriol, guano or untanned hides. Sale of spirits to passengers on board was forbidden. On arrival, passengers were entitled to remain on board for two days and be fed during that time, before being safely landed with their luggage at the shipowners' expense.

At the beginning of the gold rush, three alternatives were proposed for the construction of better port facilities for Melbourne.

The first option, suggested by Colonial Architect Henry Ginn in December 1851, was for a two-mile canal to be cut through low-lying land in today's South Melbourne, straight to Liardet's Beach at Port Melbourne. Ships could, it was thought, then sail straight through to Queen's Wharf.

The second alternative envisaged the fuller development of Williams-town, the original anchorage from which Melbourne was settled. By comparison with the mercantile bustle of Melbourne, Williamstown had become a crime-ridden backwater during the 1840s. It won new importance during the gold rush, being the closest landing point to the deep water anchorage of Hobson's Bay.

The s.s. Great Britain, *which brought 630 gold immigrants to Melbourne in 1852, was the mightiest ship of her time. The 322-ft iron vessel, driven both by wind and a 15-ft propellor, often made the England to Melbourne trip in less than sixty days. Later she was found rusting away as a coal hulk in the Falkland Islands, but was salvaged and restored after 1970 to become a maritime museum in Bristol. (Painting by E. W. Bell in La Trobe Collection).*

Edmund Thomas's painting of the end of Bay Street, Port Melbourne, in 1853 shows today's busy shopping centre to have been a sandy, waterlogged exit to the bay. Clippers of the gold-rush era can be seen at anchor. (La Trobe Collection).

David Lennox as Superintendent of Bridges made plans for a bigger jetty at Williamstown, and even found a builder for the job. However, said Lennox, when engineer Samuel Brees of the new Central Road Board took control, 'he made some alterations in the plan, and the contractor threw up his contract'. The timber already purchased, added Lennox, was left 'lying about in different places'.

The work was passed over to a new Colonial Engineer, Captain Charles Pasley, who quickly completed the jetty and a breakwater. By the mid-1850s, Williamstown Railway Pier could accommodate seven large vessels; and Williamstown Breakwater Pier another seven. The new electric telegraph of 1854 (chapter 13) ran from the Harbour Master's office at Williamstown to Melbourne; while a black-painted wickerwork time ball dropped from the lighthouse at exactly 1 p.m. each day enabled navigators to set their chronometers.

In 1856, the government agreed to utilise deep water on one side of the Railway Pier to install a 'patent slip', capable of hauling up the largest vessels, with the possible exception of monsters like *Great Britain*. More than 80,000 cubic yards of sand and earth were removed by labourers from adjacent land at a cost of £18,000. The patent slip mechanism, originally intended for Launceston, was bought by Victoria for £60,000, at a time when a complete dry dock would have cost £200,000. Charles Chessell, a Yarra River shipwright, handled the installation for £7,000. When complete, vessels no longer had to sail on to Sydney for major repairs: an extensive shipwrights' industry developed along Williamstown shores.

The suburb elected its first municipal council in April 1856, and began spending rates and government grants to improve the locality. William Kelly found that 'the Williamstown of 1857 is really an important place, intersected with wide, regular streets, curbed, chan-nelled, and macadamised, with regular trottoirs [paved footways], fine stone and brick buildings, private houses, excellent hotels, fine shops, most spacious and well-assorted general stores, branch banks, churches of all denominations . . . and a resident population of 3,536 souls, besides an enormous floating population'. By 1862, Williamstown's population had grown to just on 4,500, including 1,400 ratepayers.

The third alternative for improvement of Melbourne shipping was accelerated development of elementary wharf facilities already in existence at Sandridge (Port Melbourne).

Encouraging though Williamstown's progress might be to its loyal inhabitants, the rival landing place of Port Melbourne shot ahead even faster. Government land sales in 1853 averaged £3,400 an acre, equal to Melbourne and far above the Williamstown average of £1,800. On to the sandy blocks of Port Melbourne moved publicans, blacksmiths, shopkeepers and butchers. Hundreds of small timber houses sprang up to accommodate labourers and artisans working on the new railway and jetties.

The government attempted to have the first Station Pier built in 1853, when the Legislative Council voted £30,000 for the work. At first it was directed by David Lennox, but when the Central Road Board was formed, Samuel Brees took over. However, as assistant engineer Thomas Rosson told a Council inquiry in November 1853, Brees left his job 'rather suddenly', to be succeeded by various officials who each spent a few days on the task before washing their hands of it. One of the problems was a variation of 600 per cent in tender prices received. Not until Charles Pasley took control in 1854 was any progress made.

At Pasley's suggestion, contractors Porter & Robertson purchased two old vessels which had been deserted by their crews, filled them with bluestone blocks, and sank them in the right position to form a foundation for the pier. When completed in 1856, the pier was 60 ft wide by 613 ft long, and could accommodate six large ships. Rails were run along the pier, so that ships' cargoes could be swung by cranes from the holds on to rail trucks, and thence taken direct to Melbourne.

The pier had to be lengthened every year thereafter: in 1857 by 253 feet, in 1858 by 131 feet, in 1859 by 312 feet, and in 1860 by 152 feet. This final extension into the bay gave a low-water depth of eighteen feet in which larger ships could dock. By this time some of the original 13-inch New Zealand kauri piles had been eaten away to only three inches, and had to be replaced by West Australian jarrah.

Meanwhile, a smaller steamboat jetty was built near the end of Bay Street, where Port Melbourne Yacht Club is situated today. Bay Street, formerly a boggy, sandy waste occupied by a few shanties, began to grow into a major commercial area.

During the gold rush, Port Melbourne won a reputation as one of the world's worst spots for the notorious practice of 'crimping'. Masters of outward-bound vessels were so desperate for crews that some willingly paid corrupt boarding-house keepers to drug and kidnap seamen and even ordinary immigrants lodging with them. According to

Francois Cogné, a French artist who arrived in 1856, drew some of the most accurate scenes of Melbourne used in this book. Here he shows the busy scene at Queen's Wharf, then the city's commercial hub. At left, behind the steamship, can be seen several hotels in William Street, and the 'pepperbox' cupola of St James Cathedral. The large building in the centre is the Custom House. Immediately behind it is the Melbourne Savings Bank

*and Western Market. On the right, facing the end of Market Street, is Temple Court,
home of solicitors and shipping agents. More hotels and merchants' buildings line the
eastern side of Market Street. The prominent building at extreme right is Richard
Goldsbrough's Wool Store, today Holyman House, with its entrance now considerably
altered. (La Trobe Collection).*

a contemporary Chamber of Commerce report, drunken men 'when helpless bundles, were carried aboard outgoing ships, and sent on voyages to anywhere. They were kicked, cuffed, and ironed, until such time as they turned to, "sailor-like", and became one of the crew'. In 1862 a Sailors' Home was erected on the corner of Collins and Spencer streets in Melbourne to give seamen a safe place to stay. But even in the 1880s, occasional cases of crimping were still known at Port Melbourne.

A further problem for Port Melbourne during the gold decade was the poor state of roads connecting it with the south side of Princes Bridge and city merchants' warehouses. Today, looking at Bay Street and City Road, it is difficult to imagine that the route was once almost impassable in winter. When South Melbourne council was inaugurated, it erected toll gates, collecting sufficient revenue to build up its section of the road and even install gas lighting. At Port Melbourne, however, the government and Melbourne City Council had to help finance three timber bridges across the lagoon which flooded Bridge, Graham and Rouse streets. In other low sections, three-inch by twelve-inch hardwood planking was used to build temporary roadways.

Port Melbourne did not succeed in getting its own municipal council until 1860, when local member William Nicholson became Premier. He forced Melbourne City Council to relinquish its hold over the area. Following an election in July, local coal merchant William Morley became first chairman (mayor) of the borough. Progress after that was rapid. In 1862 Port Melbourne had 3,400 residents, of whom nearly 1,000 were ratepayers. Three miles of road had been macadamised, and eight miles of footpaths kerbed with bluestone or hardwood.

Melbourne's shipping facilities were still so disorganised in the mid-1850s that the Chamber of Commerce began agitating for a Harbour Trust to take over and unify all waterside activities. The Chamber's president, a King Street merchant named William Hammill, demanded in 1856 'a Harbour Trust constituted on a popular basis and consisting of representatives of the several classes interested in the subject'.

Two years later a Select Committee of the new Legislative Assembly examined the idea. Evidence from two past presidents of the Chamber of Commerce, Henry Farrar and James Francis, brought some convincing answers. The transfer of imported goods from ships to lighters at Williamstown was, they said, far less satisfactory than arrangements at

Melbourne gaols became so crowded during the gold rush that hundreds of convicts had to be kept on old immigrant ships, converted to hulks moored in Hobson's Bay. Some of the cells measured only thirty by sixty inches: prisoners were kept in irons to prevent escape. (Watercolour by William Strutt, Dixson Library).

Port Melbourne. Many more goods were pillaged at Williamstown. Others were 'occasionally much damaged by being thrown in heaps'. Significant time was lost: 'We are frequently kept three weeks for goods coming up the river'.

The Port Melbourne railway which opened in 1854 was able to carry imports fairly efficiently, for about 8s a ton. But those merchants able to use the steamship pier at Port Melbourne unloaded direct into horse drays, which took the goods along City Road, over Princes Bridge, and straight into warehouses. This cut landing costs to only 2s a ton. Merchants felt that the best way of achieving savings on this scale for bulk goods was to cut a canal thirty feet deep from Port Melbourne so that large vessels could sail direct to the shipping pool below William Street.

John O'Shanassy, one of the politicians examining the merchants, commented that if the canal were built, Port Melbourne 'of course would immediately fall to pieces'. Williamstown, and new railway enterprises, would be similarly affected. Charles Pasley, engineer turned

Georgiana McCrae's watercolour known as 'Batman's Hill in 1851' appears to have been painted from Flagstaff Hill looking in a south-westerly direction. The substantial houses depicted occupied the West Melbourne end of town. Behind them, on the left, was the sparsely-wooded knoll of Batman's Hill, later levelled for Spencer Street rail yards. On the

right, a paddle-steamer chugs down the Yarra River towards the bay. In Hobson's Bay, top right, can be seen a long steamship with two funnels, said to be s.s. Great Britain (one funnel was removed in 1853). Since the ship first arrived at Melbourne on 12 November 1852, the painting can probably be dated to that time. (La Trobe Collection).

politician, was also unenthusiastic about the canal proposal. He believed it would be extremely costly to construct, and would probably silt up in sandy stretches. He preferred a plan (adopted many years later) to deepen the Yarra River by constant dredging and eliminate its large curve at Humbug Reach, Fishermen's Bend. Answering questions from Peter Lalor, MLA, Pasley pointed out that the north side of the Yarra, south-west of Batman's Hill, afforded 'extraordinary facilities for the making of docks'. (This area eventually became Victoria Dock, handy to Spencer Street railway terminus). For all these reasons, the Select Committee adopted a cautious line, recommending further investigations before large amounts of public money were spent.

In 1860 the government appointed an eleven-man Royal Commission, which traversed much of the same ground. Its chairman was Charles Bright, 31-year-old inheritor of the family share in Gibbs, Bright & Co., owners of the *Great Britain* and many other vessels.

This time the investigation yielded firmer recommendations that a Harbour Trust should be given 'jurisdiction over all the shores and waters of Port Phillip . . . and rivers available for the purposes of navigation'. The commissioners thought that the Yarra should be dredged to a depth of twelve feet, at a cost of £37,000. A swing bridge should be erected over the Yarra at Spencer Street, and new wharves built on the south bank. Sites for a ship canal and graving dock should be investigated, to be capable of handling the world's largest ships.

The government accepted the recommendation for dredging the Yarra, but took little other action until a renewed economic boom in the 1870s forced establishment of a long-needed Melbourne Harbour Trust.

3

Hardships of
gold immigrants

Immigrants poured in by the thousand from almost every country on earth, jostling each other along Melbourne's soggy streets as they fought for space in overcrowded hotels, boarding-houses and restaurants. As Thomas McCombie wrote, 'The town that had accommodated twenty thousand with tolerable comfort, was suddenly called upon to provide for a hundred thousand'.

Lieutenant-Governor La Trobe reported to the Colonial Office in October 1852 that Melbourne and suburbs 'are absolutely choked with the teeming population', while 'the most extravagant rent is paid for the most indifferent accommodation'. Housing had dropped in value when Melbourne was emptied during the first rushes, but now all kinds of temporary canvas and 'broad paling' structures were being joined together to make quick profits.

When Richard Horne arrived in September 1852, he was forced to rent a room overlooking 'a narrow patch of yard all bestrown with shattered things . . . with a mad conglomerate on one side emitting typhoid odours'. That side was 'all mud and cesspool, the other all wretchedness and squalor', including the body of a dead monkey. William Kelly's brother paid £9 a week for a tiny house 'in a back slum called Bank Place, behind the Bank of Australasia', which was 'finished in the rudest style, with a filthy yard'. A few days later he was offered £2,200 to 'walk out and give up possession'.

Lodging-houses were crammed to bursting point. Alexander Finlay, a 33-year-old Scot who arrived in 1852, complained that gently-raised families were being forced to sleep in foetid rooms 'with no chance whatever of selecting their companions'. One Melbourne merchant, more benign than most, accommodated 150 people each night free of charge in his partly-built store: each morning he found that even

The overcrowded state of Melbourne lodging houses in 1852 is shown in this sardonic watercolour by William Strutt. The result was the passing of the Common Lodging Houses Act of 1854, limiting the number of residents and ensuring that the bedrooms were disinfected regularly. (Victorian Parliamentary Library).

upturned carts in the yard had been occupied by homeless families.

So rapidly did disease spread in these conditions that in 1854 the Legislative Council passed the first 'Act for the Well-Ordering of Common Lodging Houses'. Henceforth, all landlords of such houses or tents had to be registered and inspected. They were supposed to separate the sexes, keep their premises clean and well-ventilated, and notify the authorities immediately of any sickness.

Still the migrants came. The fittest quickly took themselves off to the diggings, leaving behind a large number of weak, sick or simply penniless migrants. Most of the newcomers were undoubtedly active, adventurous people, but according to Dr Mingay Syder, gold also attracted 'the idle, dissipated, scrofulous, phthysical, dyspeptic, hypochondriac, neuralgic, worn-out constitutions', as well as 'the prostitutes and other fungi of Europe'.

To help shelter them, an increasingly beleaguered La Trobe in 1852 authorised erection of a 'Canvas Town' on the south side of the Yarra, on the spot where the Arts Centre now caters for more fortunate generations. Surveyors laid out rough streets, where migrants were allowed to pitch tents in rows on payment of 5s a week. Few facilities were offered, apart from the doubtful privilege of dipping water buckets into the polluted Yarra.

All kinds of enterprises developed as the population of Canvas Town reached 5,000. Seweryn Korzelinski, who pitched his tent there, recorded that bakers delivered bread and 'a girl comes with milk well watered down'. William Kelly noticed a Mr Scott, hairdresser, who 'set razors, drew teeth, and bled' (that is, extracted cups of blood from patients to relieve illness). Coffee could be bought for 'threepence the half pint'. The government refused to allow a public house, but 'the hecatombs of bottles, flasks, and gin jars strewed about, proved that there was a most unlimited, unlicensed consumption of ardent spirits'.

Strutt's watercolour 'Hard Up!' depicts penniless immigrants forced to sell their belongings in Flinders Street near the wharves. A regular 'Rag Fair' sprang up, until, wrote William Kelly, 'the envious Jews [shopkeepers] stepped in, compelling the passive authorities to repress the practice of unlicensed auctioneering'. (Victorian Parliamentary Library).

Edmund Thomas's sharp pen depicted the squalor of life for immigrant gold-seekers in the muddy surroundings of what he called 'Canvass Town' in South Melbourne. Storekeepers followed the custom of flying flags to show their location. (La Trobe Collection).

One notable observer, the poet Richard Horne, pitched his two tents, then thought he might treat himself to a meal at a large tent named 'National Dining Rooms'. This was managed by 'a dirty girl of sixteen, and a remarkably dirty little Irish boy, of about twelve'. Inside, beds and tables were covered with 'odiously dirty and torn blankets', strewn with 'islands of stale mustard, grease, grime, and grit of cooking ashes'.

Many families had been left in Canvas Town by husbands who imagined they would return in a week or two with bags of gold. Melbourne merchant Patrick Just described 'delicately brought-up women . . . roughing it in the frail canvas tent—no privacy, no comfort'. On the swampy land, disease spread rapidly. When parents or their children fell ill, little help was available. Richard Horne noticed that one tent remained laced up for some days. Peering in, he saw a family of three 'lying dead among some dry rushes—of want, slow fever, broken hearts'.

The government made intermittent attempts to improve conditions in Canvas Town. By the end of 1852, it had spent £4,500 on erecting and fencing a two-acre quadrangle of timber buildings close to the Yarra, with police quarters and a store for migrants' baggage. In a report to London, La Trobe described this first shelter as 'nothing beyond a mere shell constructed of ordinary scantling, with broad paling walls'. Nevertheless, it could house about 400 of the most desperate mothers and children in comparative safety.

A year later, when thousands of new dwellings had been built throughout Melbourne, La Trobe ordered that Canvas Town itself should be closed down and its occupants given notice to rent elsewhere. To cope with pauper migrants still arriving, the government took over the disused council abattoirs below Batman's Hill, had them cleansed and subdivided into fifty small rooms, and offered the space at a low daily fee.

Immigrants thrown suddenly into extreme poverty had to sell belongings for whatever they would fetch. A recognised trading spot known as 'Rag Fair', named after the market in Rosemary Lane, London, sprang up in Flinders Street near Queen's Wharf. Every morning, valuable possessions were sacrificed. James Armour saw one

[47]

One of the most fondly remembered early coastal steamers was the s.s. Edina, built on the Clyde and used as a troopship during the Crimean War in the mid-1850s. Transferred to Australia, it began a Melbourne-Warrnambool service in the early 1860s. As the vessel

aged, it was used as a bay ferry between Melbourne and Geelong, carrying up to 800 passengers at a time. It continued this service right up to 1939, before coming to rest as a hulk in the Maribyrnong River. (La Trobe Collection).

man and his small daughter, 'their bodies drooping with weariness and disappointment', vainly trying to sell a violin, fishing rod and walking sticks. William Strutt described the 'pleading, despairing look, sad indeed to behold', with which such paupers tried to persuade people to buy.

After protests from Flinders Street merchants who were losing business, the City Council suppressed Rag Fair in February 1853. However, Town Clerk Edmund FitzGibbon told a later parliamentary inquiry that about eighty poor immigrants were allowed to erect their tents and shacks along vacant frontages at the Western and Eastern markets and continue trading. 'They were occupied by shoe-vendors and general dealers, and one or two lodging and eating-house keepers, who provided accommodation for the poorer classes', said FitzGibbon. These establishments too became such a 'nuisance' that they were removed in August 1855.

The constant emergencies of the early gold rush period, and belief in the efficacy of leaving as much as possible to private enterprise, prevented the government from doing more to relieve immigrants' sufferings at this time. Private charities were left to cope as best they could.

First in the field was the Wesleyan Church, which organised appeals during 1852. One meeting was addressed by 30-year-old Flinders Street ironmonger Walter Powell, who had profited so greatly from the sale of diggers' implements that he was able to open two more city stores. Shaking with emotion, Powell recounted how he had seen a young woman, newly-arrived to join her husband on the diggings, reduced to tears because she had been compelled to spend a night among riff-raff on the wharf. Such people needed safe quarters.

The Wesleyans raised £2,000, to which La Trobe added a government subsidy of £1,000. The money was spent on building a large timber shelter on the north side of La Trobe Street, near the original Supreme Court building, between Swanston and Russell streets (today the Royal Melbourne Institute of Technology). It could hold 400 immigrants, and in 1853 was advertised as being 'Now open to members of the Wesleyan Church and other respectable persons'.

Other churches stirred themselves, and in May 1853 formed a non-denominational Immigrants' Aid Society. La Trobe promised an injection of public funds, and granted a temporary lease of several acres opposite Canvas Town, on the area now the Queen Victoria and Alexandra

Dr James Harcourt of Birmingham, well-known for his work in lunatic asylums, took charge of the Immigrants' Aid Society buildings in St Kilda Road in 1859.

Detective Walter Randall was brought from London in 1853 by Melbourne City Council to keep watch over Chinese in Little Bourke Street. Randall was drowned in 1859.

Gardens. Here a collection of timber buildings called the 'Public Houseless Immigrants' Home' was erected, able to accommodate about 400 people, with kitchens, washroom, dispensary and sick ward. Shelter and three meals were provided for a standard rate of 4s a day.

Within a year, the buildings were required for military reinforcements arriving in Melbourne to deal with disorder on the goldfields. The government refunded most of the money raised, and gave the Immigrants' Aid Society possession of the rough timber buildings still standing beside the Canvas Town site. These structures became the equivalent of a poorhouse, although preference was still given to new immigrants. In 1857 they were partly converted to house hundreds of destitute children.

By 1860 the troops were able to move on to the newly-built Victoria Barracks site. The Immigrants' Society was permitted to reoccupy its original buildings, with the addition of mains gas and piped water. The move was opportune, for the Yarra floods of 1863 inundated and swept away the old Canvas Town site.

The Immigrants' Society's superintendent, 43-year-old Englishman Dr James Harcourt, arrived in Melbourne in 1856, followed by his wife and ten children. At first he established a private lunatic asylum at Pascoe Vale, but in 1859 was placed in charge of the Society's buildings in St Kilda Road. At that time about 1,500 inmates a year were being cared for. When an economic slump hit Melbourne, the numbers increased to 2,300 in 1860, 5,500 in 1861, and 6,500 in 1862, including casuals who patronised the Society's free soup kitchen.

Food was so cheap in the late 1850s that only 6s a week had to be spent on maintaining each residential pauper. Nevertheless, Harcourt

Samuel Brees painted this fine picture of Chinese gold-seekers passing through Flemington in 1854. He depicted a hardware store at left, Flemington Hotel at right, and early houses in the middle distance. When the Chinese gold-seekers returned to Melbourne, they set up enclaves which aroused much suspicion among the white population. (La Trobe Collection).

insisted that every able-bodied male inmate had to break stone as gravel
for the roads, in quantities sufficient to cover his rations. Women had to
perform laundry and sewing duties, while 300 children were given
elementary education and religious instruction. The government's
charity commissioners of 1863 concluded that the home was 'one of the
best managed, and at the same time one of the most economical, which
we have anywhere visited', giving 'well-timed assistance without
encouraging pauperism'.

The immigration system itself had been largely overhauled by 1860.
Ships from Liverpool bringing some 3,000 assisted emigrants arrived in
Melbourne that year 'in a most satisfactory state of cleanliness and
order', according to Government Immigration Agent John Tyler. Only
seven deaths occurred during voyages in 1861. An independent witness,
Daniel Puseley, was able to write that 'Swindling, dissipation, and other
relative vices are not so openly and impudently practised' by migrants.
Travel was safer, accommodation improved, and even alcoholism
diminished.

A severe imbalance of the sexes still existed. Many single men
departed after trying out the diggings, but permanent immigration into
Victoria between 1852 and 1860, most of it from Britain, comprised
183,000 males compared with only 120,000 females.

To help equalise numbers of men and women, the government gave
priority with free or assisted passages to skilled female domestic
servants 'of good moral character', importing about 2,500 a year.
Officials insisted on the women 'accepting a fair rate of wages, if
offered by respectable parties'. Immediately each government migrant
ship arrived, employers thronged the Female Immigration Depot on the
west side of King Street, near Collins Street, to engage servants who
looked reasonably clean and trustworthy.

The first family reunion scheme was introduced in 1861 to assist the
normalisation process. Any Victorian resident could apply for government assistance in bringing healthy relatives from Britain, contributing
£5 for males and £2 for females aged between twelve and forty. So
sudden was the rush for passage warrants that Parliament's vote of
£25,000 for the scheme was spent in eight weeks. By the end of 1861,
more than 1,160 males and 1,930 females had been reunited with their
families in Melbourne.

Chinese gold-seekers began to arrive in considerable numbers after 1853, increasing to about 20,000 in 1855 and 40,000 three years later. Most of these immigrants headed straight for the diggings, but a few hundred remained in Melbourne, forming a distinctive community in and around Little Bourke Street.

Most white people feared and hated them. To William Howitt in 1853 they appeared 'a very worthless class of immigrants'. The *Age* in 1857 called them 'a very undesirable race'. But the Chinese continued to flood in, to the point where they formed one in five of the adult male population. Melbourne merchant William Westgarth wrote that 'Victoria had somewhat of the disconcerted feeling that the mother-country might experience on learning that a couple of millions or so of the dusky sons of Confucius had determinedly seated themselves among the industrial hives of York and Lancashire'.

Dark rumours spread about Chinese gambling, opium-smoking, and immorality. Detective-Inspector Charles Nicholson told an 1857 Legislative Council inquiry chaired by J. P. Fawkner that although the 300 Chinese then in Melbourne were 'remarkably quiet people', he had sometimes seen up to seventy gambling in a large room above one of the main Chinese stores in Little Bourke Street. 'I very seldom go into their houses without seeing them smoking opium', Nicholson added. All who could afford it were 'very much given to going with the lowest class of women about town'.

As the police broke up each Chinese gambling den, other locations sprang up. Detective Walter Randall (also known as Rendell), employed by Melbourne City Council to watch over the Chinese, told the 1857 inquiry that they were always law-abiding except when gambling. On one occasion, when caught playing Chinese Hazard in the premises of a white man named Minett, they rushed Randall and the police head first: 'After a very severe fight we arrested seventeen of them'.

Dr Robert Bowie, Inspector of Lodging Houses, told the same inquiry there were about fifteen Chinese boarding houses in Melbourne. Most were 'orderly and well conducted'. Two proprietors had married white women.

At this time the Chinese population was concentrated around the Theatre Royal's stage door in Little Bourke Street, between Swanston and Russell streets. On the north side of Little Bourke were ten lodging houses, two Chinese grocers, and a cabinet maker. On the south side were another four lodging houses, and eight Chinese merchants, including the prominent shipowner and tea importer Lowe Kong Meng. Dr Bowie told the inquiry that the Chinese were fast extending into the brothel area between Russell and Exhibition streets, 'taking the houses as they fall vacant'.

Leaders of the Chinese community in Melbourne pleaded in vain for understanding. In a petition to the Legislative Assembly in 1857 they tried to explain that 'we Chinamen bring no wives or children to this country' because they had to stay at home to care for aged parents. Wives with bound feet found it difficult to sail, for 'when Chinese women go into ships they cannot walk or stand'. The petition was greeted by parliamentarians with jeers and laughter.

The government had already tried to halt Chinese immigration by imposing a £10 head tax (Act 18 Vic. No. 39, 12 June 1855). This failed when the newcomers simply landed in South Australia and walked overland to the diggings. In 1859, when the Chinese population reached 42,000, the government added a miners' residence fee of £4 a year (Act No. LXXX, 24 February 1859). Collection was rigidly enforced. Only 600 Chinese arrived that year, but more than 3,000 departed rather than pay heavy taxes.

Immigration Agent Tyler reported in 1861 that the Chinese influx had practically ceased. Nearly 2,500 miners returned to China that year 'with the golden fruits of their labour'. The number of Chinese in Victoria was now down to 25,000, and kept on falling. Some managed to merge into the general population. Rev. William Young's government report of 1868 noted that about fifty or so Chinese had married European women, and produced about 130 mixed-blood children. These formed part of the foundation of today's still strongly-knit Chinese community.

FACING PAGE:
Charles Joseph La Trobe, wearing the ornate Lieutenant-Governor's uniform in which he opened Victoria's first Legislative Council sittings on 13 November 1851. (Oil painting by Sir Francis Grant, in the La Trobe Collection).

4

The rocky path
to democracy

Before the gold rush, Port Phillip District was ruled with a scarcely-concealed iron fist by its first Police Magistrate, Captain William Lonsdale (from 1836 to 1839) and more gently by its first Superintendent, Charles Joseph La Trobe (from late 1839 to early 1851). Both men were instructed to refer important policy matters to Sydney, but had the right to make hundreds of daily decisions affecting the lives of ordinary people. The only check on their almost dictatorial powers lay with a branch of the Supreme Court established in 1841, and the limited duties of Melbourne City Council, elected by ratepayers from 1842.

From this to a fully representative form of government was a giant step, which would normally have taken many decades to achieve. Fortunately the British government in 1850 was anxious to grant parliamentary institutions to any colonies which had become economically self-supporting. By any test, Port Phillip fitted this description. With the Queen's approval, Victoria was chosen as the name for the newly-independent colony, and arrangements made to set up its first Legislative Council after separation from New South Wales in 1851.

This was not democracy as we know it today. London retained the power to nominate the 50-year-old La Trobe as Victoria's first Lieutenant-Governor. Working with him as a kind of advisory 'cabinet' was a four-man nominated Executive Council, with 51-year-old William Lonsdale retained as first Colonial Secretary.

Most of the heads of La Trobe's previous divisions of government were promoted to take charge of new Victorian departments. As named in July 1851, they were Redmond Barry, Solicitor-General; J. H. N. Cassell, Collector of Customs; C. H. Ebden, Auditor-General; Henry Ginn, Colonial Architect; H. F. Gurner, Crown Solicitor; Robert Hoddle, Surveyor-General; Alastair Mackenzie, Colonial Treasurer;

W. F. Stawell, Attorney-General; and Dr John Sullivan, Colonial Surgeon.

To enable government to continue during this transition period, the NSW Legislative Council on 1 May 1851 passed a special Act to provide that all existing laws should continue in force in Victoria until altered by the Victorian legislature.

The new Act for establishment of a thirty-man Legislative Council provided that ten members were to be nominated, in effect by La Trobe and his Executive Council. The remaining twenty members were to be elected by adult male property-holders who wished to register as voters.

Victoria was divided into sixteen electorates. Melbourne, with a population of 23,000 at the beginning of 1851, was allowed to elect three members. The County of Bourke outside Melbourne had 13,000 people north of the Yarra and 4,400 south of the Yarra, enabling voters there to elect two members. Geelong, with 8,000 population, was also allowed two members.

Rural districts at this time averaged less than 2,200 population each, but were allowed to elect the remaining thirteen members. These figures mean that the election was heavily gerrymandered in favour of rural property-holders—particularly since members of parliament in those days were not paid, and needed an independent income. And so it turned out. Pastoralists and other wealthy men dominated the Legislative Council from the outset, and for many years did their utmost to balk reformist legislation intended to benefit the bulk of the population.

In 1851, the only Melbourne building large enough to accommodate meetings of the Legislative Council was St Patrick's Hall, built two years earlier in Bourke Street on the site of today's Law Institute of Victoria.

Colonial Architect Henry Ginn converted the ground floor of the rented building into offices for the Clerk of Council, 36-year-old squatter-lawyer John Barker, and his small staff. The first floor was used as Council chamber, with tiny galleries for press and public. This area was fairly dark, so Ginn had part of the roof removed and converted into Australia's first glass ceiling. William Strutt, who sketched the scene (pages 60-61), thought the building had been 'nicely fitted up and made a very respectable Legislative Chamber'. Merchant G. F. Train criticised the 'little *henroost*' of a public gallery, and the fact

William Strutt's annotated sketch of the official opening of the first Legislative Council session in St Patrick's Hall on 13 November 1851. 'The beauty and fashion of the Melbourne of that day were present in full force', wrote the artist. But when Council

members refused to pay for a finished painting, Strutt's work remained at the stage shown
here, instead of becoming a magnificent permanent record of a political milestone.
(*Victorian Parliamentary Library*).

that members had 'no desk for writing, nor any place to put their papers'.

On 11 November 1851, a drizzly day, the new legislative councillors assembled at St Patrick's Hall for the swearing-in ceremony and election of their first Speaker, former wine merchant and mayor Dr J. F. Palmer. The official opening was held two days later. Melbourne's leading citizens and their wives gathered to watch, and the army's ancient cannons boomed forth. In strode C. J. La Trobe, all six-foot one-inch of him resplendent in dark blue uniform with scarlet and gilt collar and cuffs, silver epaulettes, oak leaves and acorns, and vice-regal headpiece ornamented with white and scarlet feathers, attracting a mixture of admiration and muffled jeers.

In a typically moderate speech, La Trobe said he hoped that the current gold discoveries would not harm 'the agricultural nor the pastoral interest'. The legislature faced a responsible and noble task, he added: prudent laws were needed, for 'What we sow our children will reap'.

After the Council's work began, William Westgarth, elected to represent Melbourne, admitted that 'We were all, confessedly, terribly raw in all matters of Parliamentary form'. Discovery of gold meant that 'the vast incessant tide of business thrust upon the colony made it hardly possible to spare any time' for other concerns. Every day and most of each night were taken up by a succession of 'public meetings, and deputations, Council Committees and Council sittings'.

As chaos grew in Melbourne and the diggings, La Trobe suffered virulent attacks in the press, City Council, and Legislative Council. Worried by his wife's continued illness, sickened by criticism from people to whom he had devoted the best years of his life, La Trobe resigned on 31 December 1852, although not relieved from duty by a new Governor until the middle of 1854. During this period of La Trobe's decline, the *Argus* printed a regular satirical advertisement: 'Wanted a Governor: Apply to the People of Victoria'.

Despite constant friction between nominated and elected members in the Legislative Council, the new body managed to enact a surprising number of important laws up to the election of the first Legislative Assembly in 1856. Those dealt with more fully elsewhere in this book included:

• December 1851. The first Board of Commissioners for National Education in Victoria appointed.

- September 1852. First Convicts Prevention Act, to prohibit any more transportees from entering Victoria.
- September 1852. Courts of General Sessions established to hear criminal cases and relieve pressure on the Supreme Court.
- September 1852. County Courts established to hear civil cases.
- December 1852. Residential qualification of voters for Melbourne City Council reduced from £20 to £10 a year.
- January 1853. University of Melbourne incorporated.
- January 1853. Regulations for safety of steam-powered vessels introduced.
- January 1853. Registrar of Births and Deaths appointed.
- January 1853. Police reorganisation: Chief Commissioner's post established.
- January 1853. Licensing Districts proclaimed to enforce penalties for sly-grog dealing.
- January 1853. Hulks to be proclaimed for use as additional prisons.
- January 1853. Church Act 1853. Up to £30,000 a year of public money to be spent on new church buildings.
- January 1853. Melbourne & Hobson's Bay Railway Company authorised.
- January 1853. City of Melbourne Gas & Coke Company authorised.
- February 1853. Melbourne & Mount Alexander Railway Company authorised.
- February 1853. Geelong & Melbourne Railway Company authorised.
- February 1853. Central Road Board established.
- February 1853. Commissioners of Savings Banks appointed.
- February 1853. Board of Commissioners established to improve Melbourne's drainage.
- March 1854. Bank of Victoria incorporated.
- April 1854. Electric telegraphs to be built.
- April 1854. Shipping and pilotage regulations tightened.
- November 1854. Volunteer Corps established to help defend Victoria against invasion.
- November 1854. Compulsory vaccination against smallpox enforced.
- November 1854. First Victorian Passenger Act passed to improve inward and outward shipping conditions.

- November 1854. Common lodging-houses to be registered and inspected.
- November 1854. Capital punishment to be carried out in an enclosed yard, the public excluded, and inquests to be held.
- December 1854. Health Act passed to enforce sanitary measures.
- December 1854. Municipal Institutions Act, allowing formation of new councils outside Melbourne.
- December 1854. Town and Country Police Act, to enforce municipal regulations.
- March 1855. City of Melbourne authorised to borrow £500,000 for street construction.
- May 1855. Melbourne Exchange Company authorised.
- May 1855. South Yarra Water Works Company authorised.
- June 1855. Every Chinese immigrant to pay £10 entry fee.
- June 1855. Laws passed to govern friendly societies.
- June 1855. Pollution of Yarra River above Melbourne prohibited.
- July 1855. Constitution Act, establishing two Houses of Parliament.
- March 1856. Melbourne, Mount Alexander & Murray River Railway Company authorised.
- March 1856. Bank of Australasia authorised.
- March 1856. Melbourne & Hobson's Bay Railway Company authorised to build branch line to St Kilda.
- March 1856. Studley Park Bridge Company authorised.

With the end of the pioneering era, symbolised by La Trobe's departure from Melbourne, came a new type of Governor determined to impose order on the unruly colony. In their wisdom, London officials appointed a stern disciplinarian, 48-year-old naval commodore Sir Charles Hotham, who arrived in Melbourne in June 1854.

At first Hotham was heartily welcomed by the people. William Kelly watched in astonishment as a crowd of 60,000 gathered to escort the new Governor from Port Melbourne 'in roaring triumph into town', under lines of flags and past 'window-crowded ladies', with bands blaring and singers chanting. In a brief speech at the government offices in William Street, Hotham promised the crowd that 'I shall do my duty and try to please you'.

From there Hotham and his wife Jane (daughter of Lord Bridport and grand-niece of Lord Nelson) were taken to what was meant to be a temporary Government House in St Georges Road, Toorak. The

Melbourne's first real Government House was 'Toorak House', still standing in St Georges Road. Originally it was built for merchant James Jackson. After Jackson died at sea, the government bought the mansion in 1854 for the new Governor, Sir Charles Hotham. S. T. Gill's watercolour of 1855 has captured Hotham's awkward angular figure riding up the front drive. 'We have got our house very nice', Hotham wrote laconically to his brother—but he died soon after this painting was completed. (La Trobe Collection).

This ornate design was widely published in Britain as 'the new Melbourne Town Hall'. In fact it was Knight & Kerr's prize-winning design of 1854 for a new Government House. Due to reductions in government expenditure, it was never built.

government had conducted a £500 design contest in 1853-4 for a new Government House to be built closer to the planned parliamentary buildings. The contest was won by architects John Knight and Peter Kerr with the highly-ornamented design shown on this page.* But Hotham soon made it plain that he had very different ideas.

The 'temporary' Government House, which still stands in greatly diminished grounds, had been built in 1849 by merchant James Jackson, since drowned at sea. The government purchased the leasehold for £10,300, but the house itself was in a sad state of disrepair. A new Colonial Secretary, J. L. F. Foster, failed to have the property renovated

---

*This illustration was widely published in Britain as 'The new Melbourne Town Hall', causing endless confusion among historians.

by the time the Hothams arrived. So angry was Hotham at the apparent insult that thereafter he bypassed Foster on official business as often as possible.

Tight-lipped, Hotham set about essential renovations at his own expense. Two labourers were engaged to manage 150 livestock pasturing between the house and the Yarra. Altogether Hotham spent nearly £30,000 on the property, adding a 50-ft supper room to entertain guests.

At first the Hothams did their best to get to know Melbourne's *nouveaux-riches*, as well as gentlemen immigrants with whom they had more in common. 'We have occasional dances, and the Colonists are delighted', Hotham wrote to his brother. But Lady Hotham, 'a very lady-like and rather shy person', was faced with entertaining people who, said William Kelly, had 'lately emerged from the lowest levels of the community'. Kelly added that 'poor Lady Hotham was bewildered, and Heaven knows she was to be pitied in going through the ordeal of receiving some of the stalwart dames and strapping girls . . . who went in low evening costume to make their morning calls, sopping up the nervous perspiration in the hall with thick bandanas'. Yet this was the reality of life in gold-rush Victoria.

A few weeks after his arrival, Hotham began investigating government affairs, finding much that did not accord with his ideas of proper discipline. Visiting one department in naval style without notice at 11 a.m., he saw public servants still reading the morning papers, without 'the scratch of a pen' heard from any desk.

Digging deeper, Hotham found to his horror that large amounts of public money had been squandered without audit, and the administration was dependent on bank loans to keep going. In August 1854, sidestepping his political advisors, Hotham nominated two senior officers of the Bank of Australasia, W. H. Hart and D. C. McArthur, as a 'Council of Advice' to assist the new Auditor-General, Edward Grimes, in investigating all departments. Their reports over the next nine months condemned the methods by which people were appointed to the public service, and the endemic inefficiency which existed.

New taxes had to be levied to meet a £3 million deficit, payment of miners' licence fees rigorously enforced, and more than 1,000 government employees dismissed from postal, police and maritime departments. 'The weeping and wailing and gnashing of teeth, the packing up and turning out was so general', wrote William Kelly, that even Hotham was forced to slow down his programme of reform.

*Sir Charles Hotham, the stern
naval disciplinarian and Governor,
who failed to pull wild Victorians
into line.*

The Governor provoked a renewed storm when, under instructions from the Colonial Office in London, he tried to prevent the Legislative Council from renewing the Convicts Prevention Act of 1852. Most Victorians were adamant about halting the influx of criminals who often disappeared into the anonymity of the goldfields. Huge protest meetings were held in Melbourne in October 1854, and Hotham was forced to give way.

Then, late in November 1854, came the news that miners at Ballarat were arming themselves and drilling to fight against continued payment of the hated gold licence fees. The great crisis in Victorian affairs was about to burst with stunning force over the heads of the unsuspecting Melbourne establishment.

5

Melbourne juries free
Eureka rebels

Immigrant miners were forced into armed insurrection at the Eureka stockade by the decisions of government officers in Melbourne who were remote from the realities of life on the diggings. Both La Trobe and Hotham proceeded on the assumption that the Crown possessed the exclusive right to determine how every square inch of the land should be utilised. Some was sold, much was leased to pastoralists. Minerals underneath the surface were also held to be the property of the Crown. When the gold rush began, many public facilities and extra police had to be provided. To those in power, what could be more logical than a system of paid licences for gold-seekers, so that the people who used these new facilities had to pay for them?

Unfortunately, officials overlooked the fact that for every gold-seeker who made a fortune, ten could barely scratch out a living. Stripped bare by the sharks of Melbourne, often living in pathetic circumstances, the majority of miners were driven to desperation by government policy.

La Trobe's first order of 18 August 1851 levied a monthly licence fee of thirty shillings, and instructed Commissioners of Crown Lands to ensure that the digger was 'not a person improperly absent from hired service'. Unlicensed diggers found in possession of gold were fined or imprisoned. When the full impact of gold discoveries became obvious in December 1851, the government decided that the licence fee would, 'in justice to the revenue', be doubled to £3 a month.

Huge protest meetings were immediately held at the diggings. Rallies of up to 14,000 miners attacked the harshness of goldfields Commissioners, assisted by ex-convict and Aboriginal troopers, in collecting even the existing tax. Unanimously, the miners pledged to refuse payment of the increase, whatever the results.

Surprised by the massive reaction, La Trobe withdrew the increase, but instructed officials to intensify collection of the 30s monthly fee. Squads of armed police frequently swept the diggings, destitute miners became adept at dodging them, and tension continued to rise.

Sir Charles Hotham arrived in Melbourne in June 1854 with the conviction that La Trobe had been pusillanimous, and that the law must be rigorously enforced. The new Governor was stunned to discover that out of an estimated goldfields population of 77,000 male adults, only about 44,000 paid the licence fee. In September 1854 he ordered that the hated licence searches should be carried out at least twice a week.

As police intensified their brutal methods, miners' leaders began organising a formal resistance movement. The Ballarat Reform League was established in October 1854 by a group of British Chartists promoting a programme of broad social change. Their leader was 30-year-old Welsh-born John Humffray, a vigorous orator who attempted to persuade angry miners that their best chance lay not in violence but in obtaining parliamentary representation.

By then events had gone too far for compromise. When Hotham sent all available military forces to Ballarat, they were pelted with stones by Irish diggers near the Eureka mine on 28 November 1854, and their drummer-boy was wounded by an unknown sniper. Miners' wives worked through the night to sew together a rebel flag based on the Southern Cross. Next day a large crowd gathered under the flag, many miners publicly burned their licences, and the meeting resolved to 'defend and protect them' under all circumstances.

Equally determined, 39-year-old Gold Commissioner Robert Rede next morning ordered a thorough licence hunt. Stones were thrown, Rede read the Riot Act, troops fired a volley into the air, and several diggers were taken away to gaol. That afternoon the people gathered on Bakery Hill. Peter Lalor, a 27-year-old Irish-born miner, addressed them. 'I looked around me', he later recalled. 'I saw brave and honest men, who had come thousands of miles to labour for independence. I knew that hundreds were in great poverty . . . The grievances under which we had long suffered, and the brutal attack of that day, flashed across my mind; and, with the burning feelings of an injured man, I mounted the stump and proclaimed "Liberty"'.

Hundreds enrolled in an impromptu rebel force, and began drilling inside slab and earth barricades hastily erected around the Eureka mine. For two days the miners continued organising supplies and arguing

ABOLITION

OF THE

LICENSE TAX!

GREAT OPEN AIR MEETING

TO THE PUBLIC OF BENDIGO.

GENTLEMEN, a great PUBLIC

MEETING

Will be held

ON SATURDAY NEXT, AUG. 26

IN FRONT OF THE CRITERION HOTEL, AT TWO O'CLOCK P.M.,

For the purpose of adopting proper means to effect the entire Abolition of the License Tax; and also to Elect an Anti-License Central Committee. Every Man who believes that the time has come to Abolish the License Tax is respectfully invited to attend the Meeting, and to take a part in the proceedings.

The present Anti-Gold License Movement, so far as its originators are concerned, will be conducted strictly within the limits of Law and order; but every legal means will be made use of to sweep from the Statute Book of the Nation a law which is degrading to a free people, and impolitic and oppressive in its practical operations. The great majority of the Digging Community are at present unable to pay the License tax, and therefore aught not to be compelled by the Executive Officers of the law to advance fines, or otherwise submit to an unjust and tyrannical bondage. We therefore call upon the entire Digging Community to attend the Meeting on Saturday, and show, by their presence and their unanimity, that they are determined to demand, constitutionally, from the Legislature, the immediate Repeal of the obnoxious License Tax; and that, while they are willing to pay their proper share of taxation, they are fully determined to be placed on an equal footing with the other Classes of Her Majesty's subjects in the Colony.

Abolition of the License Tax and no compromise ; Abolition of the Gold Commission, and Reduction in the Public Expenditure of the Nation ; Representation to all Classes, and equal Division of the State Taxes ; the Orders in Council revoked, and the Public Lands of the Colony thrown open to the People ; Repair of Roads and Bridges, and the immediate establishment all over the Diggings of an efficient and liberal system of National Education.

All who want the above desirable objects carried out without delay, let them one and all attend the Great Anti-License Public Meeting.

At Break of Day on Saturday let there be a universal discharge of fire-arms, to spread the news of the Meeting all over Bendigo.

DIGGERS! DO YOUR DUTY!

By Order of the Anti-License Provisional Committee,

WILLIAM D. C. DENOVAN,

HON. SEC. PRO TEM.

BENDIGO, 21st Aug., 1854.

COOK & SHERBON, PRINTERS, BENDIGO TIMES OFFICE, SANDHURST.

White miners were especially angered by the use of Aboriginal police to inspect licences. William Strutt, who painted this scene of 'Black troopers escorting a prisoner from Ballarat to Melbourne', wrote that it was 'an absurd mistake' to employ native constables who could not read printed or written instructions. (Victorian Parliamentary Library).

John Basson Humffray, Welsh-born miners' leader who supported peaceful protest against injustice. Crayon portrait by Thomas Flintoff. (La Trobe Collection).

tactics, while supporters drifted in and out. Section commanders included James Esmond, discoverer of gold at Clunes.

Commissioner Rede cleverly waited until Saturday night, 2 December 1854, when many miners left the camp for home or sly-grog tent, convinced that nothing would happen on a Sunday. But before dawn on 3 December, a force of 276 soldiers and police quietly marched from their camp and stormed the stockade. In the bayonet charge, one officer and five privates were killed. The remainder easily overwhelmed the defenders, mortally wounding about thirty diggers in a short battle. Peter Lalor escaped by a miracle, a severe gunshot wound making it necessary for his left arm to be amputated later by a friendly doctor.

Reporting the battle to London, Hotham claimed that most of the miners' leaders held 'foreign democratic opinions', wanted 'an overthrow of property and general havoc', and 'have no right to expect clemency if convicted'. The law must be preserved, however obnoxious or unpopular: 'obedience must be rendered or government is at an end'.

Antagonists in the Melbourne political battle over Eureka: Colonial Secretary J. L. F.
Foster (left) and radical Oxford-born Dr Thomas Embling (right).

Although the Eureka rebellion was so easily put down, something like
panic hit Melbourne when the news was received. 'Victoria's Hour of
Trial has come', announced the *Age* on 5 December 1854. This new
radical newspaper, which had taken over from the *Argus* as the miners'
voice, blamed 'the weak, the blundering, and the culpable Government'
for the crisis. 'How shall they answer to the misgoverned colonists, to
the insulted majesty of the British Law, and to the British Crown, to
their own consciences, and to Heaven, for their share in this fearful
business?'

Hotham's first concern was to stop the revolt from spreading,
particularly when rumours came from Clunes that 1,000 armed miners
were preparing to march to their comrades' assistance. Hotham sent an
urgent message to Hobart asking for reinforcements from the 99th
Regiment: 300 troops arrived a few days later by special steamer and
were lodged in the immigrant barracks.

On Monday, 4 December 1854, 1,500 special constables were sworn
in at Melbourne and armed with batons to prevent civil disorder. Next
day, mayor J. T. Smith called a public meeting at the Mechanics'
Institute to plan the defence of Melbourne against any further uprising.
More than 3,000 people turned up and filled that section of Collins
Street. When official speakers tried to defend the government's actions,
spectators began to mutter angrily. They installed their own chairman,
the radical 40-year-old Dr Thomas Embling, and passed by acclamation
a resolution blaming the unpopular Colonial Secretary, J. L. F. Foster,
for causing the crisis by giving misleading advice to the government.

An even larger meeting on 6 December, held on the site of the

Butler Cole Aspinall, one of several
Melbourne barristers who defended
Eureka rebels free of charge.

J. M. Grant, solicitor who organised
legal defence for the Eureka rebels, ten
years later became a radical Premier.

future St Paul's Cathedral, was addressed by David Blair of the *Age*,
who warned of similarities between the miners' grievances and American
colonists just before their revolution. Hotham now had Foster's enforced
resignation in his hand, and was able to pacify public anger by
appointing in his place the elected MLC for Geelong district, a 44-year-
old surgeon and farmer named William Haines.

Meanwhile, committal hearings were being held at Ballarat on diggers
who had survived the Eureka battle. Due to conflicting evidence,
the magistrates dismissed charges against most of the men, but sent
thirteen to stand trial in Melbourne. Hotham refused all appeals for a
general amnesty, saying that the law must take its course. Again he
misread the state of public opinion, and put himself in line for further
humiliation.

The treason trials, carrying a possible death penalty, began in the
old Supreme Court building in La Trobe Street before Chief Justice
William à Beckett on 22 February 1855. Defence barristers, who acted
free of charge, were organised by James Grant, 33-year-old Scottish-
born solicitor who had helped to guarantee Ebenezer Syme's purchase
of the *Age* and transform it into a radical voice.

The first man to be put up for trial was John Joseph, a Boston negro.
His counsel, Henry Chapman and Butler Cole Aspinall, went to great
lengths to challenge as juror anyone who looked or dressed like an
officer or gentleman. Finally a 12-man jury of small tradesmen and
artisans was empanelled: William Wallen, Frederick Waters, William

After discovery of gold, the Eureka rebellion near Ballarat was the most important single event of the 1850s in Australia, setting the scene for the rapid development of democratic principles. In this re-creation of Eureka by John Henderson, a 27-year-old artist who

claimed to have witnessed the attack, red-coated British troops showed no mercy in
subduing and killing the rebellious miners. (*Mitchell Library*).

Barrister Archibald Michie ably defended journalist John Manning against charges of treason. Michie became a prominent politician in the 1870s. (VPL).

Formerly of Middle Temple, London, barrister Thomas Cope emigrated during the gold rush and conducted the main defence of rebel leader Timothy Hayes in Melbourne. (VPL).

Watts, James Westwood, William Whitmore, James Willey, Edward Wills, Charles Wilson, Samson Wise, Jacob Wood, James Wood, and Henry Woodsworth.

The prosecution, conducted by Attorney-General W. F. Stawell and Solicitor-General Robert Molesworth, relied mainly on the evidence of soldiers who had been disguised as civilians to spy on miners' meetings at Ballarat. Trooper Andrew Peters, who posed as a store-keeper, said he had seen John Joseph being drilled under arms. Private Patrick Synott of the 40th Regiment, who took part in the bayonet charge at Eureka, claimed he recognised the 'nigger rebel' as the man who killed Captain Wise with shots from his double-barrelled gun. But under rigorous cross-examination, Sergeant Daniel Hagerty admitted that Joseph was unarmed and 300 feet away at the time.

B. C. Aspinall, a former *Herald* editor, and still only twenty-five years old, made an emotional appeal to the jury. He pointed out that 'No collision of any kind ever would have occurred had not the authorities forced it on', and asked sarcastically, 'Surely, gentlemen of the jury, you won't hesitate to hang a trifling nigger to oblige the Attorney-General?'

After a 40-minute retirement, the jury unanimously found Joseph not guilty. Cheering in the courtroom was so prolonged that a flushed Justice à Beckett ordered staff to identify the worst offenders: George Gorton and John Keogh were gaoled for seven days for contempt.

The next man tried was John Manning, reporter on the *Ballarat Times*. Manning had advocated forcible resistance to licence fee col-

The ageing J. P. Fawkner, one of
Melbourne's pioneers, spent much energy
as a goldfields Royal Commissioner to
bring down a report favouring the miners'
case. (Photograph by G. W. Perry).

Irish-born Richard Ireland acted as junior
counsel in the successful defence of
Timothy Hayes. For the next twenty
years he was Victoria's leading criminal
barrister. (VPL).

lection, and had allegedly been armed with a pike inside the Eureka
stockade. He was put up for trial on 26 February 1855, and defended by
42-year-old Archibald Michie, soon to become Victoria's first Queen's
Counsel.

The same prosecution witnesses gave the same sort of evidence as
before. In scorching cross-examination, Michie elicited the damaging
facts that troops had been issued with raw spirits just before the battle,
and that 'no deaths would have occurred but for their conduct'. The
existence of government spies in the miners' ranks made it likely that
the first shots from the stockade had been fired by design, giving the
drunken troops an excuse to charge.

After retiring for forty minutes, this second jury found the accused
man not guilty. 'Every manly, honest, and independent heart in Victoria
cordially echoes the verdict', said the *Age* next morning. 'The
discomfiture of the Government is complete'.

Trials of the remaining miners were delayed for a month while the
Crown revised its approach. The vital case of rebel leader Timothy
Hayes came before Justice Redmond Barry on 19 March 1855. This time
the jury consisted of three storekeepers, two farmers, a mason, a carter,
a butcher, a brewer, a gardener, a grocer, and a horse dealer.

On the surface, prosecution evidence seemed impregnable. Trooper
Henry Goodenough and others swore they saw Hayes at the barricade
with a double-barrelled gun. But defence barristers Richard Ireland and
Thomas Cope soon had the court roaring with laughter at police
witnesses' tangled replies. The jury retired for only twenty-five minutes

No Melbourne jury could be found to convict the thirteen Eureka rebels tried separately for high treason in the Supreme Court. As drawn by Sam Calvert for the Age *of 23 February 1855, they were (from left): Timothy Hayes, 34; James Campbell, 20;*

before judging Hayes not guilty. A crowd of thousands waiting outside the court cheered as Hayes was lifted on his friends' shoulders and carried triumphantly down Exhibition Street.

Next morning, an *Age* editorial headed 'The State Farce!' said that Hotham and his advisers 'seem to be inflicted with an incapacity for doing right'. And next day: 'The Czar of Toorak may command his law generals to conquer, but fate is against them'.

Amazingly, the government persevered, using the same discredited witnesses. On 21 March 1855 the Italian rebel Raffaello Carboni was brought up, under the false name 'Charles Raffeles'. Again a jury of tradesmen and farmers found the accused not guilty. Noting that forty-eight citizens in four juries had unanimously thrown out the cases, the *Age* concluded that 'The heart of the people is sound; it is only the heart of the Government that is rotten'.

Raffaello Carboni, 40; Jacob Sorenson, 38 (heavily tattooed); John Manning, 35; John Phelan, 24; Thomas Dignum, 22; John Joseph, 39 (negro, first man acquitted); James Beattie, 24; William Molloy, 25; John Fenwick, 31; Michael Taby, 22; and Henry Read, 50.

Next day, the hapless prosecution charged John Fenwick (*aka* Jan Vannick) and James Beattie. Again an acquittal, although this time the jury took an hour to reach its decision. On 23 March, another jury took fifty minutes to acquit Michael Taby (*aka* Tuhey). A *nolle prosequi* was entered for Thomas Dignum when no evidence at all could be produced against him.

On 27 March, the remaining five defendants were put up together. They were Henry Read, James Mcfie Campbell, William Molloy, Jacob Sorenson, and John Phelan. Again the charade of police-spy evidence was gone through. This time the jury took exactly seven minutes to acquit the lot. 'The People have triumphed', said the *Age*.

While the treason trials were proceeding, a six-man Royal Commission investigated the validity of miners' complaints. Merchant William

Westgarth acted as chairman, but the commission's outstanding member was John Pascoe Fawkner. 'Already in his 63rd year', Westgarth recalled, 'in broken health, and certainly the weakest physically of the membership, Fawkner was the most active of all, ever running full tilt into every abuse or fault or complaint'.

In March 1855 the commission presented a plan for complete reorganisation of goldfields administration. With treason charges thrown out of court, the government had no alternative but to accept the recommendations.

The monthly miner's licence was replaced by an annual 'miner's right' costing only £1. By the end of 1855, more than 50,000 such rights had been issued. The revenue gap was filled by a tax of 2s 6d an ounce on gold exports, levying the impost where it should have been made in the first place. Control of the diggings was removed from the despised police force, and given to elected wardens' courts.

To meet the miners' political claims, the Legislative Council was enlarged by twelve members, five of whom were elected by holders of miner's rights. The one-armed Peter Lalor came out of hiding, and was elected unopposed for Ballarat, along with J. B. Humffray. Compensation was paid to those who had suffered at Eureka. Only one of the miners' demands could not yet be met: 'unlocking the land' to provide smallholdings for miners anxious to become farmers.

Hotham's self-confidence was shattered by these events. His autocratic cast of mind could not accept the fact that Victoria had embarked on a course of rapid democratisation. The *Age* described Hotham in August 1855 as an 'ignorant, half-pay captain' guilty of 'false pretences' in continuing to accept his £10,000 a year salary. William Kelly watched the Governor riding sadly through Melbourne streets 'without any recognition save the angry stare of some political foe'. The man was obviously deteriorating fast. 'It soon became evident', wrote Kelly, 'that the grim lines of care and anxiety were furrowing deeply on his brow, that the writhings of a tortured mind were shedding from within their haggard hues on his countenance, and spreading their wasting influence over his entire frame'.

By November 1855 Hotham could stand the colonists' scorn no longer, and sent his resignation to London. A few weeks later he caught pneumonia after opening Melbourne's first gasworks. At 'Toorak House', which only eighteen months earlier had resounded with the gaiety of

One of the miners' leaders, a 27-year-old former railway engineer named Peter Lalor, turned back to respectability after recovering from serious wounds received at Eureka. Here a Melbourne Punch cartoon shows him as Inspector of Railways in 1856.

welcoming citizens, Hotham tossed feverishly in bed, ignored by the whole of Melbourne. He declined into a coma and died, still in office, on 31 December 1855, aged only forty-nine. The childless Lady Hotham, ten years younger, had nursed him devotedly: when all was done, she quietly crept back to Britain.

The post of Administrator of the colony fell to 67-year-old Lieutenant-Colonel Edward Macarthur, eldest son of that extraordinary Sydney couple John and Elizabeth Macarthur. As local military commander, Edward Macarthur had assisted in the pacification of Ballarat after Eureka, his calm and approachable manner winning him many supporters even among the working class. As Administrator, he carefully remained in the background and allowed his ministers to handle most political questions during 1856.

Macarthur was relieved in December 1856 by 41-year-old Scottish-born Sir Henry Barkly, former Governor of Jamaica. By this time, responsible government with a new Legislative Assembly had been established in Victoria. The gentlemanly, rather retiring Barkly realised that as constitutional Governor of an explosive colony, his safest course was not to interfere in current debate, but merely to 'consult, advise and warn'. For this reason his seven-year term was comparatively free of controversy, although storms raged constantly as radicals and conservatives fought for political ascendancy.

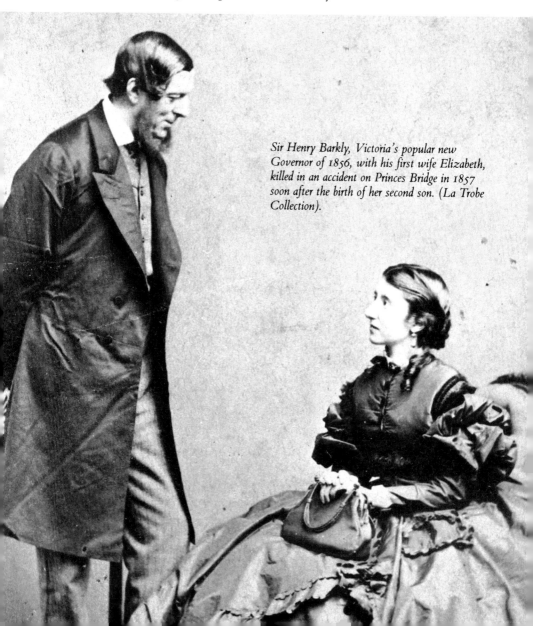

Sir Henry Barkly, Victoria's popular new Governor of 1856, with his first wife Elizabeth, killed in an accident on Princes Bridge in 1857 soon after the birth of her second son. (La Trobe Collection).

6

The new Parliament
is built

The imaginative British Act of 1850 which gave Victoria its Legislative Council also allowed the new colony to frame its own constitution. The basic model was to be the British Parliament with two houses. Since there was no hereditary aristocracy in Victoria to form a House of Lords, the colony could vary its constitution to suit local conditions.

Late in 1853 the Legislative Council, dominated by government nominees and retired squatters, passed a Constitution Act which set up a 'Lower House'—the Legislative Assembly—but attempted to ensure that it too would be dominated by conservative interests. Under this Act, members of the 60-man Assembly had to possess at least £2,000 worth of freehold property, and Council members at least £5,000 worth.

Voting rights for the public were also restricted. To vote for the 30-member Legislative Council, a man had to possess £1,000 in freehold, or be a recognised professional (lawyer, doctor, etc.). To vote in Assembly elections, a man had to own real estate worth £50, or hold a lease worth £10 a year. The bulk of urban immigrants and the working class, as well as all women, were thus excluded from parliamentary representation. The only amelioration came after Eureka, when miners were allowed to vote for goldfields representatives, allowing at least some political outlet for some of the general populace.

London's approval of the new constitution was delayed by the Crimean War. It finally arrived in Melbourne in October 1855. The following Premiers (called Chief Secretaries) took office during the remainder of the 1850s and early 1860s:

W. C. Haines   30.11.1855 to 11.3.1857
John O'Shanassy   11.3.1857 to 29.4.1857

English-born William Haines, first Premier of Victoria under responsible government in 1856, was a former surgeon and farmer who tried to accommodate the vigorous reform movement of the gold-rush period.

John O'Shanassy, an immigrant from Tipperary, was a successful Melbourne draper and supporter of goldminers' rights. With age he became more conservative. Three times Premier, he often compromised with the Legislative Council.

W. C. Haines	29.4.1857 to 10.3.1858
John O'Shanassy	10.3.1858 to 27.10.1859
William Nicholson	27.10.1859 to 26.11.1860
Richard Heales	26.11.1860 to 14.11.1861

Under this 'responsible' but barely representative form of government, Victoria's first Premier was 45-year-old William Clark Haines, a Cambridge-educated surgeon who had taken up farming near Geelong, and was a government nominee in the first Legislative Council. Essentially conservative, Haines was able to adapt sufficiently to the radical tide to be returned again to office in 1857. '"Honest Haines",' wrote William Kelly, 'makes a praiseworthy routine public officer'.

One of Premier Haines's first conundrums was the question of whether electors should be able to vote secretly. Up to that time, candidates had worked through polling agents, who presented a card to each elector with his roll number and 'I vote for ----' written on it. This open system made it easy for employers to exert pressure on tenants, employees, and even traders.

The idea of a secret ballot was invented in 1855 by 52-year-old London-born barrister Henry Chapman, who had successfully defended some of the Eureka rebels. Chapman's idea was taken up by 39-year-old

William Nicholson, prosperous Melbourne grocer and mayor, became Premier in 1859, but was unable to solve the land settlement problem.

Londoner Richard Heales, Premier in 1861, helped to smarten up the Civil Service, but failed to subdue the Legislative Council.

Henry Chapman, a barrister who settled in Melbourne in 1854, invented the world's first practical system of secret ballots for use in elections, widely copied overseas.

The conservative Anglo-Irish Attorney-General W. F. Stawell, who thankfully quit the chaos of Victorian politics in 1857 to become Chief Justice for nearly thirty years.

Above is the ornate interior of the Parliamentary Library, one of the most attractive but least-seen sections of the Victorian Parliament.

At right is the original design for Parliament House, as envisaged by architects Peter Kerr and John Knight. The core, consisting of two bluestone chambers, was built in 1856 just in time for the Legislative Assembly's first sittings. The main entrance, Queen's Hall and Vestibule, were not completed until 1879. The western facade facing Bourke Street was finished in 1892, but the colonnades intended to encircle the entire building were never completed. Nor was the magnificent 150-foot dome shown in this painting ever built. (La Trobe Collection).

William Nicholson, a humbly-born Englishman who had succeeded as a grocer in Flinders Street and as a mayor of Melbourne. Even when elected MLC for North Bourke, recalled William Westgarth, Nicholson 'was ever the plain, unassuming William Nicholson, and when Mayor or MLC both he and his wife [Sarah] would be found in their shop as usual'.

Late in December 1855, Nicholson proposed to the Legislative Council that secret ballots would be preferable to open voting. He was heatedly opposed by Attorney-General William Stawell, still smarting over his humiliating defeats in the Eureka trials. Nevertheless, the proposal was adopted for future elections. It became known and copied through the democratic world as 'the Victorian Ballot'.

William Kelly, perhaps optimistically, cheered the move. Secret ballots, he forecast, would eliminate 'the base dissembling and hollow protestations' of canvassing for votes. It would also relieve the candidates 'from the mean artifices of kissing squalid children, flattering slatternly housewives, and cajoling partial fathers'.

Unlike today's speedy polling, the first elections for the new parliament took place over several weeks from August to October 1856. The result in the Legislative Council, as might have been expected from the high property qualification, was an even greater majority of wealthy pastoral and mercantile representatives. In the Assembly, for which miners and small property-holders were permitted to vote, the result was more balanced. A considerable number of radical candidates won seats, and were able to begin their long campaign for wider suffrage, abolition of the gerrymander, abolition of state aid to religion, 'unlocking the land', and reform of the Upper House.

The main sections of a new Parliament House were ready just in time for the first meetings of Council and Assembly on 21 November 1856. A commanding site for the structure had been chosen seven years earlier by La Trobe, who reserved most of the east side of Spring Street in 1849. La Trobe's intention was that government buildings would face and dominate the ends of both Bourke and Collins streets.

The government announced a design competition for the new Parliament in April 1853. None of the entries was considered entirely satisfactory. The task was passed over to the new Colonial Engineer, 29-year-old British Army Captain Charles Pasley, whose rather conventional design was accepted in April 1854. A few months later,

London-born architect John Knight emigrated in 1852, and four years later helped to design the Victorian Parliament.

Details of Parliament House were planned by Scottish architect Peter Kerr, who also arrived in 1852.

Pasley volunteered to help lead the attack on the Eureka stockade, a fact which did not endear him to radical politicians.

At the end of 1855, Pasley's design was rejected, and a second competition held. This time a more imaginative plan prepared by two civilian architects was accepted. One of them, 29-year-old Londoner John Knight, was a visionary town planner who founded the Victorian Institute of Architects. His partner, 35-year-old Scottish-born Peter Kerr, had helped to design the new Parliament buildings at Westminster before emigrating in 1852. Knight passed most of the detailed work in Melbourne over to Kerr, who later emphasised that 'The designs for the Council and Assembly Chambers and for the library were prepared by me with my own hands and the drawings are still in existence to speak for themselves'.

Kerr's design envisaged a massively-facaded building facing Bourke Street, with the Legislative Assembly occupying the north section and the Council occupying the south end. The two chambers were to be linked by a great hall and vestibule in the middle. A substantial library across the rear was controlled by Charles Ridgway, paid the remarkable salary of £700 a year plus free accommodation. Soaring above the whole structure was to be a magnificent tower, symbolically unifying Parliament into one organism. To the shame of Victoria and its legislators, this tower has never been built. In the 1850s, total cost of the scheme was estimated at £400,000, but only £166,000 was spent up to 1860.

Henry Gritten, a 35-year-old London-born landscape artist who arrived in Melbourne in 1853, drew this scene from Albert Street, East Melbourne, in the early 1860s. At left can be seen part of St Peter's Anglican Church, which still stands. The next building, directly above the Chinese water-carrier, is today's Parliamentary Library—the first section of Parliament to be faced in Tasmanian freestone. Almost adjoining, with frontage to Spring Street, is the original Parliament House, rather ugly without its present facing stone and colonnades. Across Spring Street can be seen the Old White Hart Hotel (today site of the Windsor Hotel); and in the middle distance, the spire of Scots Church. On the north-east corner of Bourke and Spring streets is today's Imperial Hotel, built about 1862. The two-storey building alongside, which still stands, was built by Dr William Mackie Turnbull as his residence and surgery in 1854: it later became Melbourne's first Eye and Ear Hospital. On the right is the Royal Princess Theatre, rebuilt in 1886 as today's Princess Theatre. The centre of the picture is occupied by the Parliamentary Gardens. All told, a Melbourne scene with few basic changes today. (La Trobe Collection).

The contract for the basic bluestone structure was awarded to W. C. Cornish, a 41-year-old Cornwall-born builder who had successfully completed new post offices in Melbourne and Geelong. James Burgoyne supplied the prepared stone from his masonry works on the north-east corner of Spencer Street and Flinders Lane.

Troubles began early, when stonemasons insisted on working an eight-hour day instead of the ten hours worked up to this time. They were in a strong position, as the government was pushing hard for completion so that both chambers could be occupied by November 1856. Cornish held out so adamantly against the union that the government was forced to pay him £1,700 compensation to cover extra wage costs. Parliament was ready just in time, although internal decoration was not finished.

The building's beautiful library, built between 1858 and 1860, linked the two chambers at the rear, but the entrance hall so admired by visitors today was not completed until 1879. Meanwhile both library and parliamentary frontage were faced with Bacchus Marsh freestone at a cost of nearly £130,000. The stone decayed rapidly, and had to be pulled off and replaced with Tasmanian stone of the same hue.

To William Kelly, the Lower House seemed 'the *beau ideal* of an assembly chamber, imposing in its fine proportions' and finished with 'sober chasteness and elegance'. Its dimensions were the same as the House of Commons, but had to accommodate only one-tenth the number of members, giving 'extraordinary profuseness of room'. The Upper House, with its 'florid, barbaric style of crimson, gilding, and cut glass', was 'altogether superlative in its character'.

The official opening of Parliament was delayed a few days while the paint dried. On 25 November 1856, soldiers paraded, bands played, and flags flew from most Melbourne establishments. Judges, city councillors, and foreign consuls trooped in to join wives in the public galleries, and await the arrival of Administrator Sir Edward Macarthur.

After formal opening ceremonies and noble speeches were done, the Parliament got down to practical business. It soon became obvious that distinct groups would emerge on public questions, especially in the Assembly—a generally conservative strain consisting mostly of government ministers and gentry, and a radical party led mainly by Chartist and Irish immigrants.

Some visitors to the Assembly were not impressed by the newcomers.

J. P. Fawkner asked William Strutt to paint the historic opening of Victoria's first Legislative Assembly in 1856. Strutt agreed, and again made a working sketch of the scene—but again the government refused to pay for a finished picture. Strutt left his drawings and photographs of individual members in the hands of Fawkner, who gave them to the Parliamentary Library. The Strutt sketch reproduced here shows (top, from left): Justice William à Beckett of the Supreme Court; the wealthy W. J. T. Clarke, MLC; early settler John Hodgson, MLC; (bottom) surgeon Francis Murphy, first Speaker; and lawyer John Barker, first Clerk of the Legislative Assembly.

'Such a common-looking set of raggamuffins I never saw', exclaimed Anne Baxter, wife of a 50th Regiment officer. She thought that Charles Gavan Duffy, an Irish-born radical fighting to 'unlock the land', had 'a very bad voice, quite like a broken one, and his appearance is anything but good'. William Kelly observed that many members had been 'jerked from very humble grades indeed', and were 'everlastingly stumbling into ludicrous errors'. John O'Shanassy's rough brogue was sometimes impossible to understand. To the conservative banker-historian H. G. Turner, who arrived in Melbourne at the time of Eureka, many members of the new Parliament were infected with 'red radicalism'. Their main objective, he snorted, was to coerce the Upper House 'into accepting the decision of the popular chamber as final'.

Yet these untutored savages, always with the forceful assistance of the *Age*, were to lead Victoria into the democratic era faster than any other nation. Countries such as France, Germany and the USA had experimented with different aspects of democracy: only in Victoria did the elements come together so quickly, for better or worse, to form a colony with institutions almost indistinguishable from today's.

The first major victory for radical members was abolition of the property qualification for Legislative Assembly candidates. This meant that any British male resident over thirty could stand for Parliament even if he had no assets. Perhaps conservatives thought this would further lower the standard of their opponents: they allowed Duffy's bill* to pass both houses in August 1857 and become law (Act 21 Vic. No. 12).

Next came the historic move towards universal manhood suffrage for the Lower House. The Haines government had never been happy about the hasty earlier Act which allowed holders of miners' rights to vote. Conservatives feared that radicals could 'swamp' any electorate by registering supporters as miners regardless of their true occupations. As a counterweight, Haines introduced an electoral bill giving multiple votes to landholders, and imposing a minimum of six months residence in an electorate.

Most of the general public was outraged, spurred on by daily *Age* attacks on a government 'seeking to retain the restricted franchise which debars one-half of the colonists from admission to the polls'. Fearing another violent outbreak by miners, Haines gave way: in November 1857 the Universal Manhood Suffrage Act promised a vote in Assembly elections to all adult males. Two months later, another radical demand was met when parliamentary terms were reduced from five to three years, allowing unpopular governments to be dismissed with greater speed.

The Haines ministry was finally defeated in February 1858 on details of a bill to equalise the number of electors in each district. The Irish-born draper John O'Shanassy was able to form a government with a large proportion of radical ministers. They succeeded in passing a measure (Act 22 Vic. No. 64) which increased the Assembly from sixty to seventy-eight members, and partly removed the electoral gerry-mander. The property qualification for Legislative Council electors was also reduced.

---

* Duffy himself possessed nothing like the £2,000 in real estate originally necessary to stand for the Assembly, and had to rely on subscriptions from admirers to make up the amount.

Although the political stalemate reduced releases of Crown land, large numbers of subdivisional sales were held during the 1850s. Private owners who had bought broad acres during earlier slumps reaped large profits. S. T. Gill's watercolour of 'Provident Diggers in Melbourne' show men prepared to invest their gold in small blocks of freehold land rather than fritter it away. (La Trobe Collection).

Charles Gavan Duffy, famous Irish nationalist who tried to 'unlock the land' for Victorian miners and farmers. (VPL).

C. J. Don, Melbourne stonemason who became the first artisan elected to Parliament in 1859, died only seven years later. (VPL).

With a wider franchise available for the 1859 elections, the moderately-reformist grocer William Nicholson took office as Premier on a salary of £2,000 a year. Elected to the same legislature was 39-year-old Charles Don, a Scottish-born stonemason, who claimed to be the first artisan elected to any parliament in the British Empire. Don received no salary, for until 1870 only parliamentary officers were paid.* So Don had to work on extensions to Parliament House during the day, and take his seat as a member at night. His stressful life, heavy drinking, and stone-dusted lungs killed him seven years later.

The great political question at the end of the gold decade was how to 'unlock' fertile land from the squatters' grasp and turn it into productive farms. So far the squatters had enjoyed first claim on the land, with 14-year leases or cheap freehold acquisitions. Sheep and cattle roamed over thirty million acres of Victoria—more than half its total area. Only 300,000 acres, equal to one per cent of the squatters' lands, were under cultivation in 1859. Thousands of miners who wanted farms were either clogging the towns with their destitute families, or were panning a meagre living from what alluvial gold remained.

The most significant radical force in the colony was now an unofficial 'Land Convention', set up in Melbourne in 1857 with the dream of settling each family on an agricultural holding of about 320

---

*In 1860, for instance, former Eureka rebel Peter Lalor, MLA, was being paid £800 a year to act as Chairman of Committees.

acres (half a square mile), and thus converting a depressed proletariat into a productive class of smallholders. So blinkered and selfish were the conservative forces that they could not see what enormous social benefits this would bring.

The Convention met each week at the Eastern Market on the south-west corner of Bourke and Exhibition streets (today the Southern Cross Hotel). Here, recalled *Melbourne Punch* editor James Smith in his reactionary later years, 'Any political adventurer who wanted to bring himself before the public had only to mount an empty hay-van, illuminated by cotton wicks burning in tin dishes of tallow, and to commence a noisy harangue on the wrongs of the people'.

Among the orators was a young South Yarra grocer, Graham Berry, who had served on one of the Eureka juries and would later become a radical Premier of Victoria.* Inflamed by the speeches, a Melbourne man named William Osborne set off with several mates to take possession of the squatters' acres by force: they got only as far as a pub at Flemington. James Smith met Osborne again years later, to find he had 'blossomed' into a pillar of bourgeois respectability, sporting a silver-mounted walking stick.

In May 1858 the conventioneers organised a giant rally of about 10,000 marchers, preceded by brass bands playing the Marseillaise, and carrying banners with slogans saying 'When justice is denied, allegiance ceases to be duty'. Passing the Melbourne Club and the now-conservative *Argus* office, the procession gave three groans for squatters, then assembled around Parliament House to chant 'Britons never shall be slaves'.

Over the next two years, the Legislative Council dug in its heels, rejecting all attempts by the Assembly to reform the land laws. Losing patience, thousands of people gathered again at the Eastern Market on 27 August 1860 to hear what their leaders proposed. Graham Berry and Charles Don condemned Governor Barkly for refusing an election on the land question. A 45-year-old Chartist named John Crews, soon to become Prahran's first mayor, organised another mass demonstration outside Parliament House for the following evening, to show support for William Nicholson's new land bill.

After sunset on 28 August, thousands of men, some wearing the red

---

*On 'Black Wednesday', 8 January 1878, when Supply was rejected by a Legislative Council refusing continued payment of MPs, Berry sacked many public servants and judges to conserve funds.

Heated political meetings in the Eastern Market, as depicted in this old engraving, culminated in a riotous attack on Parliament House on the evening of 28 August 1860.

ribbon of revolution, crushed into the yard between the Legislative Assembly and Council, shouting for 'a vote, a rifle, and a farm'. When elderly Gippsland squatter Robert Thomson emerged from the Council building, he was, said the *Age*, 'grappled by the mob, his clothes almost torn off his back, and his hat jumped upon'. Others in the crowd tried to force their way into the parliamentary buildings, and were barely kept out by police reinforcements. The ground was littered with building rubble: some demonstrators began throwing rocks at the police and broke all the Assembly windows. By mid-evening about ninety foot police and six mounted troopers had arrived. Forming a wedge, they made three charges into the crowd, 'using their batons with fearful effect', said the *Argus*. With 'shrieks and cries of terror', the crowd fled through the city. By 10 p.m. it was all over, with eight wounded constables and dozens of demonstrators lying in hospital with severe injuries.

An immediate result of the riot was the passage of an 'Act for Securing the Freedom of the Deliberations of Parliament'. This prohibited public meetings of more than fifty people within a 200-yard radius of Parliament House. Later, when the parliamentary yard was built over, rifle slots were inserted above the main entrance, giving an extensive field of fire down Bourke Street.

This serious clash, a jarring reminder of the Eureka uprising six years before, had unexpected results. The entire middle class of Melbourne united to defend the status quo. As in the riots which followed the police strike of 1923, hundreds of special constables were enrolled to help public order. Nicholson's land bill was totally perverted by the Legislative Council, to allow anyone to purchase up to 640 acres every year. Wealthy squatters rushed to buy this amount of freehold for themselves, and often for every member of their families. Poor men who wanted to become farmers still had little chance to acquire land. Disgustedly, Nicholson resigned in November 1860.

Nicholson was followed as Premier by 39-year-old Richard Heales,

The pioneer Melbourne Club developed into an exclusive gentlemen's club after its present building at 36 Collins Street was built in 1858.

a former coachbuilder and renowned temperance worker. Faced with the recalcitrant Legislative Council, Heales attempted to issue occupation licences to smallholders, in the same way that leases had been issued to squatters. But the ultra-conservative Sir William Stawell, recently the recipient of one of Victoria's first knighthoods, had been appointed Chief Justice: his Supreme Court took pleasure in declaring the proposed smallholders' licences illegal.

The elections of August 1861 swept Heales and his democratic supporters back into power in the Assembly, but their attempts to reform the Legislative Council and to pass land laws which would favour selectors instead of squatters again failed. In 1865, J. M. Grant, who had organised legal defence of the Eureka rebels, managed as Minister for Lands to inaugurate a system of free selection for smallholders, under which they could take ten years to pay £1 an acre for farms of up to 320 acres. This victory, achieved mainly by Melbourne radicals, marked the real beginning of permanent farming communities in Victoria.

The convulsions of the 1850s may have partly democratised the Parliament, but in ordinary life they helped to cement divisions between social classes. After the first careless rapture of the search for gold, where every man appeared to have equal opportunities, property owners dug in solidly to defend their assets, while all around them swirled the mass of immigrants who owned nothing and never would.

An awkward interim period occurred when a number of wealthy but unsophisticated newcomers insisted on joining the ranks of the gentry. Many snubs and disappointments were endured by those trying to force themselves into a 'higher' social sphere. The merchant Patrick Just, writing in 1859, thought that Melbourne's upper class presented 'an incongruous nature', where 'the power exercised by women of refined education and manners is almost neutralised by an amount of vulgarity and ignorance which wealth has forced into the more educated ranks'. The writer observed that the wives of *nouveau-riche* miners 'vie with each other in lavish expenditure, without any reference to good taste or propriety'. He hoped that their numerous social blunders would eventually 'give way before the education and training of their families'.

The wealthy conservative class enjoyed many other resources beyond the reconstituted Legislative Council. For upper-class males, the Melbourne Club changed from a loose association of roistering young squatters into a symbol of exclusivity, particularly when it erected its present building at the eastern end of Collins Street near the new Treasury. The club bought the 88-ft by 313-ft site in 1858 for £8,000, and engaged architect Leonard Terry to design a magnificent Italianate three-storey building costing £21,000. The brothers Abraham and James Linacre set to work immediately, digging a huge basement for kitchen and servants' quarters (today mainly a wine cellar), and erecting above it a spacious vestibule, impressive staircase, extensive dining rooms, library, offices and members' bedrooms. Melbourne's first flushing water closets were installed on all floors.

The club opened with a grand ball on 6 October 1859, when 300 members brought their wives to one of the rare occasions when women were admitted to the hallowed precincts. Servants in full livery offered iced champagne and a twelve-course dinner to leading judges, civil servants, and others who had joined wealthy pastoralists in Melbourne's most exclusive and influential private organisation of the time.

Annoyed by use of the 'blackball' device for keeping people out of the Melbourne Club, a group of lesser merchants, lawyers, politicians and editors decided in 1856 to set up new clubrooms which would admit members (but not women) on 'a basis as popular as it is compatible with respectability'. Their Victoria Club opened that year in a vacant building on the south side of Bourke Street between Queen and William streets, and rapidly filled with members.

The Victoria Club made a bad mistake by appointing a newly-arrived Dublin-born clerk, 34-year-old James McGuire, as its manager. Over the next two years, McGuire embezzled most of the club's funds, forcing it to close its doors. Justice Redmond Barry angrily sentenced McGuire to eight years hard labour, and he was despatched in irons to the Williamstown hulks. After this scandal, no other gentlemen's clubs were able to open in Melbourne until the 1860s.

One of the first effects of the gold rushes was a severe shortage of labour, and increase in wages which (in the minds of conservatives) gave workingmen an inflated idea of their importance. Many merchants had to send their office clerks to perform labourers' work on the wharves: some proprietors even drove their own drays. William Howitt found Melbourne workmen of 1853 'very independent, and very unceremonious', writing that 'they seem to think when they get out here that they may do just as they please'.

*Thomas Smith, first president of
the Operative Stonemasons'
Society, helped to achieve the
Eight-Hour Day for members.*

*James Stephens, Welsh-born
Chartist, led the march of 21
April 1856 which clinched the
Eight-Hour Day.*

A more tolerant Mary Stawell, wife of Chief Justice Sir William Stawell, observed that 'the free and wild life they led made them feel that we were not on different planes, and it first brought home to me what the Brotherhood of humanity might be'. A barely-literate workman named John Goodrich, who set up business as a pawnbroker in Collingwood, wrote home: 'I Feel Confident with The many advantages the Colony holds Out to the Industrus a man may Soon make himself Indepentant of the Graspin Tyrant'.

The idea that 'Jack is as good as his master' was reinforced by the sight of hundreds of well-educated people who failed on the diggings and stumbled back to Melbourne. R. M. Thomas observed in 1853 that 'the lower classes are the masters, and the ladies and gentlemen their servants'. He had seen 'young men of highly respectable connections, acting as messengers . . . wheeling water, selling lemonade, portering on the quay . . . or repairing the roads like common convicts'. Worse still, 'Ladies advertise as washerwomen', while 'gentlemen become as servile as slaves'.

Like these unsuccessful diggers, sections of the working class suffered severely during periodic slumps. Fortunately downturns were usually short-lived. Time and time again the colony was rescued by new injections of gold and hopeful immigrants. In this setting, workers gained enough confidence to form the first permanent trade unions. Fired with passionate idealism for a better life in a new land, they succeeded in winning notable victories on wages and working hours.

About half a dozen reasonably strong unions were in operation by the mid-1850s, mainly among stonemasons, printers, engineers and metal workers. Some unions registered themselves under a new Friendly Societies Act (18 Vic. No. 41, 12 June 1855), so that members could be assisted when they fell ill. Within seven years, John Lascelles, Registrar of Friendly Societies, was able to report that the societies comprised

11,000 members, who paid weekly subscriptions usually of one shilling, and when ill received free medical advice as well as allowances of 10s to 20s a week. The biggest societies were the still-extant Manchester Unity (6,000 members) and Foresters (3,500 members).

Early in 1856, when Melbourne was in the midst of a building boom, skilled stonemasons decided to try for a world first: an eight-hour day, equivalent to a 48-hour week. The union's leaders included James Galloway, a 28-year-old Scottish-born mason; and James Stephens, a 35-year-old Welsh-born mason who had attended one Chartist meeting in Britain when troops shot and killed twenty demonstrators.

Galloway and Stephens, both gold-rush immigrants, met members of their branch at Thomas McVea's Mac's Hotel at 164 Smith Street, Collingwood. On 4 February 1856 they decided to urge the Operative Stonemasons' Society to demand an eight-hour day. The union's president, 33-year-old Englishman Thomas Smith, who had worked with Stephens on the new Houses of Parliament in London, arranged conferences with employers.

Most of the large contractors, who had themselves been masons, and knew what it was like to work all day under the hot Australian sun, readily agreed to the experiment. However, three employers refused to reduce their working week from sixty hours. They were George Cornwall, who was building Melbourne Grammar; W. C. Cornish, builder of Parliament House in Spring Street; and George Holmes, contractor for the new Western Market. The union organised a large demonstration for 21 April 1856, during which employees of recalcitrant contractors downed tools and joined the march. All employers were forced to give way before this united front. During the next few years, the eight-hour principle spread to printing, foundries, and other manufacturing trades. Eight Hours Day became Melbourne's greatest annual procession, until supplanted by so-called 'Moomba Day' in 1954.

Trade unions continued to grow in strength during the late 1850s, about twenty unions organising their trades, and the stonemasons alone achieving 3,000 members. At the urging of Benjamin Douglass, 28-year-old president of the Operative Plasterers' Society, moves began to build a Trades Hall where workmen could hold union meetings, listen to lectures, and offer a lending library for self-educational purposes. In 1858 the government granted an acre of land on the north-east corner of Victoria and Lygon streets. Here a temporary weatherboard building was opened on 29 May 1859, to be replaced two decades later by Joseph Reed's existing stone edifice.

7

New buildings for
public servants

The gold rush threw Victoria's building programme into chaos, delaying many public works at a time when they were more desperately needed than ever. Colonial Architect Henry Ginn grappled as best he could with shortages of labour and materials. When the gold madness made it impossible to obtain reliable tenders from contractors, Ginn was forced into the 'objectionable course' of employing day labour himself at high rates. To get scarce building materials, he broke regulations by paying cash on the spot.

Even so the hapless official could not cope with many urgent demands. In March 1853 La Trobe removed new police and goldfields buildings from his control, allowing officers on the spot to proceed without expert supervision. A few weeks later, the 35-year-old Ginn resigned, complaining that he could not carry on 'with respect or honour'.

No immediate replacement could be found for Ginn. La Trobe called upon David Lennox, a 65-year-old Scot who had designed the first Princes Bridge across the Yarra, and was superintendent of the colony's bridges and roads. Although on the point of retirement, Lennox agreed to assist with other projects. 'The stress was so great that several public works were left off', he later recalled. He found La Trobe 'most anxious' to complete urgent works, but 'there never has been money enough on hand to do this'.

When Lennox bought expensive materials because none other were available, the Auditor-General commented: 'If Mr Lennox is going to spend money in this way, the sooner we get shut of him the better'. Reacting bitterly after long years of arduous service to various Australian colonies, Lennox too threw in his hand, and retired to live at Parramatta.

The next man to tackle the impossible task was James Balmain,

*Captain Charles Pasley,
who at 29 inaugurated
Melbourne's most
important era of
government building.
(VPL).*

former overseer of works. Balmain had shown vigour in designing and quickly erecting the first Government Printing Office in William Street. He was appointed Acting Colonial Architect after the departure of Ginn and Lennox.

Balmain gave evidence to a Legislative Council inquiry into the state of public works late in 1853. He described how La Trobe blithely gave verbal instructions for large works to commence, but Colonial Secretaries Lonsdale and Foster failed to follow up with written details. On the most urgent task of building extensions to Melbourne Post Office to cope with immense gold-rush crowds, 'I think that we had half finished the work before we received the regular instructions to commence', said Balmain.

Balmain gave the inquiry a list of public works in progress at September 1853. Yarra Bend Asylum was being extended to cope with lunatics among gold-rush immigrants. Melbourne Gaol in Russell Street was being enlarged, but so far only one wall was complete. Several corrugated iron buildings were being erected to house additional prisoners at Pentridge stockade. Military officers' quarters in Melbourne had been completed 'in a permanent manner' in corrugated iron, with the addition of a verandah taken from the old post office.

To assist shipping, said Balmain, the quarantine station at Portsea and pilots' quarters at Queenscliff were being built. A gauging shed at the Custom House was complete: although built in timber, 'I look upon it as a permanent structure', he added.

Police Commissioner William Mitchell took advantage of Ginn's and Lennox's departure to build several goldfields lockups, most of which have since fallen down. However, permanent stone police stations were erected in 1853 at Port Melbourne, St Kilda, Brighton and

Melbourne's first purpose-built government offices, on the south-east corner of William and Lonsdale streets (today the Supreme Court site), were thought to be sufficient for many years when erected in 1845. After the gold rush, however, much larger government facilities had to be provided at the other end of town. This anonymous painting shows the

scene in William Street about 1855, with the original Exhibition Building at left. A row of housing for public servants can be seen behind the flagpole. A sentry-box was provided near the corner of the main government offices. The two-roomed weatherboard structure at right was the first Melbourne electric telegraph office. (La Trobe Collection).

Heidelberg, at a cost of £800 each. Prahran police were given a corrugated iron station costing £600.

Builder Samuel Ramsden, who put up the Customs gauging shed and the military barracks in Melbourne, told the inquiry in November 1853 that the labour market had at last begun to stabilise. 'Wages of weak laboring men are not higher, but strong men—men who carry bricks up a ladder, are in demand, and get 20s a day; common laborers get 11s to 12s a day; masons get 33s; and carpenters from 25s to 30s a day', said Ramsden. 'Mechanics will come and ask for work now'.

So when a bulging-eyed young captain of Royal Engineers named Charles Pasley was appointed Colonial Engineer of Victoria and landed in Melbourne about this time, the worst shortages of labour and materials appeared to be over. Pasley successfully reorganised his chaotic department, to the point where he was nominated to the Legislative Council in October 1854, and was even free to march off to war against the Eureka rebels two months later.

Under the new Constitution, Pasley was appointed Victoria's first Minister (Commissioner) of Public Works in 1855, while continuing to act as professional head of the department. He began a vast new building programme, which saw every important government office rehoused in a manner befitting the wealth of the world's great gold centre.

During most of the gold-rush years, the Governor and some of his executive officers occupied a two-storey granite building erected in 1845 on the south-eastern corner of William and Lonsdale streets, where the Supreme Court building stands today. Weatherboard accommodation was provided alongside for civil servants and the Government Printer.

On every working day, La Trobe used to ride from his home at Jolimont through the city to these offices. Governor Hotham was faced with an even longer daily expedition from 'Toorak House' to William Street.

With the construction of Parliament House in the mid-1850s, the centre of gravity for government activities began to shift eastwards. Pasley's new public works programme aimed to accommodate the growing number of civil servants closer to the scene of political activity.

The most urgent of these works was a bigger Government Printing

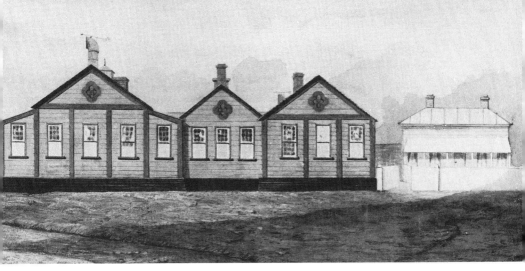

The first Government Printing Office in William Street, originally built for a Governor's Ball in 1853. Government Printer John Ferres lived with his wife Mary and their six children in the cottage at right. (La Trobe Collection).

Office. So many Acts were being approved, so much evidence was pouring out from select committees, and so many official forms were required, that printing facilities in William Street were overwhelmed.

The single-storey weatherboard printery alongside the old government offices was originally run up in time for the Governor's Ball of 24 May 1853. Although the builders worked a night shift and were paid double rates, James Balmain said the 'spirit of emulation begotten in the men' made it one of the cheapest buildings ever erected in Melbourne, costing only 1s 3d per cubic foot. As soon as the dancers moved out, 35-year-old Government Printer John Ferres moved in with his half-dozen presses and hundreds of fonts of hand-set type, to begin printing the 'immense number' of gold licences required. In June 1854, two wings were added, one to enable the *Government Gazette* to be published bi-weekly, the other as a bookbinding department. When the two Houses of Parliament began operating from 1856, the need for printed matter became even greater. 'The work frequently rushed into the office like an avalanche', Ferres later recalled.

Charles Pasley put his most promising draftsman, an 18-year-old Liverpool-born gold immigrant named John Clark, to work on designing a new printing office. A large site was allotted in the paddocks between the Treasury Gardens and Parliament, where Macarthur Street runs today. Between 1856 and 1858 a large functional three-storey stuccoed stone building arose at a cost of £29,000. It still stands today, although hemmed in by later buildings.

Democratic government meant a huge increase in the amount of official printed matter required. Parliamentary bills alone required thousands of pages of hand-set type kept standing. A new Government Printing Office was just as urgently needed as the construction of Parliament itself. The result was this historic building, commenced in 1855 and opened for business on 29 May 1858. (Newsletter of Australasia, September 1859). At right, the building still stands south of Parliament House in Macarthur Street, East Melbourne, although technological change in recent years has forced government printing into other premises.

The Crown Lands Office on the north-west corner of La Trobe and Queen streets, completed in 1857, also housed the beginnings of a National Museum.

The basement was used for Australia's first steam-powered lithographic presses, where thousands of coloured maps and government loan debenture certificates were run off. Upstairs were five huge cylinder presses operated by steam, nine smaller presses worked by hand, and a steam-powered bindery. All told, the equipment could produce 6,600 printed sheets per hour. Just as well, for by 1860, nearly seven million copies of government printing jobs were being produced each year by a staff of several hundred workers.

The next urgent need was a Crown Lands Office, completed in 1857 on the north-west corner of La Trobe and Queen streets. The *Argus* of 25 September 1857 thought that the stuccoed stone building resembled 'one of those solidly respectable family mausoleums in which London merchants used to bury themselves in the reign of Queen Anne'. Nevertheless it was increasingly vital to government operations. During 1859 alone it collected £750,000 from the sale of Crown land, plus £260,000 in occupation licences and stock assessments. The department was also preparing itself for an onslaught of selectors' claims when the land was finally 'unlocked'.

For a time the building housed the Treasury's Assay Section. When that moved, the space was given over to items intended for the first National Museum.

In the absence of any income tax, enlargement of the Custom House in Flinders Street was essential to protect government revenue. By the end of the gold decade, import duties on alcoholic beverages were running at about £1 million a year. Duty on tobacco and cigars netted £170,000 a year. Duties on tea and coffee raised £150,000. Imports of sugar and molasses were levied at £130,000, while duties on opium imports yielded £5,000.

Hugh Childers, related to Earl Grey, became Collector of Customs in Melbourne in 1853 when only 26 years old.

Below: The Custom House in Flinders Street, as rebuilt in 1858. Additions in the early 1870s produced the historic structure which stands today.

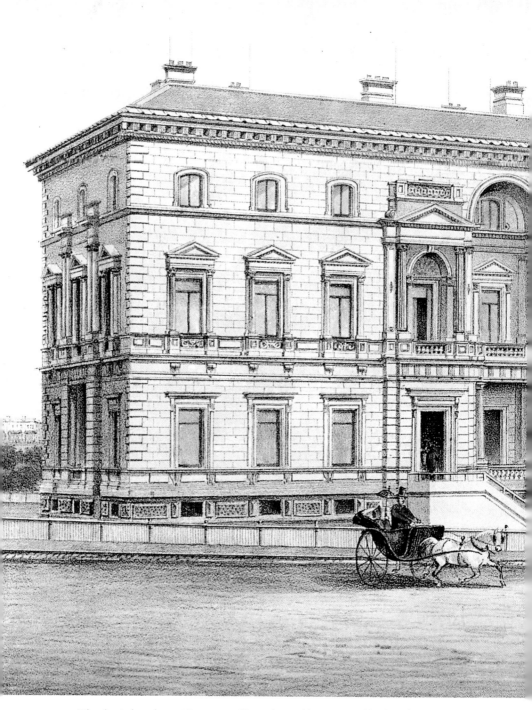

The classical sandstone Treasury Building, designed by 19-year-old John Clark and built between 1859 and 1862 at a cost of about £70,000, still graces Spring Street at the eastern end of Collins Street. Completion of the 200-foot building enabled all Treasury

functions to be moved from the William Street area and centralised close to Parliament House. Ten strong vaults in the basement held gold deliveries, and were later used to store government archives. Lithograph by Francois Cogné (La Trobe Collection).

In addition, port and harbour fees raised more than £25,000 for government coffers; while use of the patent slip at Williamstown yielded £6,000. Imposition of a £10 head tax on Chinese residents contributed more than £50,000 a year. The export duty on gold was also administered by the Customs Department: this yielded £350,000 in 1859. All told, Customs officials raised nearly £2 million each year for government purposes—far more than any other department.

Fortunately the original Custom House, built in brownstone during the 1840s, had a large open area on the Flinders Street frontage. Architects John Knight and Thomas Kemp designed a combined new Custom House and Melbourne Exchange to fill the space in 1854.

Early the following year, Governor Hotham came into bitter conflict with the pudgy Collector of Customs, 28-year-old Cambridge-educated Hugh Childers. Hotham's well-meant attempts to streamline the Customs Department caused Childers to accuse the Governor of 'treachery'. Hotham asked London to dismiss Childers, but was rebuffed by Sir William Molesworth, new Secretary of State for the Colonies.

Exasperated by the delays caused by this confrontation, merchants decided to build their own Melbourne Exchange in Flinders Lane. Knight and Kemp's plans for a new Custom House were abandoned, and the chaotic old methods of clearing imports continued.

By 1858, architect Peter Kerr had completed most of his work on the new Parliament House, and was able to join Knight and Kemp in preparing yet another Custom House design. Fresh tenders were called, and the building was able to open for business in 1859 although still incomplete. During the 1870s it was again redesigned by John Clark, and rebuilt in the form in which it stands today. Clark's reward was to be dismissed during Graham Berry's 'Black Wednesday' purge of 1878.

Melbourne's most impressive official structure of the gold-rush era was a new Treasury Building, which still stands in Spring Street at the eastern end of Collins Street. This noble edifice was designed by government draftsman John Clark when he was only nineteen years old.

The building was urgently needed, for government escorts were still delivering large quantities of gold to Melbourne. At first the precious metal had been kept in banks' strongrooms, but they soon ran out of space. In 1852 La Trobe ordered construction of a large strong-room at the original Treasury building, a three-storey bluestone structure erected in 1851 near the north-west corner of William and Lonsdale streets, diagonally opposite his own offices.

The three-storey building at left, near the north-west corner of William and Lonsdale streets, was the original Treasury of 1851 to which early gold consignments were delivered. Gold escort troopers can be seen in front. Next door was Frederick Cooper's cottage and three-storey bonded warehouse. (S. T. Gill sketch: La Trobe Collection).

A mounted company of the 40th Regiment took over gold escort duties from May 1853 to January 1857, and during that period delivered a total of six million ounces of gold, valued then at £24 million. This huge amount strained even the government's storage resources. To hold the overflow, it leased mayor J. T. Smith's two-storey Georgian stone town-house at today's 300 Queen Street. The house had been built with eight rooms and cellar about 1850, and was enlarged with an extra storey in 1858-9. The original Treasury in William Street has long since disappeared, but Smith's house still stands.

In order to centralise gold storage, and thus reduce the number of troops needed for round-the-clock guards, the government instructed Public Works Commissioner Pasley to prepare plans for the new Treasury in Spring Street.

Among private houses which survive from the gold-rush era, one of the grandest is J. T. Smith's residence at 300 Queen Street, designed by Charles Laing about 1850. Smith, a publican, was mayor of Melbourne seven times between 1851 and 1864. The house was originally two storeys: architect David Ross added the third storey in 1858–9, when the Treasury used the building as an additional gold receiving office. The government purchased the house in 1950 for the Mental Hygiene Authority.

Pasley had been stung by criticism in the *Argus* that government buildings were not being designed with much 'taste, experience or originality'. He gave young John Clark his head: drawings for a beautiful and elaborate Renaissance-style building to be faced in Bacchus Marsh freestone were complete by 1858. Even the *Argus* was impressed, admitting on 30 March 1859 that the building would be 'a material addition to the architectural ornaments of the city'.

The initial contract for constructing foundations, to incorporate large vaults for storing gold, was won by James Lawrence, a Collingwood builder. He used bluestone from Footscray, and charged £30,000 for the work. Walls and freestone ornamentation were constructed by Robert Huckson, an East Melbourne contractor, at a cost of £41,000. Roofing and other work was completed in 1862 by Collingwood carpenters Alexander Cairns and Henry Mills. Clara Aspinall, visiting her barrister brother in Melbourne, thought the construction had been

W. H. Archer, brilliant young Londoner, controlled the statistical work of the Registrar-General's Department.

Professor W. E. Hearn of Melbourne University was rebuffed by politicians when he tried to reform the Civil Service in 1856.

completed in quick time: 'Buildings here spring up like magic when they are set about in good earnest'.

Completion of the new Treasury enabled the central forces of officialdom to move out of the government offices in William Street. The Premier's Department of those days, with its tiny staff, cost only £8,000 a year to run: it occupied the first floor of the new building. On the same floor, in the south wing, was a lavishly decorated and furnished Executive Council chamber, with separate offices for Governor, aide-de-camp and secretary.

On the second floor was located the important Registrar-General's Department, under 37-year-old London-born statistician W. H. Archer and his twelve permanent employees, costing £14,000 a year to run. The Treasurer's Office moved into the ground floor, where its thirty staff cost £33,000 a year. Here too sat the Auditor-General, who was able to inspect every application for government money *before* it was spent, not afterwards as applies today. Outside the building, armed troops guarded the consignments of gold safely stored in the basement vaults: no successful thefts were ever recorded.

What became of the general run of men (but no women in those days) who would occupy these new government buildings and attempt to carry out the directions of Parliament?

The gold rush brought great changes, not all for the better, to the Civil Service. The days had passed when La Trobe could coolly inform his subordinates that they were on call seven days a week, twenty-four hours a day, without extra pay. During the emergencies of the gold rush, La Trobe was forced to appoint anyone who could call himself a 'gentleman', or present a convincing letter of introduction from Britain. Nepotism was rampant, and responsibility almost non-existent. 'A government billet in those days was about the softest thing a fellow could drop into', recalled one former civil servant.

One of La Trobe's worst mistakes had been to appoint an old friend, Major Envidale Campbell of the 90th Foot Regiment, as his private secretary in 1852 and as Victoria's first Registrar-General in 1853. The *Argus* called the appointment 'outrageous . . . wanton destruction of the efficiency of a department for the purpose of securing a snug berth for a friend'. Major Campbell was wise enough to leave most practical operations to his deputy, W. H. Archer, who succeeded to the top post when Campbell died suddenly six years later.

After Governor Hotham's discovery in 1854 that many official 'gentlemen' scarcely began work by 11 a.m., and often finished in mid-afternoon so they could go drinking or promenading, the new Parliament decided in 1856 to appoint a Board of Inquiry. Its chairman was 30-year-old Irish-born William Hearn, first professor of history and political economy at the new University of Melbourne. Hearn's report thoroughly analysed the reasons for bureaucratic ineptitude, and made a number of suggestions for improvement which, if adopted, would have put the Victorian public service ahead of anything else in the world.

'The present condition of the Civil Service is far from satisfactory', Hearn reported. He disclosed that an attempt had been made to introduce entrance examinations, but these were abandoned in 1853. Appointments were now made principally by the head of each department, 'or by the recommendation of his personal friends'.

Hearn proposed formation of a Public Service Board, independent of Parliament, so that 'Public appointments are matters not of private or of political patronage, but of solemn national trust'. Such a board, he thought, would result in 'freedom from the degrading system of patronage', and would 'tend to raise the character of the service'.

One of the board's major tasks, said Hearn, would be to remedy 'shameful deficiencies' in civil servants' spelling, penmanship and arithmetic, through a central system of competitive examination for entry to the service. Those who survived this test should undergo further examination 'on a wider range of subjects' of their own choice.

Even successful candidates should be placed on probation for six months at half salary. This would enable those who suffered from 'faults

Richard Grice, chairman of the Civil Service Royal Commission in 1859, thought public servants should be fined for making mistakes.

of temper, a tendency to insubordination or disagreeable habits' to be weeded out.

For those confirmed in their posts, said Hearn, further advancement should be by merit rather than seniority. Under the old system, 'the industrious official has little hope of promotion; the careless and inefficient little fear of degradation'.

The politicians disregarded Hearn's farsighted recommendations. Nothing further was done until 1859, when the O'Shanassy government appointed a Royal Commission to investigate renewed fears that the Civil Service was 'in an excessive degree over-manned and over-paid'. Chairman of the inquiry was a wealthy 46-year-old squatter and merchant, Richard Grice.

In its report, the Grice Commission defended the number of civil servants employed, on the ground that Victoria had undertaken 'extra-ordinary functions' beyond the normal duties of government in more settled countries. It was 'compelled to conduct the business of a great landowner', construct roads and bridges, form railways and electric telegraphs, establish lighthouses, and so on. These unusual functions accounted for about £2.5 million of the colony's £3.5 million annual government expenditure.

Positive recommendations of the Grice Commission largely repeated Hearn's earlier ideas, but watered them down. Perhaps its strongest new suggestion was that in any case of carelessness by a public servant, his departmental head should inflict 'a small fine', deductible from his next salary payment.

Some of the ideas from both these inquiries were incorporated into the first Public Service Act in 1862. Unfortunately the key proposal of competitive examination was not adopted. Twenty years later, out of 17,500 appointments to the service, only 1,700 persons had won their jobs by passing an elementary qualifying exam. In practice, most appointments remained in the gift of politicians who could influence departmental heads, and that meant the employment of many inferior bureaucrats.

Edward Gilks, a Melbourne engraver, drew this scene of the south end of Elizabeth Street from Flinders Lane about 1863. At left is the solid headquarters of the English, Scottish & Australasian Chartered Bank. Most of the buildings between the bank and Collins Street were erected by importers and merchants. Still on the western side, over Collins Street, can be seen the London Tavern (still standing but altered) and the Age office of that time. The eastern side of Elizabeth Street was largely occupied by agents, drapers, insurance companies, the Clarence Family Hotel, and at extreme right, Isaac Younghusband's huge stone warehouse. (La Trobe Collection).

8

Improvements in
urban streets

'I look upon the City Council as a school of liberty', the shrewd 44-year-old financier Henry Miller told a Legislative Council inquiry into municipal government in 1853. It was true that many Victorian politicians cut their teeth on parochial affairs, but Miller's comment was one of the few kind things said about Melbourne City Council during its formative years.

An early Act of the Legislative Council (16 Vic. No. 18, 3 December 1852) reduced the qualification for voting in City Council elections from £20 to £10 annual occupancy of a dwelling or commercial establishment within Melbourne's wide boundaries. The legislators hoped this would make the corporation more widely representative of small business interests. In practice it allowed a group of city publicans to organise voting among residents, especially those who were Roman Catholics, and control the corporation's expenditure for most of the gold decade.

The publicans' leader was John Thomas Smith, a jovial young man from Sydney who married a daughter of pioneer pub-keeper Michael Pender, and took over several of the family's hotels in Melbourne. During the 1850s and early 1860s, Smith became mayor of Melbourne seven times, winning him the title of 'Melbourne's Dick Whittington'.

The most urgent task facing the corporation was to complete the reconstruction of Melbourne streets to cope with heavy gold-rush traffic. Bitumen or concrete surfacing was unknown in those days, but during the 1840s, a few major streets had been levelled and 'macadamised'—that is, covered with a layer of compressed gravel.

A main drain built by the council down Elizabeth Street was supposed to carry storm water into the Yarra. But one day in 1853, William Kelly stepped out of the Argus Dining Rooms in Collins Street

Once Melbourne streets were macadamised with compressed gravel, it was possible for council workmen to scrape them free of horse manure and rubbish. A sketch by Henry Glover in the mid-1850s.

to see both Elizabeth and Swanston streets 'complete rivers, running in volumes, with a velocity that was startling to look at'. The water roared past, 'empty cases, coffee tins, old hats, sardine boxes, discarded clothes, tattered mats, butchers' offal, and all varieties of household filth careering frantically on its bosom'. Outside the Bank of Australasia, Kelly saw horses 'sunk to their chests in the mire, with their chins patiently resting on the kerbstones'. When the rain stopped, shopkeepers used rickety planks to provide foot crossings for customers.

To cure these problems required large municipal works, which City Surveyor James Blackburn estimated in 1853 would cost about £600,000, or about ten times the council's current revenue. Since future generations would reap the benefit of this expenditure, councillors suggested to the government that they should be allowed to raise an overseas loan, using the security of future rate collections. The government's response was to appoint a committee of inquiry. This produced extraordinary evidence in its report of 28 March 1854.

J. M. Smith, an Elizabeth Street solicitor who came to Melbourne in 1839, attacked the council vigorously. Smith believed that the gold boom had left the best men with 'little leisure to think about political matters'. The publicans' clique, he said, had brought the council into such disrepute that no respectable men were willing to offer for election and 'bear any portion of the odium that attaches to the body'. It would, Smith added, be 'most imprudent' to trust the corporation with

a large sum of borrowed money. Many individual councillors were 'totally unfit' to have any voice in its management.

William Hull of Little Collins Street, who had been a magistrate in Melbourne for ten years, said that when he arrived in 1842, the streets were 'partially broken up, and intersected with stumps of trees, deep holes, and gullies'. Some had been improved since then. But, said Hull, he too was unwilling to trust the existing corporation to spend loan

Lonsdale Street, looking east from Elizabeth Street in this 1863 lithograph by Francois Cogné, remained a comparatively quiet backwater after the gold rush. St Francis, Melbourne's oldest church, still stands at left, on the north-east corner. Behind it can be seen the first stage of the Melbourne Public Library. On the right-hand side, White's Bedding Factory and other small mills are in the space now occupied by the giant Daimaru store. Behind them on the skyline can be seen the original Melbourne Hospital buildings. On the corner of Swanston Street is John Walker's Britannia Hotel. Further up Lonsdale Street is the spire of Wesley Church, still standing today. (La Trobe Collection).

J. T. Smith became mayor seven times between 1851 and 1863. Smith married Ellen Pender, of Irish convict descent: Governor Barkly refused to receive her at Government House.

Edmund FitzGibbon, a gold immigrant of 1852, became Town Clerk after William Kerr's disgrace in 1856, and was appointed chairman of the Board of Works in 1891.

money wisely. He suggested adoption of the procedure followed in England, where salaried commissioners were appointed by the government to carry out all public works, free from political interference.

The pioneer John Pascoe Fawkner told the inquiry that the existing City Council had 'altogether lost the confidence and good opinion of the public'. City publicans had 'manipulated' the polls to win a majority. Since there was no secret ballot, it was easy to bully and threaten opposition candidates and voters. When a respectable merchant, Henry Mortimer, stood for office, the mob had hoisted a dripping bullock's head over the polling place. If large loans were raised, said Fawkner, he was sure that councillors would 'appropriate the public money for private purposes'. Already they had spent £12,000 on a lavish new town hall: 'monstrous while the city wanted a supply of water'.*

An Italian-born financier, Antonio Gabrielli, employed by the secretive Rothschild group†, gave evidence to the Legislative Council inquiry. Gabrielli gave the colonists a few brutal lessons in international finance. Low-interest loans for new countries, he said, were difficult to raise. In Britain, six per cent interest 'would be considered a very good investment', but because of the risky nature of colonial investment, the

*James Blackburn estimated before the gold rush that the town hall should cost £2,600. By the time it was ready for meetings in 1854, it had cost £26,000.

†Some historians have doubted this, but an authorised history of the Rothschilds mentions the 'Gabriel' family as being important in its railway schemes.

regular rate of interest was from ten to fifteen per cent. Nor was it possible to raise much money locally: 'This community, as a body, is too much engrossed in private enterprise . . . people here find better returns for their capital in building and commercial undertakings'.

The need in Melbourne was certainly great, said Gabrielli. Comparatively little had been done towards making improvements or comfort: 'There are no roads, no accommodation, no public buildings of any importance'. But there was a solution. If the corporation spent a large proportion of a loan on building markets, abattoirs and the like, this 'would give a permanent large revenue to the town, and consequently greater security'. Gabrielli coyly suggested that if the rates were raised by only sixpence in the pound, this would yield extra revenue of £25,000 a year, sufficient to pay the interest.

In the end, the government agreed to guarantee Gabrielli's loans of £525,000 to Melbourne and £200,000 to Geelong. The interest rate was publicised as only six per cent, but the bonds were issued to Gabrielli at 95% of their face value, yielding him a total of eleven per cent interest in the first year.

Within a few days of issue, the bonds were selling in Melbourne at a four per cent premium, giving Gabrielli an immediate windfall profit of about £25,000. William Howitt wrote scornfully that Gabrielli had been able to 'sell this scrip at a premium to the very merchants who should have done all this themselves . . . instead of letting their money lie, as gratuitous deposits, in the banks'. More than that, Gabrielli 'has returned home with the grateful acknowledgements of the Melbourne public for easing them of this sum, and pronounced by the newspapers as a public benefactor'.

Wasteful though these arrangements were, the immediate result of the Gabrielli loan was a huge increase in civic works throughout Melbourne. Arrival of the money coincided with a marked drop in goldfields output: many unsuccessful diggers made their way back to Melbourne and probably would have starved or left for overseas had not immediate work been available on the roads.

By June 1854 William Howitt was able to report that 'Mr Gabrielli's money has done miracles. Hundreds of men are in full employ, actively blasting stone along the river, carting it into town, breaking it, and laying the streets'. Such labour was particularly suitable for strong men with mining experience.

*Henry Burn painted this exceptionally clear view of Melbourne from Princes Bridge in
1862. At left is the just-completed Princes Bridge Hotel (today Young & Jackson's).
Across Swanston Street can be seen the tower of the original Melbourne Town Hall.
Coming south down Swanston Street was Damman's tobacco shop, the Bank of Victoria,
and the Prince of Wales Hotel on the corner of Flinders Lane. In the middle of the picture,
the twin-towered structure was St Paul's School, opened in 1857. It adjoined St Paul's
Church, predecessor of today's St Paul's Cathedral. On the right side of St Paul's was
the residence of the Anglican Rev. Septimus Chase, followed by a series of boarding
houses, with Scots Church on the horizon. The square building in front of St Paul's was
the original City Morgue and Registry of Births, Deaths and Marriages. To the right was
the Melbourne & Suburban Railway Company's city terminus. (La Trobe Collection).*

William Kelly saw Melbourne 'emerging from the grub state to that of the resplendent butterfly'. Macadamised roads on solid foundations began 'creeping out from the centre all round to the suburbs'. Bluestone gutters and kerbs were constructed in the busiest streets. Flush with money, the council even had portable metal bridges built to enable pedestrians to cross gutters during floods. Kelly thought the bridges served mainly to obstruct the water—Melbourne he said could boast of not one 'Bridge of Sighs' but hundreds. More successful were mechanical street-cleansing machines with rotating brushes, imported from London to sweep horse manure from macadamised roads.

Totally disregarded, however, was a plea by Peter Kerr, president of the new Institute of Victorian Architects, for better overall planning of the city's expenditure. Kerr was more than a century ahead of his time, telling an Institute meeting in 1856 that 'If we are to have an architectural city, with its terraces, arcades, crescents, squares, gardens and fountains, with any pretension to uniformity, style and subordination to one grand system and effect, then must a special Department of the State exercise a complete surveillance over all the principal localities'.

With the completion of works in central Collins Street, the area became a fashionable meeting place. 'Collins Street amazed me', wrote Clara Aspinall on her arrival in March 1858. 'Here all things are conducted calmly, quietly, and harmoniously. Beautiful ladies may be seen gliding out of one shop into another, bright with the hope of meeting some of their fair friends, who, like themselves, have come in from the suburbs'.

Collins Street also became the spot to meet eligible men: 'Beaux of the most elegant description may be seen from two to four o'clock in the afternoon marching up and down', wrote the visitor. At this fashionable time there was 'great display' of gay equipages on the newly-smoothed road: 'Barouches drawn by milk-white steeds or magnificent bays; mail-phaetons, pony carriages, and American buggies of every description'.

But, warned Clara Aspinall, few ladies ever ventured into other streets, for there an objectionable 'American, go-ahead spirit' held sway. The western hill of Bourke Street, wrote William Kelly, was full of noisy squatters, horse dealers, and auctioneers' touts, 'all either vomiting smoke or swallowing brandy'. Here was George Kirk's original horse bazaar, bought by squatter W. C. Yuille at the time of the first gold rushes, and leased to a noted Irish-born huntsman, G. J. Watson. Kelly was almost knocked off his feet by 'crowds of half-broken horses' and bullock teams 'charging under the thongs and curses of their semi-civilised drivers'.

By 1856 the corporation had spent £400,000 of its Gabrielli loan. Of this, about £150,000 represented expenditure on materials—£86,000 for road metal, £34,000 for flagstones, £19,000 for rubble, and £12,000 for

Peter Davis, reformist mayor in
1856-7, struggled vainly against the
'publican clique' in Melbourne City
Council.

Dr Richard Eades, an 1852
immigrant, became mayor in 1859-
60. He read the Riot Act when
protesters stormed Parliament House.

bluestone pitchers. Major streets constructed, and the amounts spent on
building them, were:

	£		£
King Street	18,000	Napier Street, Fitzroy	6,000
St Kilda streets	13,000	Swanston Street	6,000
Elizabeth Street	11,000	Victoria Street	6,000
La Trobe Street	10,000	Russell Street	6,000
Flinders Street	10,000	Spencer Street	5,500
William Street	9,000	Madeline Street, Carlton	5,500
Lonsdale Street	9,000	Victoria Parade	4,000
Spring Street	9,000	Wellington Parade	3,000
Port Melbourne streets	8,000	Market Street	3,000
Gisborne Street	8,000	Bourke Street	3,000
Exhibition Street	7,000	Lygon Street, Carlton	2,600
Collins Street	6,000	Flinders Lane	2,500

A notable feature of this list was that the highest expenditure
occurred in King Street, where merchants were erecting substantial
bluestone warehouses; and in St Kilda, where the same merchants were
building their private mansions.

But hidden penalties often accompany borrowed money. With cash
so plentiful, jobbery and corruption became commonplace. As early as
19 October 1854, the *Age* began criticising the 'clique of publicans' on
the City Council who were bringing it into 'profound contempt'.
Instead of 'honorably discharging the duties of their trusteeship', they
were merely enriching their friends, squandering public funds, and
indulging in nepotism.

A. Robertson's painting of 1853 from Flagstaff Hill gives a good idea of what a low-rise city Melbourne was just after the gold discoveries. On the left horizon is St Peter's Church, Eastern Hill. Directly above the hay wagon is St John's School, on the north-west corner of La Trobe and Elizabeth streets. (La Trobe Collection).

The *Argus* attacked Cr Robert Bowden, a Spencer Street merchant, who arranged with other councillors to have construction of their streets given priority, thus 'obtaining as much as possible of the public money to increase the value of the properties of their immediate friends and supporters'. An unusually honest Collins Street auctioneer, Cr Peter Davis, tried to prohibit the appointment of councillors' relatives to corporation positions, but his motion was defeated.

A further Legislative Council inquiry of 1857 chaired by J. P. Fawkner concluded that in the expenditure of Gabrielli funds, 'a large amount of recklessness and want of judgment characterized the conduct of the City Council'.

During this period of financial mismanagement, the only person punished was an extraordinary character named William Kerr. Born in Scotland, Kerr had started the *Argus* newspaper in Melbourne in 1846 at the age of thirty-four. He was bankrupted by libel suits, but continued as a radical editor until appointed Town Clerk by his publican friends in 1851.

When the Gabrielli money became available, the council voted to pay half the cost of importing heavy flagstones from Caithness in Scotland: merchants and shopkeepers paid the remainder so that footpaths in front of their establishments could be constructed. As Town Clerk, William Kerr accepted their payments, but failed to account to the City Treasurer for some of the money. Instead, he used it to help finance an insurance company in which he held shares. Cr Davis investigated, and insisted on Kerr's resignation. The only job which

Kerr's friends could now find for him was as station-master at Sunbury, where he died three years later.

So the Gabrielli money, although it did much good, continued in part to be frittered away. Giving evidence to a parliamentary inquiry in 1863, Town Clerk Edmund FitzGibbon pointed out that during the gold boom, 'road metal cost 40s per cubic yard, it now costs 4s 11d'. Labour costs had been extortionate: 'A man with a horse and cart then earned 40s per day, now from 9s 6d to 12s. Kerbing, which cost 30s, now costs 4s 6d; and earthwork, which was then paid for at 8s per yard, can now be done for 1s.'

Interest costs on the Gabrielli loans were also huge in nineteenth-century terms. FitzGibbon said that interest, running at about £20,000 a year, absorbed fully two-thirds of all city rate payments. Geelong paid a further £8,000 a year interest on its loan. By the time the loans were extinguished in 1875, Melbourne paid more than £320,000 in interest, as well as having to repay the principal by means of special government grants.

During the first years of the gold decade, Melbourne streets were lit in a flickering fashion by a couple of hundred sperm oil lamps. Yet Sydney enjoyed the benefits of gas lighting since 1841. What was the matter with Melbourne enterprise? *Melbourne Punch* lamented that

> For many weary years alas!
> We looked and longed in vain for gas.

A gas service for Melbourne had been proposed in 1850, when the entrepreneurial Rev. John Allen resigned as secretary of Melbourne Hospital so he could organise the Melbourne Gas & Coke Company. Labour shortages during the gold rush interrupted the company's plans, until William Westgarth, one of the main promoters, went to England in 1853 and signed up Alexander Smith on a five-year contract. Smith, then only twenty-nine, and one of the numerous race of Scottish engineers, had successfully built gas works in Devon.

Even before his arrival in April 1854, Smith condemned a one-acre freehold site the company had bought at the western end of Collins Street. The directors applied for a free grant of five swampy acres on the Yarra below Batman's Hill. Instead, the government leased the land for twenty-one years at nominal rent, on condition that the company install a dock and bridgeworks.

*Ambrose Kyte, wealthy
Fitzroy landlord, was
chairman of the first successful
competitor to Melbourne Gas Co.*

*Scottish-born engineer
Alexander Smith built
Melbourne's first public gas
works in the mid-1850s.*

By the end of 1854, construction had reached the stage where the foundation stone could be laid. The usual town procession was organised, but the 40th Regimental Band was suddenly withdrawn and despatched to take part in storming the Eureka stockade. The remaining police, shareholders, contractors and masons silently continued the march in heavy rain, to watch Mayor J. T. Smith tap the stone into place.

In mid-1855, the massive retort house, purifying house and gasometer were complete, and a tall brick chimney was steadily rising. Total cost of these works was estimated at £40,000. A further £6,000 was spent in cutting a dock from the Yarra, 254 ft long by 54 ft wide, allowing colliers drawing nine feet of water to unload coal direct to the retort.

A curious ceremony to celebrate completion of the 195-ft chimney took place on 24 October 1855. More than twenty guests were lifted to the top 'by means of a small steam engine', to be entertained by directors in a temporary apartment built for the purpose. Later, photographer G. W. Perry and his bulky equipment were hoisted to the top to take photographs of shipping along the Yarra.

Meanwhile the City Council's beautiful new streets were being dug up again to allow installation of gas mains. Alexander Smith planned these on a grandiose scale, with 24-inch pipes able to transmit nine times as much gas as the old Sydney mains. Nineteen miles of pipes were imported, and a tunnel driven through Batman's Hill to reach Spencer Street. By the end of 1855 most of central Melbourne had been connected.

A week before Christmas, Governor Hotham lit the first fire in the retort. He caught a chill doing it, and died on 31 December 1855, the day before the gas was turned on. The following night, newspapermen wrote their reports under hissing gaslight for the first time. Public celebrations were postponed for a week because of Hotham's death, but

then burst forth at the Criterion Hotel with a gas-fired 'large star and a horizontal bar studded with jets', while outside Michael Cashmore's drapery in Elizabeth Street there blazed 'a crown in jets of gas'.

For Melburnians, however, gas supply did not come cheaply. In England the average price to consumers was 7s 6d per thousand cubic feet, but in Melbourne the company began by charging 25s per thousand. Alexander Smith blamed the difference on large establishment costs, smaller market, and the high price of imported coal. Labour costs were also much higher, for in Melbourne the men had already achieved an eight-hour working day, as against ten hours in Britain. Furthermore, British labourers received only 12s a week, but in Melbourne, said Smith, they had to be paid the same amount *per day*.

Painting by an unknown artist with the initials 'M. G. W.' shows the original Melbourne Gas Company's gasworks about 1856. The location was swampy ground below Batman's Hill in West Melbourne, where coal and timber could be landed cheaply from lighters using the Yarra River. The 130-foot retort house had a chimney 195 feet high, and the gasometer was 80 feet high. Nineteen miles of piping delivered gas to most of the city area from 1 January 1856. (La Trobe Collection).

Despite these costs, Melbourne establishments soon came to regard gas lighting as essential. In March 1856 the *Argus* surveyed the city, and disclosed the following number of lights installed (number of establishments in brackets):

Hotels (96 establishments)	1,617 lights
Places of amusement (7)	452
Merchants and grocers (51)	419
Drapers (36)	363
Churches (6)	215
Butchers (15)	159
Stationers (8)	140
Restaurants (11)	119

Ironmongers (7)	119
Tobacconists (14)	114
Jewellers (13)	104
Shoemakers (17)	99
Chemists (15)	80
Pastrycooks (9)	67
Fancy goods (6)	67
Tailors (5)	48

With the addition of a few smaller shops, the survey gave a total of more than 4,300 gas lights already installed.

The gas company was also negotiating with the City Council to install street lamps, assisted no doubt by the fact that five councillors were directors of the company. Other councillors raised some objections on costs, but agreement was finally reached in 1856 to import 300 iron lamp posts and light them each night for a cost of £18 per lamp per year. Melbourne streets were lit by gas for the first time on 10 August 1857: the following year another forty-eight lamps were erected on the Yarra wharves. On grounds of public safety, the *Argus* was ecstatic: 'We want more policemen, and they must be made of gas', it proclaimed.

The company's first extensions beyond the city were made eastwards in 1856, to light up the new Parliament House, St Peter's Church, Chalmers Church, Victoria Parade, Lygon Street in Carlton, Brunswick Street in Fitzroy, and a few main streets in Collingwood.

By the next parliamentary inquiry in July 1857, the gas company was already making good profits, and planning further extensions of the mains. Alfred Priestley, company secretary, told the parliamentarians that annual income was now £27,000 a year but working expenditure only £13,000. This allowed dividends to be doubled from four to eight per cent, and the price of gas to be lowered by ten per cent.

Pleased with this progress, Parliament approved raising an extra £150,000 in share capital, to finance further expansion to eastern and southern suburbs. Forty miles of 12-inch pipes were ordered from England, and the company's West Melbourne plant expanded.

By January 1858, Wellington Parade was being dug up, and gas mains were snaking out along Bridge Road to serve most of Richmond. At Church Street the mains turned south, crossing the river with a nine-inch pipe to reach as far as Prahran Town Hall.

Another main was laid over Princes Bridge and along St Kilda

Road, enabling street lights to be installed, and both South Melbourne and St Kilda lit up. The company laid smaller pipes along Toorak Road and in North Melbourne, thus covering most of the inner suburbs by 1859. To the north, Flemington, Brunswick and Coburg (including Pentridge Gaol) were supplied.

At the end of 1859, the Melbourne Gas Co. controlled 160 miles of piping, was supplying gas for 800 street lamps and 22,000 lights in buildings, and was paying a 12% dividend. Alfred Priestley told another parliamentary inquiry in March 1860 that the company now had nearly 2,800 individual customers, about half of them in Melbourne itself.

This remarkably fast spread of a profitable gas service naturally inspired competition. Rev. John Allen, the company's original secretary, formed the Collingwood, Fitzroy & District Gas Co. early in 1859. He persuaded Ambrose Kyte, a wealthy 38-year-old Irish-born merchant, who owned about thirty shops and dwellings in the area, to act as chairman. With this kind of support, the necessary capital was quickly raised. 'I sold an amazing quantity of shares in an unprecedentedly short time', Allen told the 1860 inquiry.

Allen and Kyte engaged an English engineer named Stephen Hutchinson, who had operated gas works in Plymouth and London before joining the gold rush in 1852. Hutchinson erected a retort on the south-eastern corner of Smith Street and Reilly Street (now Alexandra Parade), Collingwood, and succeeded in supplying gas to many areas which had not already been covered by the Melbourne Gas Co.

Perturbed by competition, the larger company immediately reduced the price of its gas to 17s 6d, and offered to connect households free of charge. Even this did not knock out the competition. The Collingwood company was able to continue and make good profits, supported by fierce suburban loyalties which were now developing.

Similarly in South Melbourne, the local council decided that it preferred the business to go to local men. In 1861 it authorised 33-year-old hardware dealer John Danks to form the South Melbourne Gas Company and build a gasometer on the south-west corner of Graham and Pickles streets, Port Melbourne. Danks Street nearby still commemorates this successful venture.

Many other local gas companies were formed as suburbs continued to grow in population and financial strength during the 1860s. Until the coming of natural gas supplies, their gasometers remained prominent landmarks all over Melbourne.

Opposite Melbourne Hospital, John Black's Tattersall's Horse Repository took up much of the south side of Lonsdale Street between Swanston and Russell streets. This S. T. Gill engraving of 1853 shows the new structure, occupying 66 by 360 feet. Along the covered rides were carriage stands, stalls and loose boxes accommodating 200 horses. Above were haylofts and granaries, covered by a corrugated iron roof 35 feet above ground level. At the Little Bourke Street exit were blacksmiths' forges, veterinary stalls and

harness rooms. In Lonsdale Street, William Disher's three-storey Tattersall's Hotel was built alongside in the mid-1850s. William Kelly wrote that the whole establishment 'impressed every visitor with wonder and admiration'. The structure was considerably altered in 1858 to become the American Hippodrome circus and concert hall. In 1860 it was changed to the Prince of Wales Theatre and in 1863 to the Lyceum Theatre. Today the area is occupied mainly by small Greek shops and restaurants. (La Trobe Collection).

9

Melbourne's horse and buggy age

It was one thing to give Melbourne roads a solid gravel surface, quite another to keep them clean. Dozens of bullock teams and thousands of horses thronged the streets: their manure had to be constantly swept up by council workers and transported to dumping grounds on the city's outskirts. No picture of Melbourne in the 1850s would be complete without the realisation that this kind of pollution hung constantly in the air. Residents simply accepted it as part of life, along with the stench from their own privies.

By 1860 there were more than 70,000 horses in rural areas of Victoria, compared with only 16,000 a decade earlier. No figures are available for horses stabled in Melbourne and suburbs, but at least another 20,000 were used by Melburnians in 1860. To help care for these animals, 130 full-time blacksmiths and farriers, and 70 saddlers, conducted business in the city and inner suburbs alone.

With the spread of suburban settlement, hire services were established to help horseless people towards their destinations. Clara Aspinall described small hansom cabs which could carry one or two people, but these were often expensive. 'I have seen ladies paying a pound for a cab to take them to pay a ceremonious visit', she wrote. According to the *Argus*, the usual rate in 1856 was 4s a mile. The newspaper described the cries of cab-drivers touting for business in Swanston Street: 'emrld-ill' (Emerald Hill), 'pooran-pooran' (Prahran), and 'S'killed-'er' (St Kilda).

Among wealthier people, William Kelly found in 1857 that private equipages were 'decidedly on the increase'. Lumbering English coaches and landaus had gone out of fashion. Melburnians now preferred light American buggies: despite their 'slim, spider-like, and apparently unsubstantial construction', they enabled owners to traverse difficult roads with comparative ease.

Henry Glover's sketch shows the crowded omnibus which plied between Bourke Street and Prahran from 1853. In the background are the Bull & Mouth Hotel, and Cobb & Co's first booking office. Gentlemen of the town parade at right.

Omnibuses were the cheapest method of horse transport, plying between the city and most nearby suburbs for 6d to 2s 6d per passenger. They were 'the most draughty things imaginable', wrote Clara Aspinall, but women were often 'thankful to get into one of them after an exhausting walk into the town'.

Typical of these suburban services was a two-horse omnibus which plied between Prahran and Melbourne from 1853. It started from the Duke of York Hotel in Prahran at 8.30 a.m. and returned from Melbourne at 5 p.m., charging 5s for the two-way trip. A competing service established in 1857 by Sol Davis charged only 2s for a return ticket.

By 1860, eighteen competing omnibus companies operated services between Bourke Street and the suburbs. An official timekeeper used a whistle to ensure regular departures and reduce congestion.

The most prominent omnibus proprietors in the city were F. B. Clapp in Bourke Street and William Brewer in Collins Street. Four

Only because of the gold rush do we get this action-packed painting of the Liardet family's four-in-hand coach named 'Defiance', which normally ran a service between Melbourne and Port Melbourne. In 1851, the Liardet sons thought they could make more money by

taking gold-seekers to Ballarat. William Strutt sketched the scene, but wrote 'I do not think the coach ran long: the roads were too heavy and rough for such a vehicle'. (Victorian Parliamentary Library).

coachmen operated from Collingwood—Patrick Donohoe, John Lambell, James Shannon, and Josiah Williams. Most other suburbs had only one resident cab proprietor, operating anything up to twenty or thirty runs per day. St Kilda proprietor Richard Edwards offered the best service, using several 'buses in 1860 to make fifty runs a day.

Coach services from Melbourne to the diggings began almost immediately after the discovery of gold. Seeing the possibility of large profits, young Frank Liardet, son of a Port Melbourne pioneer publican, took the family's four-horse English coach off the suburban run to Melbourne in 1851, and attempted to begin a passenger service to the diggings. The roads were so frightful that the heavy carriage often became bogged, and the service was soon discontinued.

Other attempts to start passenger services out of Melbourne in 1852 met a similar fate. William Kelly and a friend tried one coach, and found that 'it required all the muscular powers of our arms to retain our places'. He described the 'violent oscillation of these oblong vehicles . . . the fearful way in which they plunge and dip in uneven ground, and the heart-heaving bounds they cause in clearing blind drains and broken tree-limbs'. Passengers who had paid exorbitant fares 'were at least three times on every stage politely asked to alight and walk hip deep through the mire'.

A number of young Americans who emigrated in 1853 to seek their fortunes in Victoria were able to revolutionise coaching. Foremost among them was George Mowton, who established a branch of the famous Adams 'American Express' Line of Wagons in Collins Street in 1853.

Another immigrant on the same ship was 23-year-old Massachusetts-born Freeman Cobb, who had worked for the Adams company in California. Cobb decided to strike out for himself, and established his first Cobb & Co. office in Bourke Street, assisted by three other young Americans named John Peck, James Swanton, and John Lamber. The firm imported the first lightweight Concord coaches to be seen in Australia. Instead of resting on solid axles like the old-style coaches, the Concord bodies rocked on leather 'thoroughbrace' supports, easing passengers' agony over potholed roads.

As gold immigrants continued to pour in, plenty of passenger business was available between Port Melbourne and Melbourne, where Cobb began operations along City Road in July 1853. Six months later

*Although lame, the young American
Freeman Cobb helped many
Victorians to travel by starting Cobb
& Co. in Melbourne in 1853.*

*John Peck, 23-year-old Connecticut
man who helped Cobb begin a coach
service from Melbourne to the diggings
in January 1854.*

the partners inaugurated services between Melbourne, Bendigo and
Castlemaine, flying along rough bush tracks past heavier vehicles
bogged on the main roads.

Cobb himself sold out and returned to America in 1856. The
business was bought by another Massachusetts man, 23-year-old F. B.
Clapp, who was already operating suburban services in Melbourne. By
1859, Clapp had built Cobb & Co. into Victoria's biggest mail contractor.
Two years later he sold the profitable firm to a 33-year-old Scottish-
born carrier, Alexander Robertson, who continued to run Cobb & Co.
in partnership with Canadian-born John Wagner for many years. The
name Cobb & Co. became a legend during the rapid expansion of
coastal and inland towns after the 1860s.

In a colony of frequent rain, roads and bridges became matters of
passionate concern for people who depended on getting perishable
goods quickly to market, or who wished to visit business and personal
acquaintances.

Victoria's population expanded so rapidly during the gold decade
that the problem of providing decent roads to all areas within reasonable
time was simply unsolvable. Once away from Melbourne's central
streets, much improved through the Gabrielli loan, most roads soon
deteriorated into mere tracks and bogs.

A partial solution was found with the imposition of tolls, based on
the principle that those who used roads should pay for their improvement. By the mid-1850s, toll gates had been erected on all main outlets

A typical mixture of city enterprises is shown in this S. T. Gill lithograph of part of the north side of Collins Street, between Queen and Elizabeth streets, in 1853. The building at left was occupied by Smith & Adamson, seedsmen and florists. Ground floor of the centre building was occupied by Robert H. Adams's American Express Line of Wagons, one of which is seen ready to start for the goldfields. Upstairs was the P. & O. shipping company, soon to move to the south end of Elizabeth Street. Its offices were taken over by the Lloyds Association of Underwriters, gold-buyer Edward Khull, and the short-lived Diggers' Bank. The premises at right were soon occupied by Sanders & Levy, clothiers; and F. P. Hunt, hat manufacturers. (La Trobe Collection).

The toll gate in St Kilda Road, about a mile from the city, yielded £24,000 in revenue between 1853 and 1856, paying most of the cost of constructing the road.

from Melbourne. One-horse gigs and buggies were allowed through for 6d; loaded drays for 1s. Revenue derived from metropolitan tolls during the four years 1853-6 comprised:

Mount Alexander Road, and other roads to goldfields	£92,000
Melbourne Central District	£54,000
Sydney Road	£17,000

This income covered nearly half the cost of improving urban roads during the same period.

Along outlets to the goldfields, toll bars were erected at Flemington and Keilor in 1854. In Sydney Road, tolls were exacted at Brunswick, Campbellfield and Kinlochewe. In the Central District, nine toll gates were installed, in St Kilda Road, Deep Creek Road, Pascoe Vale Road, Punt Road, Bridge Road, City Road, Victoria Street, Studley Road, and Plenty Road. By the end of the gold decade, another toll gate installed at Heidelberg was collecting £1,700 a year; while one at Eltham raised £200 a year.

Responsibility for constructing main roads around Melbourne at first rested with the Central Road Board, established in February 1853 by Legislative Council Act 16 Vic. No. 40. Dr Francis Murphy, 44-year-old Irish-born surgeon and squatter, was appointed president of the new body.

The Legislative Council held an inquiry into the progress of roads at the end of 1853. Dr Murphy said that in deciding how to spend the

£450,000 allotted by the government for all roads, his board examined the amount of traffic already carried, and the amount of new country which would be opened up. Mount Alexander and Sydney roads were considered the most important, but cost up to £9,000 a mile to construct because of the great number of cuttings and bridges required. St Kilda Road was cheaper, but even here contractors had submitted tenders ranging from £4 to £45 per running yard.

George Harris, Inspector-General of Roads, told the inquiry that 'all great lines of communication' had to be properly constructed, using a foundation of eight-inch bluestone pitchers. Above that was laid bluestone broken to 2.5-inch gauge, to allow drainage, with finer stone compressed to form a hard surface. The depth of stone should be eighteen inches at the centre, sloping down to about nine inches at the edges.

Labour costs were high. Harris claimed that English navvies could remove about ten cubic yards of soil per day from the route. In Melbourne, however, 'one-half of that quantity might be taken as the extreme amount of what they could do'. In breaking up road metal with a sledgehammer, 'the utmost that the best man could do here' was about two yards of hard stone.

One of the Road Board's first works was to macadamise most of Bridge Road, Richmond, from the end of Wellington Parade. This was extremely convenient for president Murphy, who lived in the delightful house 'Mayfield' on the Yarra River at Collingwood. Voters also approved his efforts: he switched from the Legislative Council to the first Assembly, and remained its Speaker for fifteen years, with an allowance of £1,000 a year.

By 1857, the Road Board had spent £1,666,000 in forming or completing 340 miles of road. The main items included:

Ballarat Road (Melbourne end)
  2 miles formed; cost £8,000; 10 bridges built, cost £3,700.

Bridge Road/Hawthorn Road
  3 miles formed, cost £23,000; 3 bridges being built.

Brighton Road
  7 miles formed, cost £58,400.

Bulleen Road
  3 miles formed, cost £19,000.

Church Street, Richmond
  1 mile formed, approaches to bridge made, cost £10,000.

City Road, South Melbourne
  2 miles formed, cost £38,200; 1 bridge built.

Dandenong Road
  2 miles formed from junction with Brighton Road, cost £14,000.

Deep Creek Road, Bulla
  6 miles formed, cost £31,000; 2 bridges built (Bulla and Sunbury), cost £6,000.

Geelong Road, Footscray
  10 miles formed, including 2.5 miles planked road, cost £45,000.

Heidelberg Road
  5 miles formed, cost £20,000; 3 bridges built, cost £12,000.

This first timber bridge across the Moonee Ponds Creek at Flemington took gold-seekers on the road to the diggings. Sketched from the south-east by William H. Jarrett, 1851. (Mitchell Library).

Mount Alexander Road
> 70 miles formed, including 5 miles metalled, 3 miles planked, cost £690,000; 23 bridges built, cost £39,000.

Pascoe Vale Road
> 3 miles formed, cost £10,600; 2 bridges built, cost £2,000.

Plenty Road
> 4 miles formed, cost £45,000; 1 bridge built, cost £900.

Point Nepean Road
> 8 miles formed, from Brighton towards Cheltenham, cost £8,000; 2 bridges built, cost £3,000.

Punt Road, Richmond
   1 mile formed, cost £7,100.

Sydney Road (Melbourne end)
   37 miles formed, cost £258,000.

Toorak Road, Prahran
   3 miles formed, cost £36,000.

Victoria Street, Collingwood
   1.5 miles formed, cost £9,100.

Late in 1857 the Central Road Board was abolished, its functions being incorporated into a new Board of Land and Works. This body centralised all government activities concerned with roads, bridges, public works, Crown lands, survey, railways, sewerage, water supply, and electric telegraphs.

The first Inspector-General of Roads and Bridges under the new regime was Thomas Higinbotham, a 39-year-old Irish engineer who emigrated to Melbourne in 1857 to join his better-known brother, editor, politician and later Chief Justice, George Higinbotham.

During 1859-60, Thomas Higinbotham connected unmetalled sections of Dandenong Road at a cost of £10,000; and spent £4,000 on extensions to Nicholson Street, Fitzroy.

Higinbotham found that he had to spend more than £100,000 on repairing faulty work performed by fraudulent contractors during the 1853-6 period. Sydney Road was the worst: inspectors discovered that its foundations had been laid with 'a sort of rotten granite', and spread with road metal in 'one coat of about four inches in thickness'.

More than good roads were needed to tie the scattered suburbs to the metropolis. Melbourne was surrounded by watercourses almost uncrossable by horse traffic: the Yarra River winding to the south, east and north-east; the Plenty River and Merri Creek draining from the north; the Moonee Ponds Creek and Maribyrnong River approaching from the north-west. At places these streams could be forded; scores of punts could carry traffic slowly and expensively; but what was really needed was a huge programme of bridge construction to join up the new roadways.

Ambitious Melburnians were equal to the task. Already in 1850 one of the world's biggest single-arch stone bridges, the first Princes

Bridge, leaped over the Yarra at a cost of £20,000 to join Swanston Street and St Kilda Road. During the five-year period of the Central Road Board, 1853-7, no fewer than 225 large and small bridges costing £420,000 were constructed throughout Victoria.

Many of these bridges were built on the goldfields, and were often little more than temporary timber constructions. However, many important bridges were built in Melbourne suburbs. In Flemington, a 16-foot timber and stone bridge costing £2,300 crossed what was then known as Brickmakers' Gully. A 25-foot timber bridge crossed the Moonee Ponds Creek on the main route to the diggings, joining Flemington Road to Mount Alexander Road. The first bridge across the Moonee Ponds Creek at Broadmeadows was built in 1854 at a cost of £1,700.

Further to the north-west, at Keilor, a massive stone and timber viaduct and box bridge was built by Road Board engineer Samuel Brees in 1853 to cross the ravine cut by Steele's Creek. During construction the bridge girders broke and fell into the creek, and Brees hurriedly left the government service.

Along Plenty and Heidelberg roads, four timber and stone bridges were built in 1854 to cross Merri Creek, the Plenty River, Diamond Creek, and Darebin Creek, at a total cost of £13,000.

To assist in construction of Point Nepean Road, two timber bridges were built across Mordialloc Creek and Kananook Creek in 1855 for a total of £3,000.

Four government bridges were built to the east of Melbourne up to 1854 to enable easier crossing of the Yarra River into what would become the heavily-populated eastern suburbs. The first, a rather elaborate timber bridge at the end of Bridge Road, Richmond, was built in ten bays of thirty feet each, supporting a 21-foot roadway. Completed in 1851, it cost £5,270. The roads approaching it were completed in 1859 at a cost of £15,000. Two smaller bridges were built across the Yarra at Hawthorn from 1852-4, one to connect Victoria Street to Barkers Road, the other to connect Swan Street to Riversdale Road.

Johnston Street, Abbotsford, was connected to Studley Park Road, Kew, by a temporary timber bridge built in 1854. It became known as the 'Penny Bridge', partly because that was the toll for pedestrians, but also because the keeper was Thomas Halfpenny, retired as Chief Constable of Horsham. A larger new bridge nearby, built at a cost of £17,000, was opened by Governor Barkly in 1857.

A timber bridge was thrown across 'the Falls' in the Yarra River in

Deep ravines near Keilor, en route to the diggings, gave colonial engineers many difficulties. This 135-foot stone and timber box bridge was completed in 1853 at a cost of £11,400. The 145-foot timber viaduct at left was built the same year for £5,300. Tolls

were charged to defray these costs: the tollkeeper's cottage can be seen at right. From a
contemporary watercolour by Samuel Brees, government engineer who designed the bridge.
(La Trobe Collection).

This laminated timber bridge of 1860 gave direct connection from Richmond to the Botanic Gardens in South Yarra. Sam Calvert sketched the view on Regatta Day, later known as Henley-on-Yarra. (Newsletter of Australasia, June 1860).

1860 to replace the impractical solid dam of the 1840s which aggravated floods in South Melbourne. Melbourne and South Melbourne councils shared the £5,000 cost of the new bridge, and soon the end of Queen Street was connected to Queensbridge Street. Toll returns showed that hundreds of thousands of pedestrians, vehicles, horses, sheep and cattle used the bridge each year.

The most unusual suburban bridge of the gold decade was built in 1856-7 to link Church Street, Richmond, with Chapel Street, South Yarra. In March 1856 the Legislative Council approved formation of a £12,000 company to build the bridge and charge tolls. Its directors were three pioneer Melbourne businessmen: John Hodgson, MLC; W. F. A. Rucker; and John Carson. They negotiated with the British government to purchase an immense 210-foot iron bridge built for use in the Crimean War. This had solid riveted iron walls, ten feet high, designed

to prevent Russian snipers from picking off British troops using the bridge.

The whole thing was dismantled for shipping to Melbourne, and rebuilt as a single span, supported by huge stone buttresses on both sides of the river. Altogether the company and local councils spent £57,000 on constructing the bridge and its approaches. The result was so solid that it carried vast amounts of horse and tram traffic, until demolished in 1923 so that today's bridge could be built.

A more attractive bridge was built by the government in 1860 to link what used to be known as 'the Government Paddock' (now Olympic Park) in Richmond to the newly-established Botanic Gardens in South Yarra. The bridge rose in a graceful arc of laminated timber supported by cross-girders, enabling thousands of pleasure-seekers as well as goods traffic to cross from Swan Street to Anderson Street.

Looking back from the 1860s on the marvellous decade of gold, residents could scarcely complain that the authorities had not done a great deal towards wrenching order out of the transport chaos which once plagued Melbourne.

Australia's first steam train service began on 12 September 1854 when the Melbourne & Hobson's Bay Railway Company's little engine and carriages rolled out of the first Flinders Street station facing Elizabeth Street. This S. T. Gill lithograph of 1854 shows rail workers at left, shipping masts in the Yarra, and men waiting to board the train. (La Trobe Collection).

10

The great railway boom
and collapse

Ever since George Stephenson and his son Robert built the first travelling steam engines at the end of the Napoleonic Wars, daily life in Britain had begun to change radically under the influence of this first mechanised means of transport. It took forty years and the gold rush to bring the railway revolution to Australia. Several Stephenson employees migrated to Melbourne in the 1850s, providing engineering skills which gave Victoria the first railways in Australia, and assisted greatly in the extension of Melbourne suburbs.

A Legislative Council select committee in 1852 concluded that the government should concentrate its funds on building roads, leaving all rail construction to private enterprise. However, railway routes should be surveyed and entrepreneurs assisted with land grants, loans and guarantees. This may have been generous, even foolish, but aroused little criticism at the time. Politicians were not paid salaries and had to make a living in some way. They became directors and major share-holders in companies whose intention was to make large profits from speculation in land along rail routes.

Another basic decision with damaging long-term results concerned the gauge, or distance between rails. This problem began in New South Wales, where the Sydney Railway Company, slowly building a line between Sydney and Parramatta, decided on the wide Irish 5ft 3in. gauge instead of the English standard 4ft 8.5in. Victoria began building to the wider gauge just as Sydney changed its mind and converted back to the English gauge.

A Legislative Council committee chaired by entrepreneur John Hodgson, MLC, inquired into the gauge question in October 1853. The hearings were told by W. S. Chauncey, engineer of the Melbourne & Hobson's Bay Railway Co., that the wider gauge enabled trains to be

Engineer James Moore improvised the first steam-powered engine to travel along an Australian railway, used on the Port Melbourne line in 1854.

Scottish-born J. V. A. Bruce was the successful tenderer for building the Melbourne-Sunbury-Bendigo railway in 1858.

run more safely and at greater speed: 'The carriages could be built higher, and more goods could be placed on the trucks'. Frederick Christy, locomotive engineer, said that the wider gauge greatly simplified engine design. The committee concluded that 'numerous evils' attended narrower gauges. So Victoria and New South Wales each went their own way, with the result that interstate rail transport remained uneconomic for many years.

Three railway companies were floated in Melbourne in 1852. The first proposed a two-mile railway from Port Melbourne to Melbourne. The second wanted to build a western line from Melbourne to Geelong. The third scheme envisaged a northern railway from Melbourne to the goldfields. Under the law of the day, any company seeking public subscriptions had to undergo Legislative Council examination and have a special Act passed.

Flushed with enthusiasm, the Melbourne & Hobson's Bay Railway Co. floated in August 1852 with capital of £100,000 and William Nicholson, MLC, as chairman. The Legislative Council allowed it to proceed by an Act dated 20 January 1853, which granted free of charge a strip of land 100 yards wide from Melbourne to Port Melbourne railway pier. A further ten acres were granted on the south side of Flinders Street, facing the end of Elizabeth Street, for a station and marshalling yards. All that the government required in return was half-price travel for military and police forces.

The line was soon laid along the flat ground, a special bridge built over the Yarra, and a test run made on 2 June 1854 with an engine improvised by company engineer James Moore from a steam pile-driver

By Christmas 1860, when this sketch was drawn for the Newsletter of Australasia, *Melburnians had become accustomed to rushing for the train with a hamper of food so they could spend a day on the beach.*

mounted on a truck. Although primitive, this was the first travelling steam-powered railway engine used in Australia.

Meanwhile, Robert Langlands's Port Phillip Foundry was building the boiler for the first regular locomotive, constructed in Melbourne by the firm of Robertson, Martin & Smith. The six-wheeled engine was rated at 30 h.p. and said to be capable of 25 m.p.h. while hauling a load of 130 tons.

Large crowds gathered in Flinders Street on 12 September 1854 to watch the first train leave. At noon, Governor and Lady Hotham arrived with their retinue, and were seated in two 'handsomely painted' first-class carriages. The 40th Regiment band played in an open third-class carriage at the rear. In a blare of steam, music, cinders and whistles, driver William Pattinson took the first train away. The trip to Port Melbourne was made in a few minutes at about 15 m.p.h. Ships in the bay fired welcoming salutes. The train brought two more loads of passengers, who joined in a lavish banquet held in a corrugated-iron engine shed at Port Melbourne.

John Sadleir, officer in charge of the police detachment, recalled that on the return trip the engine 'stuck fast and refused to budge an inch'. With Sir Charles Hotham 'scowling and stern as if he were dealing with a mutiny', twenty police were summoned to push the train along the line until the engine fired again.

The line achieved considerable success, particularly after its first five Stephenson locomotives arrived from England. By the end of the company's first year, it had carried 270,000 passengers and 28,000 tons of goods. Additional finance of £40,000 was borrowed from the English & Scottish Bank at 7% interest so that the single line could be duplicated, and an additional railway bridge built over the Yarra.

One unexpected difficulty arose at the long railway pier at Port Melbourne. Local boatmen believed they had lost business because most ships could now dock alongside. Piermaster James Vines reported that 'The boatmen were continually rushing up the pier and knocking down passengers', and 'obstructing the steps so that ladies would have to clamber over five or six boats' to get ashore. When Vines interfered, the boatmen threatened to murder him: one night his head was cut open with a knife, and on another occasion he was stabbed with a boat hook. He named his assailants as Hopkins, Stafford and Alexander Daniels, and their watermen's licences were cancelled.

The second railway group to be floated, entitled the Geelong & Melbourne Railway Co., was authorised by the Legislative Council on 8 February 1853. The name was slightly misleading, for the company's line terminated for some years at Greenwich Pier, Newport.

The project was strongly backed by Geelong businessmen, and successfully floated with £350,000 capital. Initial backers included Charles Thorne (chairman); Dr Alexander Thomson, MLC; J. H. Mercer, MLC; and J. F. Strachan, MLC. The government assisted by granting a 100-yard strip of land all the way to Geelong, guaranteeing 5% interest on shares, and donating £1,000 towards a preliminary survey.

The survey was carried out in 1852-3 by 32-year-old Edward Snell, who described in his diary how he got 'tolerably totty' on board the *Selina* at Williamstown and saturated when landing his gear through the surf. Engaging a runaway sailor and other hands, Snell worked 'knee deep in mud' to survey a route through swamps and creeks. On New Year's Day 1853 he visited Geelong friends to dine on 'champagne, sherry, bottled stout and no end of grub'. After completing the survey, the colorful Snell contracted to supervise the line as engineer for a generous fee of five per cent of construction costs.

By 20 September 1853, the company was ready to lay the foundation stone at its Geelong station. La Trobe sailed down for the occasion, and was welcomed with 'a great flare up'—a dinner and ball in the carriage shed, decorated for the occasion with drapes and flowers.

The company's first locomotive, called 'Ariel', was built in 1854 by Geelong engineers Walker & Munro. All other locomotives were imported from England. As further calls were made on shares, the company's single line reached out from Geelong, thirty miles to Werribee being opened on 1 July 1856. Labour was again hard to find: to help construct the final section to Newport, the government allowed convicts from the *Sacramento* hulk to be employed.

Edward Snell, now Engineer-in-Chief, described to a parliamentary inquiry in June 1857 some of the difficulties experienced in building the line. It had been costed at £250,000, based on wages of 8s a day to mechanics and 5s a day to labourers. However, double these amounts were necessary to attract men to work from 6 a.m. to 6 p.m. More than 720,000 cubic yards of earth had to be shifted by hand, and 100,000 cubic yards of stone excavated.

One contractor named Allan de Lacey went bankrupt, and transferred his contract to Musson, Ross & Leslie. A man named Mackintosh was contracted for plate-laying but proved incompetent: 'He is now an inspector in the employ of the Government', Snell added slyly. Eleven bridges were built of Baltic pine with stone abutments. The 1,000-foot rail jetty at Newport gave great trouble to contractor Henry Attrill, being built in nearly thirty feet of soft mud, 'into which the piles sunk of their own weight'.

At last, on 25 June 1857, the line was completed. Governor Barkly went to Geelong to accompany hundreds of residents on a ceremonial trip back to Newport. At Cowie's Creek bridge, locomotive superintendent Henry Walter leaned out to wave to people cheering from the Ocean Child Hotel, struck his head on a projecting beam, and was killed. Rather subdued, the residents returned to Geelong for a grand banquet attended by the Governor, Premier Haines, Anglican Bishop Perry, and 3,000 lesser guests.

Regular services began the following week. Melburnians wishing to travel to Geelong could catch the paddle-steamer *Citizen* from Queen's

Wharf three times a day, to board the train at Newport. Return fares were £1 first class, 16s second class, and 10s third class.

The third and most ambitious railway float was called the Melbourne, Mount Alexander & Murray River Railway Co. Its purpose was to build a line from Spencer Street, through the hilly country of the gold diggings, and ultimately on to Echuca on the Murray.

A Legislative Council Act of 8 February 1853 approved the raising of £1 million capital, on condition that shareholders would be liable for twice the amount of their shares if the company were unable to meet its debts. In return, the company was granted not only the normal 100-yard strip of land along its route, but also fifty acres of valuable land on the western side of Spencer Street for its station and yards.

Scenting good pickings, the financier Antonio Gabrielli hurried to Melbourne to give evidence before a select committee inquiry in September 1853. Gabrielli warned the committee that the shares with their double liability would be valueless if floated in Melbourne. 'They will not be negotiable in London, nor anywhere else', said Gabrielli. 'Unless this undertaking be placed before the English public in a plain way, there are no means of raising so much as a sixpence on your scrip'.

Gabrielli of course was an interested party, wanting to float loans on the high-interest basis which he achieved a few months later with the City Council. But his advice on railway flotation was rejected by colonial know-alls, who proceeded optimistically with the Melbourne float.

Former Colonial Architect Henry Ginn, who had quit the government service in a rage, bobbed up as managing director of the Mount Alexander company. He told the committee that plans had been drawn to build the line from Melbourne, with a branch line from Williamstown, to run via Bacchus Marsh, Ballarat, Mount Alexander and Bendigo. However, nothing was finally approved by the government while it awaited the arrival of its new Colonial Engineer, Captain Pasley.

C. H. Ebden, himself an extremely wealthy squatter, went to London in 1854 to try to find more capital for the railway. As Gabrielli had forecast, he failed miserably. All told, only £130,000 could be raised in Melbourne, with not a penny coming from Europe.

By 1856, all three rail companies were in considerable financial trouble. The Melbourne-Port Melbourne line had cost £180,000 to lay and

Fervent efforts were made by Geelong businessmen to finance a railway from their city to Newport. S. T. Gill sketched the laying of the foundation stone near Corio Bay in September 1853. Rejoicing gave way to lengthy delays, and the line was not opened until June 1857. Financial problems forced the government to nationalise the undertaking in 1860. (La Trobe Collection).

equip. The *Age* thought it should have cost about £10,000, for nowhere could 'two miles of easier railway-making be found'. To William Kelly, the line seemed a flagrant instance of 'infamous engineering and reckless expenditure'. Nevertheless this company was able to survive for the moment, and even plan an extension to St Kilda.

The Mount Alexander line had spent most of its meagre capital on preparatory work, and had little prospect of raising more. In this case the Legislative Council moved quickly, passing an Act on 19 March 1856 'to enable the Government of Victoria to purchase all the property and other interests possessed by the Melbourne, Mount Alexander and Murray River Railway Company'. This was one of the world's first examples of nationalisation of a privately-owned public facility. Yet it was not so ironic that capitalists in the Legislative Council should have brought it about: there was need for haste before the first Legislative Assembly could be elected later that year and probably grant less favourable terms. As it was, the government paid £68,000 for the company through an issue of 5% debentures, and took over current works on which a further £57,000 was owing. In other words, the taxpayer paid for the mistakes already made.

The company building the Geelong-Melbourne line was also in serious difficulties, having spent the £350,000 raised by its share issue and a further £262,500 raised from private debentures. Robert Russell, Melbourne's pioneer surveyor and contractor for the first nine miles of the line, told a Legislative Assembly inquiry in June 1857 that he had visited England the previous year to offer shares in the company: 'I sold them at a premium in London, and they jumped at them'. Now all the money was gone, and earnings were not even sufficient to pay the interest.

The Melbourne-Geelong company finally collapsed in February 1858, when the directors pleaded with the Haines government to take over its assets and liabilities. Government engineers Charles Pasley, George Darbyshire and Thomas Higinbotham prepared a damning report. This showed that the line was mostly unfenced, allowing cattle to wander in front of trains. Cuttings and embankments had not been made wide enough to take a double line. Drainage had been 'almost entirely neglected', and the line already damaged in several places by flood waters. Every bridge except the long timber bridge over the Werribee River was in a dangerous state. Inferior gravel instead of broken bluestone had been used to ballast the line. One-tenth of the sleepers needed immediate replacement, and the remainder within four years. The line had no signal system, essential to safe operation. In a word, Edward Snell's and Robert Russell's work had been appalling.

A good deal of haggling followed this report. It was not until an Act of June 1860 that the government agreed to take control of the line, paying out £600,000 for assets and debts.

Select committees of both Houses of Parliament pondered railways policy throughout 1856-7. Towards the end of the year they agreed that 'the State must necessarily be entrusted with the formation of the main lines of Railway'. To finance them, Victoria would raise 25-year debentures, paying 6% guaranteed interest, up to a total of £8 million.

Antonio Gabrielli again appeared on the scene with offers of finance, but was rebuffed in the Legislative Council report, signed by Henry Miller, MLC, chairman of the Bank of Victoria. Miller claimed that Gabrielli had 'improperly' forced a considerable discount on his large loan to the City Council in 1854.

C. H. Ebden, now Treasurer in the Haines cabinet, visited London again to try to arrange the huge rail loan with famed financiers Baring Brothers & Co. Then the Haines government fell. The new Premier, John O'Shanassy, himself chairman of the Colonial Bank, obtained finance from six major local banks early in 1858.

To handle its rapidly increasing responsibility for transport, the government set up its first Railways Department in 1856. In the beginning it was headed by Peter Lalor, MLC, who had worked as an engineer on the Geelong line before taking part in the Eureka rebellion. As head of railways, Lalor was paid a salary of £600 a year, but was forced to resign when a law was passed prohibiting civil servants from sitting in Parliament. He was replaced by Joseph Ward as permanent Secretary for Railways. The Chief Engineer was George Darbyshire, who had worked for the Manchester & Buxton Rail Co. in England before emigrating. J. K. Brunel was appointed Inspecting Engineer.

With politicians and public demanding quick action to finalise major lines, the Railways Department appointed forty additional engineers and draftsmen to prepare surveys and plans. Unfortunately most of them became afflicted with the government stroke. David Ross, an experienced private architect, told a parliamentary inquiry that many drawings which government draftsmen had spent ten days preparing should have been completed in two days at most. One series

To enable trains to cross the Maribyrnong River and reach the goldfields, this 200-foot tubular iron bridge was erected at a cost of £50,000. It was begun by the Melbourne, Mount Alexander & Murray River Railway Company, which faced insolvency after three years and had to be nationalised in 1856. Spencer Street station was built as the city terminus for trains on this line. (My Note Book, January 1859).

of drawings had taken eight times the normal period to complete. Chief Engineer Darbyshire could only reply weakly that detailed survey maps were not available for country to be traversed.

Tenders were at last called in 1858 for a government line through Sunbury and Kyneton to Bendigo. W. C. Cornish, builder of Parliament House, joined a 36-year-old Scot named John Bruce in a successful £3,357,000 tender to build the entire Melbourne-Bendigo line. They employed several thousand navvies, and by 13 January 1859 reached Sunbury.

Governor Barkly performed the opening ceremony, although the branch line to Williamstown was not ready for business until 17 January 1859. Stations at Digger's Rest and Sunbury were opened on 10

February. Almost immediately, 10,000 passengers a week began using the Williamstown section; and 3,000 passengers a week the Sunbury line. Arrangements were made for Victoria Stage Company horse coaches to meet passengers at Sunbury and take them on to goldfields destinations.

To operate the Williamstown and Sunbury lines, the government had ordered its first five locomotives in 1857 from George England & Co. of London. In 1859 a further ten engines were bought from Beyer, Peacock & Co. of Manchester. Williamstown Railway Workshops began operations at this time, and all the imported locomotives were assembled there under Superintendent F. C. Christy.

The private company had previously ordered a huge 200-foot iron tubular girder bridge from W. Fairbairn & Sons of Manchester to carry trains across the Maribyrnong River. The government continued this contract, agreeing in November 1856 to pay £13,000 for the bridge, plus freight to Melbourne. When finally erected in 1858, the 500-ton bridge cost £50,000.

To establish a reasonably direct route for the railway, the government had also to pay enormous compensation to landowners along the line who had bought tracts very cheaply before the gold rush. One of the worst cases was that of W. J. T. Clarke, MLC, whose holdings were scattered all along the route from Footscray to Sunbury. After much argument and arbitration, the government paid £17,000 to Clarke for 267 acres which had cost him £747 only a short time before.

The financial stability of private railways to the east of Melbourne was not much more encouraging. To provide a service in this direction, the politician John O'Shanassy floated the Melbourne & Suburban Railway Company in 1857. O'Shanassy owned a successful drapery store in Collins Street, relying on his wife Margaret to run the shop while he concentrated on larger matters. In 1853 they paid £1,200 for sixteen acres in East Hawthorn, where their magnificent mansion named 'Tara' (later 'Broughton Hall') began rising. All that was needed now was a train service.

Fortunately O'Shanassy was also chairman of the Colonial Bank. He arranged a loan of £32,000 to the rail company, getting it off to a good start. Subscribers took up another £258,000 in paid capital and £115,000 in debentures. Wealthy landowner William Highett, MLC, agreed to act as company treasurer.

With what seemed ample funds at its disposal, the company built Princes Bridge station on the north side of the Yarra River. From there, consulting engineer A. K. Smith ran a single track beside Wellington Parade and Brunton Avenue as far as Punt Road, where Richmond

William Highett, Treasurer of the Melbourne & Suburban Railway Co., whose expensive Hawthorn line went into liquidation.

John O'Shanassy, MLC, built this magnificent mansion 'Tara' at East Hawthorn in the 1850s, expecting that his railway company would soon reach the area. Even today the line between Auburn and Camberwell curves to avoid crossing Tara Street.

station was built. The line opened for business on 5 February 1859 with a banquet at which working-class gatecrashers rioted and consumed the choice food meant for official guests.

The line was extended by a bridge over Punt Road to a station at Cremorne Gardens (since vanished), then on to East Richmond and Burnley. Crossing the Yarra to hilly territory in Hawthorn brought severe difficulties: Irish-born contractor Patrick Higgins found that his men had to move more than 200,000 cubic yards of earth to make culverts and embankments.

The company's valuer, Benjamin Cowderoy, told a parliamentary inquiry that nearly £100,000 was spent on acquiring land and erecting buildings. This was £30,000 above the original estimates.

Engineer T. H. Merrett said that eleven rail bridges required at various stages of the Hawthorn line were expensive to plan and build. Bridges across Punt Road and Church Street cost nearly £5,000 each; while two major 136-foot bridges high above the Yarra River cost about £23,000 each. Instead of the £156,000 originally estimated, the company had spent £250,000 on its works. Merrett's 3.5% commission amounted to more than £8,000.

By the end of 1860, the company was carrying nearly 600,000 passengers a year, with total income running at about £15,000. Opening of the Hawthorn line on 13 April 1861 with two London-built engines named 'Hawthorn' and 'Kew' practically doubled these figures.

But the company's financial position was now parlous. Its secretary, George Lilly, told another parliamentary inquiry late in 1861 that most of the line's rolling stock was 'in a very bad state of repair'. Profits, he said, were just sufficient to pay interest on bonded debts. Phillip Johnson, the company's new chairman, agreed that the only solution was to liquidate. The property was sold by auction to a syndicate called the Melbourne Railway Company, which later amalgamated with the Hobson's Bay Company before its ultimate nationalisation.

Railways made better progress to the south of Melbourne. After many arguments about the best route to be followed, the Hobson's Bay Co. built a branch line through South Melbourne to St Kilda, opening on 13 May 1857. Travelling parallel to today's Ferrars Street and Canterbury Road, the line made the low ground of Middle Park available for suburban development.

Company engineer William Elsdon told a Legislative Assembly inquiry in 1857 that £33,000 was being spent on building the line, buying engines and carriages, and erecting stations at South Melbourne and St Kilda. Plans were in hand to erect a permanent bluestone station and warehouse at Flinders Street, to replace the ramshackle timber terminus originally provided.

Joseph Ward, Secretary for Railways, told the inquiry that the number of passengers using the St Kilda line greatly exceeded expectations, requiring platforms to be doubled in length. Horse 'buses brought many travellers from a pickup point at the Devonshire Hotel in Brighton to St Kilda. At holiday times, said the *Argus*, 'the passengers are numbered by the thousands and ten thousands'. Figures produced later to Parliament showed that in 1860, the line was carrying more than a million passengers and 170,000 tons of merchandise a year, and making good profits.

Success of the southern suburban route invited competition in the same region. While still in its period of expansionism, John O'Shanassy's Melbourne & Suburban Railway Co. decided in 1857 to run a branch line southwards from Richmond station across the Yarra River, and

The 100-foot bluestone and timber bridge which crossed St Kilda Road in 1859 to take trains from St Kilda to Windsor stations — a route abandoned in 1862.

establish new stations at South Yarra, Prahran and Windsor, finishing near the main artery of Dandenong Road.

Large new works were necessary for this enterprise. A rail bridge over the Yarra at Cremorne cost more than £30,000. Deep cuttings to take the trains below Toorak Road, Commercial Road and High Street, Prahran, cost £15,000. The terminus, Windsor station, opened in 1860.

Brighton landowners formed a competing syndicate in 1857 known as the St Kilda & Brighton Railway Co. Its secretary, estate agent George Walstab, called for investment on the basis that the railway would add greatly to local land values. More than £130,000 was soon subscribed, and additional mortgage finance obtained from the Bank of New South Wales.

Company engineer William Randle designed a five-mile loop line joining St Kilda and Windsor stations, then turning south to Brighton. The loop line was a considerable engineering feat, running parallel to Fitzroy Street on a huge blue-gum viaduct raised to avoid spillage from Albert Park lagoon. On the city side of St Kilda Junction, where Union Street runs today, a 100-foot bluestone and timber bridge took trains fifteen feet above St Kilda Road. A 66-foot bridge crossed Punt Road, enabling the line to reach Windsor station.

Southwards from Windsor, deep cuttings had to be made to take trains underneath Dandenong Road and Alma Road, with a level crossing which still exists at Inkerman Street. More bridges, tunnels and level crossings designed by engineer C. R. Swyer, took the trains to

Melbourne south of the Yarra, as shown in the Blackburn/Fairfax map of 1858
(continued from pages 2-3). This gives the routes taken by the main private railway
companies, leading to dense urban development in their areas. Note position of artillery
battery on Marine Parade (today Beaconsfield Parade). Key to numbers: 14 Powder

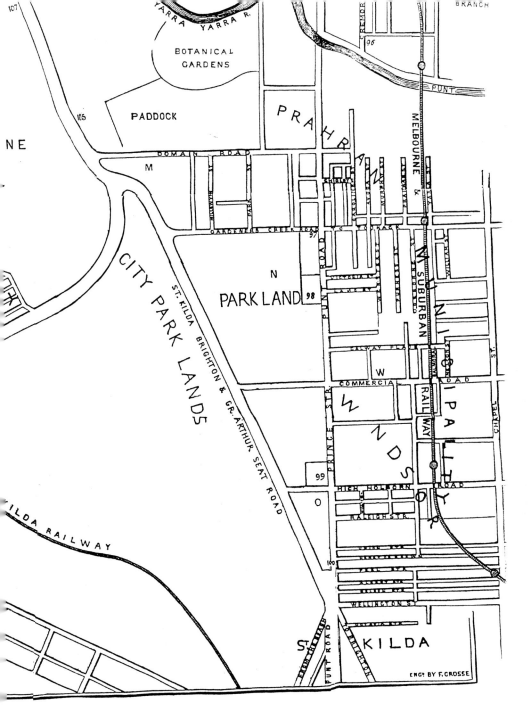

Magazine; 15 Gas Works; 16 New Dock; 17 Hughes's Wharf; 18 Raleigh's Wharf; 19 Cole's Wharf; 28 Emerald Hill Cricket Ground; 104 Protestant Orphanage; 105-106 Toll Gates; 107-108 Immigrants' Barracks.

Left: Hugh Glass, main promoter of the Melbourne to Essendon railway, owned much land along the proposed route.

Right: J. C. King, former town clerk of Melbourne, agreed to become a director of the speculative Essendon line.

today's stations of Balaclava, Elsternwick, and North Brighton. A gigantic 203-foot bowstring bridge was built to take trains twenty-five feet above Point Nepean Road. Total cost of the works to this stage was £125,000.

The single-track line was opened for public use on 19 December 1859, with trains running between Melbourne, St Kilda and Brighton every hour. The line was extended to Middle Brighton and Brighton Beach stations, with appropriate celebrations, on 21 December 1861. By that time the company was carrying nearly 200,000 passengers a year, yielding £11,000 in revenue.

However, the St Kilda-Windsor loop never justified its great expense. It was closed on 20 September 1862 and the works dismantled. The St Kilda & Brighton Railway Co. went into liquidation with losses of £70,000, and was taken over by the Melbourne & Suburban Co.

Planning began in 1858 for a short private line to be operated by the Melbourne & Essendon Railway Co. The main promoters and share-holders were three Irishmen: Hugh Glass, a wealthy landowner who lived in the magnificent 'Flemington House' on the Maribyrnong River; J. C. King, MLA and former town clerk of Melbourne; and Patrick Phelan, MLA for the Keilor area.

John King, as company secretary, told a Legislative Assembly hearing that most of the shareholders owned land along the route. Apart from the directors, they included Rawdon Greene, W. H. Tuckett, John Dinwoodie, John Brown, E. B. White, Peter McCracken, and Charles Bradshaw, MLC. King admitted that the line had been projected 'to enhance the value of their property'. Hugh Glass, giving evidence, said the proposed line ran through nearly a mile of his own property.

All this made little difference to the politicians: the line was approved by an Act dated 24 February 1859, and £75,000 capital quickly raised. Engineer Francis Bell returned from his position as manager of the Great Northern Railway in New South Wales to design the line and its stations.

Through its political friends, the company arranged to borrow some of the government's new engines and rolling stock, and to use its line already built from Spencer Street as far as North Melbourne. From there the company constructed its own four miles of single track roughly parallel to Mount Alexander Road, on the west side, establishing stations at Kensington, Newmarket, Ascot Vale, Moonee Ponds and Essendon.

Contractor George Holmes had little difficulty in building the single track for £41,000 over the comparatively flat land, with less than 70,000 cubic yards of soil being moved for cuttings and embankments. Three bridges had to be built, at Racecourse Road, Kent Street, and Maribyrnong Road, but these cost less than £7,000. Other roads were traversed by inexpensive level crossings.

The line opened to public traffic on 1 November 1860, offering eleven trips both ways each day at hourly intervals. An extension to Flemington Racecourse was added at a cost of £9,000, in time for the running of the first Melbourne Cup in 1861.

But the promoters had seriously over-estimated public demand. Although population in the Flemington to Essendon area increased by several thousand, most people preferred to catch one of the many horse 'bus services which operated in the area in the early 1860s. These 'buses ran more frequently, were cheaper, and dropped passengers in the central city area. The rail company ceased operations in 1863, their works lying idle until taken over by the government three years later.

As the government took control of each faltering private line, Victoria's indebtedness continued to grow. Politicians assuaged public fears with the theory that since future generations would benefit, most of the debt could wait.

All would have been well had a sinking fund been established to extinguish the debt within a reasonable period. But fares and freight charges were never set high enough to allow this to be done. Nor was any government wily enough to reap the real profit, which lay in the continual resale of land made extremely valuable by each rail extension. Most of that bonus went to private speculators.

11

Building a
commercial city

Every kind of trading and commercial enterprise expanded beyond recognition during the 1850s. Despite occasional slumps, the continued high production of gold gave confidence to importers and manufacturers that Melbourne was worth rebuilding into a city of substantial warehouses, shops and factories. Some of these structures survive even today.

The first essential for a growing city was to get cheap supplies of food from the farms and wharves into the hands of the people. The City Council tried to achieve this by revamping the already-established open-air Western Market. Then as the city expanded eastwards, it developed a new Eastern Market.

The Western Market occupied a site of nearly two acres directly north of the Custom House, bounded by Flinders Lane, William Street, Collins Street and Market Street, an area dominated today by the National Mutual Centre.

During most of the 1840s, the block was fenced but practically bare except for a few wooden sheds, a stand-pipe from the Yarra, and a small brick gaol. The City Council erected rows of brick stalls in 1849, but these burned down in 1853. All that remained were hovels of the survivors of 'Rag Fair'. These were peremptorily demolished in 1855. At the same time the council took the opportunity of widening this section of Flinders Lane from 33 to 50 feet, as it remains today.

The council planned to capitalise on the now-valuable Collins Street frontage by erecting impressive office buildings, supported on massive bluestone cellars facing southwards to the lower market ground. These foundations were built early in 1856 by contractor George Holmes, and used as lockup stores. But the remainder of the scheme was left unfinished. A Legislative Council inquiry chaired by J. P. Fawkner concluded in 1857 that the council had 'completely ruined this market place, and inflicted vast injury upon producers and consumers'. Market gardeners were forced to stand their carts in Collins Street, or in a small quadrangle left in the middle of the building works, where only twenty producers could find a place.

Since Melbourne was expanding rapidly to the east, most vendors quit the chaotic Western Market scene and opened stalls on ground reserved for an Eastern Market. This three-acre site bounded by Bourke, Exhibition and Little Collins streets had originally been intended for municipal buildings. However, as Melbourne Town Hall rose on its present site in Swanston Street, the eastern block became available for other purposes.

The site had been used as a hay and corn market since 1846, with a row of brick stalls built on the Exhibition Street frontage in 1847 to make a small general market. The Bourke Street frontage was divided into 30-ft square allotments, where retailers of cheap clothes, shoes and books erected temporary timber shops. These were destroyed by fire in November 1855, and replaced by rows of carts and stalls trading in the open air. The *Leader* in July 1858 thought the greatest attraction of this impromptu market was 'confectioners' stalls, blazing with light and glittering with wonderful feats in the art of making sugar candy'. Noisy vendors offered 'heating happles, three pounds a shilling', or 'brooms for a bob [one shilling]'.

Better arrangements for vendors were made in 1858, when the City Council paid John Moore £3,400 to build four long corrugated-iron arcades over most of the site. Each of these shed-like structures was 42 feet wide, with flagstones laid to protect shoppers from mud and manure. All 224 stands were occupied by market gardeners, fruit growers and general dealers by the opening date in May 1859.

The site soon became known as 'Paddy's Market', a noisy jumble of shouting tradesmen, haggling customers, squealing animals, and fervent political orators. The open-air arcades were demolished in 1877, and a much more solidly-built Eastern Market erected with regular lockup shops and gas-lit walkways. This survived until 1960, when today's Southern Cross Hotel was built over part of the area.

Import-export merchants formed the backbone of Melbourne's commercial life. Their consignments of gold and wool filled vessels departing from Melbourne. When those ships returned with new immigrants, the holds were crammed with all kinds of goods needed by the growing community.

The colony's growing agricultural strength was shown by the opening of a grand new Eastern Market on the corner of Bourke and Exhibition streets, running right back to Little Collins Street, in 1859. It replaced the old Western Market as the city's main produce site. This Gritten/Philp lithograph also shows the Treasury Building on left horizon. Below it, in Exhibition Street, are Mac's Hotel and Marsh & Grant, monumental masons. On the right-hand side, the first two-storey building on the horizon is the Female Reformatory. Coming forward to Bourke Street, Ruddell Brothers' grocery is shown, alongside C. H. Tipper's Haymarket Hotel. (La Trobe Collection).

Imports during the first part of the gold decade fluctuated wildly, as merchants tried to estimate the type and quantity of products needed over the following twelve months. A series of booms and slumps often threw their estimates astray, making mercantile speculation a perilous business, with many insolvencies of undercapitalised traders. By 1860, however, trade had settled down into a more predictable pattern. In that year, the total value of imports into Victoria was £15 million—

more than five times that of 1851. Practically all imports came from Britain, and were mostly unloaded at Melbourne in preference to other Victorian ports.

The lists of imports for 1860 given in Appendix A (page 445) may seem boring, but in fact they reveal much about the daily life of Melburnians during the gold decade. Alcohol consumption for the 125,000 people in Melbourne and 315,000 elsewhere in Victoria was still extraordinarily high. So was the consumption of tea; while vast piles of chicory were imported to adulterate coffee. Residents smoked furiously to consume huge quantities of pipe tobacco and cigars (but not cigarettes). Even the consumption of 800 lbs of snuff each year shows what a large quantity of the addictive material was sniffed.

In housing the population, imported corrugated iron and shingles were favoured for cheap roofing, but quality builders required millions of Welsh slates. Dressed timber was imported from Europe and Tas-

Entrepreneurs could start wholesale distribution in a small way during the gold decade. Here is Robert Marshall's modest warehouse and cottage on the north side of Collins Street, between Queen and William streets, as sketched by Edmund Thomas. Marshall also operated a rail parcel service in Spencer Street. (La Trobe Collection).

mania. All glass, wallpaper and paint had to be brought in. Most bricks were locally made.

To furnish the interiors of houses and offices, ironmongers and crockery importers did a roaring trade. Millions of candles and the newfangled Swedish safety matches were landed in 1860. The large quantity of imported seeds shows that suburban and market gardens were being developed with vigour. Booksellers were doing well, bringing in nearly £100,000 worth of books a year for the cultured segment of the population. Other home entertainment relied mainly on imported pianos and sheet music.

The medical world had no way of treating disease except through traditional panaceas: hence the large amount of raw drugs imported. Opium was used as the main ingredient in locally-made nostrums; no doubt much found its way into addicts' hands. Mercury was administered by doctors and quacks to mask the all-too-common symptoms of syphilis.

High expenditure on food imports indicates the failure of successive governments to open up cheap land for agriculture. In one of the world's most fertile areas, the figures shown for imports of foreign grain, flour, butter, fruit, cheese and potatoes are almost beyond belief.

Overall, the statistics show that great scope existed for replacement of imports by local production. A start was being made: imports of machinery and tools indicate that manufacturing was ready to expand. Local production of light carriages and buggies was already well established in 1860, hence the low import figure for this item. The biggest opening of all was obviously in wearing apparel, but it would be some years yet before local textile and clothing manufacturers could compete successfully, behind the shield of protective tariffs vigorously promoted by David Syme's *Age* and his dependent politicians.

The mountain of imported goods had to go somewhere, as expeditiously as possible. The Custom House and sheds even when completed could hold only a small proportion. Melbourne merchants who had ordered the goods were forced into a frenzy of warehouse building, occupying considerable lengths of street frontage near cargo discharge points on the Yarra River and railway termini.

Most warehouses were built in bluestone, for security against thieves and fire. Usually they were limited to basement and one or two storeys, for there were no hydraulic or electric lifts, steam cranes were rare, and heavy crates had to be manhandled with block and tackle.

Several merchants survived from Melbourne's pioneer period and were well-placed to exploit the opportunities of the gold rush. The best-known was an ageing former naval captain, George Ward Cole, who started building Melbourne's first large private wharf on the Yarra, near the end of King Street, in 1841. On this wharf was one of the first 'bonded warehouses', meaning that Cole paid a substantial bond and annual fee allowing him to take goods direct from vessels without submitting to Customs audit. Under this system, duties were paid as goods left the warehouse in small quantities for retail destinations.

When the government acquired Cole's Wharf in 1852 so that Queen's Wharf could be extended westwards, the captain built another bonded warehouse with capacity for 3,200 tons of goods (Customs measurement) on the south-east corner of Flinders Lane and Spencer Street, strategically placed for the northern rail systems being planned. During the 1850s Cole operated through two junior partners, W. G. Bruce and Thomas Norton, but by 1860 had resumed sole control.

Also a survivor from the 1840s was that tireless merchant, politician

Right: This two-storey bluestone warehouse at 62–6 King Street is now dwarfed by skyscrapers of the 1980s building boom. The warehouse was built in 1854 for the American firm of Andrew Newell, Samuel Hooper and Samuel Stevens, Melbourne's biggest exporters of wool to Boston. Later it became the York Butter Factory, and today is a nightclub.

Below: Only the extensive bluestone basement and ground floor of G. A. Mouritz's coal warehouse were built at 22 King Street in the 1850s. The top two floors were added in 1873. The building later became the Underground nightclub.

English-born merchant
*William Degraves (right) built
a huge warehouse in Flinders
Lane early in the 1850s, today
converted with the frontage
shown below.*

and historian William Westgarth. Westgarth built his warehouse on the east side of Market Street in partnership with Alfred Ross. James Spowers joined the firm in 1858, while Westgarth continued his political campaigning.

Another self-made merchant-politician, the near-illiterate William Nicholson, helped to float the Hobson's Bay Railway Co. in 1853, after deciding to establish his bonded warehouse in Flinders Street opposite the projected city rail terminus. By 1856 the warehouse was one of Melbourne's biggest, with capacity for 4,500 tons of goods. Nicholson left most of the mercantile work to his partner Andrew Sutherland while continuing a successful political career.

An equally remarkable mixture of occupations could be seen in the case of Dr Augustus Greeves, a practising surgeon, hotel proprietor and politician besides being a large importer of spirits and tobacco. Greeves built his warehouse in 1853 with capacity of 2,400 tons on the north-east corner of Little Collins Street and today's Royal Arcade. So successful was Greeves that he also became Minister of Trade and Customs in John O'Shanassy's government of 1857.

Another politician who made his living as a merchant was Thomas Loader, an emigrant from London during the 1852 influx. Taking a partner named Sydney James, Loader specialised in the importation of ironmongery and saddlery, with retail outlets in the lower-rental sections of King and Elizabeth streets. Loader was elected as MLA in 1859 on a radical land reform programme.

For a time, most merchants believed that the western end would remain the most important part of Melbourne, and sited their warehouses accordingly. J. C. Zander erected a two-storey bluestone warehouse in Highlander Lane (off the western end of Flinders Street) in 1853, being licensed to operate a bonded store with capacity of 2,070 tons. Zander died in 1858, after which his widow Cecilia continued the business for many years—apparently Melbourne's only example at the time of a woman operating a major mercantile business.

Adjoining the Zander establishment, with a frontage to today's 22 King Street, was a single-storey bluestone warehouse with basement built in 1853 by George Mouritz and William Poole to hold imported coal. In 1873 the Zander family took over this structure and added another two floors in faced bluestone. This completed the building known in more recent times as the Underground nightclub.

By the mid-1850s, mercantile firms were moving east. Above is the elaborate Flinders Street warehouse of F. J. Sargood (shown at left); his son who became Sir Frederick Sargood, MLC; and their partner John King. On the Swanston Street side is the house originally known as 'Hodgson's Folly', converted into the Port Phillip Club Hotel with Edward Scott as licensee, and today the site of Port Phillip Arcade.

During the gold decade, Cleve Brothers built two bluestone warehouses which survive at the western end of Melbourne. This photograph shows how goods were delivered by dray to the Lonsdale Street warehouse, and hoisted by gantry to the upper floor. (La Trobe Collection).

Further along the eastern side of King Street, at today's No. 62, another bluestone warehouse also survives today as a nightclub. This was built in 1854 by three American immigrants, Andrew Newell, Samuel Hooper, and Samuel Stevens jnr. The firm arranged monthly consignments of wool by clipper ships to Boston, and imported all kinds of American-made goods. During the 1860s the building was taken over by merchants Alison & Knight.

In William Street, one of the largest bonded warehouses was built by Frederick Cooper, next door to the Treasury and Gold Office which occupied the north-west corner of Lonsdale and William streets. Cooper's warehouse, first bonded in 1854, had a capacity of 1,620 tons.

Another bonded warehouse of 2,800 tons capacity was built in 1853 on the north side of Flinders Lane, between William and King streets, by John Alison and Andrew Knight. The partners did well: during the slump of 1854 they were able to take over another bonded store of 3,500 tons capacity built in Flinders Street West by Captain John Foxton, RN.

James Service, a Scottish-born immigrant of 1853, brought with him a large range of goods thought likely to appeal to Melburnians. He set up a warehouse on the north side of Bourke Street, between William and King streets, and prospered greatly. Service soon handed most of the daily business over to another Scot, James Ormond, and immersed himself in politics, becoming MLA in 1857, and Minister of Land and Works in 1859.

As railways were completed and roads improved, Melbourne irresistibly expanded eastwards. The result was rapid construction of warehouses in the more central sections of Flinders Street and Flinders Lane.

The biggest of these new warehouses in the early 1850s appears to be that of George and Thomas Harker. The Harkers' bonded store, capable of holding 5,800 tons of goods, was built in 1853 on the north side of Flinders Street, between Elizabeth and Queen streets.

This area soon became dominated by similar warehouses. In 1855 two German gold-rush immigrants, Moritz Michaelis and Adolphus Boyd, built their large stone store on the north-west corner of Flinders and Elizabeth streets. Michaelis later became leader of the local leather-making industry. Part of the firm's Flinders Street complex was occupied by a bonded store operated by G. R. Griffiths, William Fanning and T. J. Nankivell.

Further along Flinders Street, on the north-east corner of Bond

Street, rose a large bonded warehouse built in 1853 with a capacity of 1,900 tons by wealthy squatter Richard Grice, who took into partnership his clerks T. J. Sumner and John Benn. This firm traded successfully for many years as Grice, Sumner & Co.

About this time, a substantial three-storey warehouse faced with freestone was erected in Flinders Street by F. J. Sargood and his partner John King. The site chosen was next to the Port Phillip Club Hotel, originally built as a private house by merchant John Hodgson and popularly known as 'Hodgson's Folly'. In 1859, Sargood's son F. T. Sargood joined the softgoods firm as a partner, making sufficient profits within ten years to be able to build the mansion 'Ripponlea'. The warehouse has long since disappeared, but the mansion remains a feature of Elsternwick.

Slightly to the west of the Sargood warehouse, three American traders named George Train, Joshua Crane and George Starbuck jnr built a three-storey store in 1854, distributing mainly barrels of high-grade American flour and other foodstuffs.

The narrow street named Flinders Lane was the next selection for merchants seeking areas of cheaper land on which to erect their warehouses. First in the field was William Degraves, who with his brother Charles had bought an acre of land on the north-eastern corner of Flinders Lane and Degraves Street just before the gold rush for £2,000. At first they used the land for a large flour-mill operated by a steam engine. However, when William became a director of the Hobson's Bay Railway Co., he decided to build a huge stone bonded warehouse of five storeys plus cellar. The steam engine was used to hoist goods on an external platform to upper floors. In the mid-1850s, Degraves leased the warehouse to merchants Alfred Woolley and George Robinson, devoting himself to pastoral pursuits and conservative politics. The Degraves warehouse survives today, with an art nouveau frontage added early in the 20th century.

Another Flinders Lane warehouse of the gold-rush era which has miraculously survived was built in 1858 by Samuel Levy and George Robertson on the north-west corner of Flinders Lane and Higson Lane, between Russell and Exhibition streets. By 1860 three other Levy brothers — Lewis, Goodman and Nathaniel — had taken control, and added the top storey to make the building which still stands, intact with large cellar.

Another temporary trade slump in 1857 halted most warehouse

construction. However, a partnership of three brothers, Alfred, Daniel and Sali Cleve, built a three-storey bluestone warehouse on the south-east corner of King and Lonsdale streets about 1857. This is still in use today as Lazar's Restaurant. Architect Leonard Terry also designed for the brothers a smaller two-storey bluestone warehouse just around the corner in Lonsdale Street. Erected in 1858, the building today serves as offices.

In 1858, the woolbroking partnership of Richard Goldsbrough and

An important surviving reminder of the great days of Melbourne's western end as a mercantile centre: Holyman House, at 390-8 Flinders Street. This building began life in 1858, designed by John Gill as a bluestone wool warehouse for merchant Richard Goldsbrough (right). The frontage was drastically altered and turned into a shipping office in 1936 by William Holyman & Sons.

This rare surviving bluestone warehouse near the eastern end of Flinders Lane was built about 1858 to replace a corrugated iron store. Architects James Robertson and Thomas Hale designed the warehouse for merchants Samuel Levy and George Robinson.

Hugh Parker asked architect John Gill to design a three-storey bluestone warehouse for the south-east corner of Flinders and Market streets. This building later became a shipping agency, Holyman House, and still stands. During 1861-2, Goldsbrough built even larger wool stores, which can be seen today at the north-east corner of Bourke and William streets.

While English and Scottish merchants with substantial capital dominated the wholesale import and distribution trades, many families with smaller resources were able to build or lease shops and develop thriving small businesses.

A decade earlier, most of these busy urban activities were non-existent or in their infancy. An important result of the gold rush was to supply Melbourne with a great variety of retail and trade services which helped to change it from a frontier town into a pinnacle of colonial civilisation.

Few retail emporiums as we know them today were erected in gold-rush Melbourne. Even those that did exist have all been rebuilt, because they traded in the most popular areas. The most successful of these early retailers was Irish-born Mars Buckley, who with his wife Elizabeth and partner C. J. Nunn started a drapery business in Bourke Street in 1852 in a small rented wooden shop. Buckley & Nunn were soon able to purchase a freehold frontage of 162 ft in Bourke Street, with a depth of 300 ft. By 1861 the firm was making an extraordinary £40,000 a year profit. Mars and Elizabeth bought a 32-acre frontage on the south side of the Yarra, which later became Heyington Place, Toorak. There they built the enormous mansion 'Bealieu': in the following century this became St Catherine's School.

Many families who survived life on the diggings returned to Melbourne to settle down in a business. Since farming land was difficult to buy, hundreds put their savings into small shops. Author Robert Martin described them in 1853 as 'the shopocracy of Melbourne'.

The typical shop or office building of those times had only a small street frontage, with a long narrow ground floor public area. The tenant and his family usually lived in cramped quarters on the upstairs level, until they made enough money to move to the suburbs. A tiny backyard contained kitchen, laundry, privy, and delivery area. Opening hours were from early morning until late at night, six days a week, with the wife often taking charge as soon as her children were old enough.

Into these small spaces squeezed a remarkable variety of trades and professions. By 1860, for instance, there were 240 drapers and clothiers in Melbourne and near suburbs. Another 130 tailors and 120 dressmakers made up garments from imported cloth; while 320 shops sold footwear. Some 70 auctioneers offered allotments and buildings to the public. To design the better class of building, 60 architects vied for business.

Brisk trade was carried out in home furnishings. Melbourne had 90 ironmongers, 40 furniture shops, 30 china and glass shops, and 30 fancy goods shops. To find servants, 17 labour registry offices operated. Fifteen music stores supplied sheet music, pianos, and other instruments.

Food supply depended partly on 120 bakeries working through the

Germain Nicholson, Melbourne's best-known grocer and anti-transportation agitator of the 1850s, whose main shop was located on the site of today's Manchester Unity Building in Swanston Street.

Alfred Felton emigrated to Melbourne in 1853 and became a wholesale druggist in Swanston Street. He made many benefactions, especially to the National Gallery of Victoria.

night; while 460 grocery shops offered a fair variety of local and imported edibles. Fifty restaurants and coffee shops did a brisk trade. Wine and spirit stores, 65 in number, delivered to city and inner suburbs. Fifty tobacconists supplied pipe tobacco, cigars and snuff.

The best-known grocer in Melbourne was Germain Nicholson, an Englishman who arrived in the 1840s and expanded his tea-importing business greatly during the gold rush. A renowned philanthropist, Nicholson allowed homeless immigrants to occupy his warehouses whenever space was available. His busiest shop was located opposite the Town Hall, on the north-west corner of Collins and Swanston streets, a site occupied today by the Manchester Unity building.

Medical problems were widespread. To assist sufferers, 130 doctors, 15 dentists, 9 opticians and 100 chemists made a good living. The best-remembered of these chemists was Essex-born Alfred Felton, who emigrated in 1853 and set up a drug supply house on the west side of Swanston Street, between Collins Street and Flinders Lane. Felton, later a prominent manufacturer, established the Felton Bequest which purchased many paintings for the National Gallery of Victoria.

Personal adornment was popular during good times and bad. No fewer than 105 Melbourne jewellers supplied gems and wedding rings, and repaired clocks and watches. Sixty hairdressers made an excellent

Footwear importer John Black built this impressive Victoria Arcade on the north side of Bourke Street between Elizabeth and Swanston streets. Architects were George Wharton and J. R. Burns, while S. T. Gill drew this lively lithograph, printed by J. S. Campbell about 1854. (La Trobe Collection).

VICTORI

BLACK PROPRIETOR

ARCADE
ARCADE,

living. Thirty professional photographers supplied portraits which were sent in thousands to loved ones 'at home'.

Agents were everywhere. Men described as 'brokers and commission agents' numbered 100, while 18 brokers specialised in buying and selling mining shares. To cope with legal problems, often complex because of the distance from Europe, 120 solicitors and 90 barristers acted for clients. Forty commercial printers supplied the variety of legal, business and personal stationery required.

Transport needs were assisted by 80 saddlers and 50 livery stables, although the latter had to move continually outwards to rent cheaper land on city fringes. Fifteen nightmen worked by individual contract to remove human waste to dumping grounds which also moved further afield as population grew.

Building of arcades for small shopkeepers began in Melbourne in 1853, in order to take maximum advantage of increasingly expensive city land. The first, called Queen's Arcade, was built on a two-acre site owned by Presbyterian minister Rev. James Clow on the south-west corner of Swanston and Lonsdale streets. The Arcade, containing eighty lockup shops, occupied an area 360 ft long by 33 ft wide. When gas arrived it was lit by 'a row of splendid chandeliers'. William Kelly attended the opening ball, at which 'fanciful dresses of the most outré description abounded', with many ladies exhibiting 'an extreme of nudity' around the shoulders.

Although Queen's Arcade at first caused a sensation, it was a little too remote from the fashionable part of Collins Street. The shops soon fell into the hands of what William Kelly described as 'an associated Jewish confraternity', by which he meant the Levy brothers, Goodman, Lewis and Nathaniel; and the Lazarus brothers, Samuel and Solomon. These keen traders filled the windows with 'dolls, pictures, cigars, old clo', jewellery, toys, perfumery, bad stationery, infirm musical instruments' and so on. In the middle was an office where money was advanced at 50% interest.

Throughout its early years, Melbourne faced the constant threat of devastating fires spreading among frail timber shops and dwellings which still outnumbered those built in stone or brick.

The gold-rush city inherited an antiquated fire-fighting system whereby individually insured buildings were supposed to be protected by fire engines owned by the Victoria Insurance Co. But in November

1853 a fire destroyed several Collins Street buildings owned by Jewish shopkeepers, along with about £200,000 worth of stock.

George Train described the ludicrous scene when firefighters were summoned by the ringing of a hand alarm bell. Two water carts arrived, each holding about 200 gallons of Yarra water. This was poured into 'two or three asthmatic fire engines' so it could be pumped into the blaze. 'Had there been any wind', wrote Train, 'the whole street must have gone by the board'.

A few weeks later, in December 1853, another serious fire burned down half a dozen buildings in Flinders Lane. Train and several American friends, who had seen modern fire pumps operating in Boston, took up a subscription and raised several thousand pounds to begin a volunteer firefighting service. A large fire bell was hung in the Town Hall tower, and more powerful pumps ordered, along with sufficient hose to connect with the Yarra through a series of engines.

The insurance companies got their act together in 1855, when they agreed to combine all private brigades into a United Insurance Companies Fire Brigade. Joseph Dalton was appointed full-time super-intendent, and two new engines named 'Neptune' and 'Deluge' imported. At the same time, the government installed a steam pumping station in Spring Street, which constantly filled a 150,000-gallon tank on Eastern Hill, allowing water to run by gravity through the city and Collingwood. Barracks on the corner of Collins and King streets were converted into a central fire station, with a second station alongside the Town Hall.

Meanwhile, volunteer brigades were started in several suburbs, including South Melbourne, Collingwood and Williamstown (1854), North Melbourne, Richmond and Prahran (1855), and St Kilda (1857). A Port Melbourne brigade was started in 1855, after a huge fire in January which levelled nearly three acres of timber stores and dwellings.

Melbourne's worst fire of the decade occurred on 25 February 1859, when a North Melbourne bakery went up in flames, spreading rapidly through a block of forty wooden houses and shops, and obliterating the area bounded by Flemington Road, Wreckyn Street, Courtney Street and Villiers Street. At first the brigade could not find water plugs, which were buried under a layer of mud. Even when connected, the hoses were too short to reach the fire.

Insurance business during the early years of the gold rush was conducted by branches of about a dozen overseas and colonial companies. The

London-based People's Provident Assurance Society set itself up in Collins Street, with Michael O'Grady as secretary, but offered mainly life insurance. The Launceston-based Cornwall Fire & Marine Insurance Co. operated in Melbourne through its agent, Fulton's Foundry. The Sydney-based Australian Mutual Provident Society used its Melbourne solicitor, Henry Jennings, as agent.

By 1857, merchant James Francis estimated that premiums of '£300,000 a year leave the colony for the benefit of foreign [insurance] companies'. Yet the most pressing need, satisfactory fire insurance, was not being met. Francis told a Legislative Assembly inquiry that even in his own prosperous warehouse business, he had been unable to obtain insurance against fire.

The first insurance companies formed in Melbourne in the 1840s had gone into liquidation after paying out high and sometimes suspicious fire claims. But in the euphoria of the gold rush, several new organisations decided to take the risk.

The first to float its shares was the Colonial Insurance Co., formed in 1856 by a powerful Melbourne group which included Richard Guthridge, William Clark, D. S. Campbell, W. M. Bell, F. J. Sargood and Charles Vaughan. The company established an office on the south side of Collins Street, near Elizabeth Street, with William Green as managing director and Charles Lucas as secretary. It raised £30,000 in

Mars and Elizabeth Buckley, whose gold-rush fortune enabled them to build the large Buckley & Nunn emporium in Bourke Street (now David Jones), and the mansion 'Beaulieu' in Toorak. (La Trobe Collection).

William Strutt's painting of a hay wagon blazing in a Melbourne street in the 1850s shows the helpless terror felt by inhabitants in the face of unexpected fires. (Dixson Library).

paid-up capital, mainly from large merchants, and insured them against fire to the extent of a million pounds. The idea seemed to work: Green was able to tell a parliamentary inquiry that by July 1857 the company had made £26,000 profit.

The second local company to enter this risky field was the Australasian Fire & Life Insurance Co., which floated its shares in 1857 to the extent of £25,000. Merchant J. G. Francis was managing director. William Macredie, a partner in Matthew Lang's liquor business, was manager. Ironmonger Thomas Loader was appointed secretary. An office was established in the Hall of Commerce in Collins Street, still Melbourne's financial heartland today. This company did not like the idea of unlimited personal liability which applied to directors of the Colonial Insurance Co., and limited its payouts to double the amount of share subscriptions. Despite its caution, this company too prospered, its £1 shares being worth three times that amount within five years.

Although Melbourne merchants were in daily competition with one another, they needed a trade association to lobby government and City Council on their common needs. That multi-talented merchant William Westgarth saw the need very early in the gold rush. Almost singlehanded he formed the Melbourne Chamber of Commerce in 1851 and became its first president. J. B. Were was elected president from 1852-4, followed by A. R. Cruikshank (1854-6), James McCulloch, MLC (1856-

7), David Moore, MLA (1857-8), H. W. Farrar (1858-9), William Nicholson, MLA (1859-60), and C. E. Bright (1860-2).

The Chamber achieved a major success in 1852 when it persuaded Collector of Customs J. H. N. Cassell to abandon the complex system of levying tariffs which had been inherited from New South Wales, and impose simplified duties mainly on items like liquor and tobacco. In effect, this was the nearest that Victoria ever came to being a free-trade colony. Having won its immediate object, the Chamber of Commerce faded out for a time.

During the busiest period of the gold rush, it seemed that nothing could be done to establish a central 'news room' where merchants could obtain the latest shipping and market information. When the outspoken American trader George Train arrived in Melbourne in May 1853, he was surprised to find there was nowhere except pubs in which to discuss affairs with other merchants. Only one newspaper had 'a commercial reporter at a hall called Lloyds Room, back of the Royal Hotel', wrote Train. Eventually he located Edward Wilson, who had purchased the *Argus* with a loan of £300 and was struggling to make ends meet. But all Wilson could offer was a list of shipping arrivals and departures— nothing else to show the state of trade.

'I felt almost lost', wrote Train. He managed to persuade about fifty old and new merchants to hold informal meetings at 2 p.m. each day. In this way, said Train, 'we were enabled to compare notes regarding the markets', and even begin publication of the first regular list of merchandise prices.

Their landlord, Samuel Moss, demolished the premises to begin building the Criterion Hotel, forcing the merchants to plan their own meeting place. A company was floated to build a 'Hall of Commerce'. According to Train, gold-buyer Edward Khull was the most active promoter, raising £23,000 towards building costs. La Trobe refused to grant Crown land for private purposes, so a double allotment was purchased on the south side of Collins Street, between Elizabeth and Queen streets. Here in 1855 an impressive three-storey stone building arose, and was soon fully let. Richard Woolley, secretary of a revitalised Chamber of Commerce, was glad to take space for £250 a year, for the building was right in the middle of a thriving business community. In later years, Reuter's overseas commercial telegraph service was established in the building, giving instant access to overseas market trends. After the Hall of Commerce was demolished, Capel Court was established on the same site.

The Melbourne Exchange Building, on the south side of Flinders Lane between Market and William streets, was planned by a joint-stock company with a special Act of Parliament in 1855 allowing it to sell shares. When the company ran into difficulties, the government took over part of the building to install a Central Telegraph Station. The small structure at right was the house of Charles Jarman, Exchange Keeper.

W. G. Baillie was among the first brokers to attempt formation of a Melbourne Stock Exchange in the 1850s.

The Hall of Commerce was erected in 1855 on the south side of Collins Street, between Elizabeth and Queen streets, to accommodate a growing band of stockbrokers and financiers, as well as the Melbourne Chamber of Commerce. In later years it was renamed the Exchange Building. S. T. Gill's lithograph also shows (from left) James Blundell's

printing and bookselling establishment, where Gill had an upstairs studio. Next door is the short-lived Imperial Hotel, soon converted into offices. On the west side of the Hall of Commerce was W. M. Tennent's auction rooms, and the Union Bank on the corner of Queen Street. (La Trobe Collection).

The ebullient early years of the gold rush and flotation of joint-stock companies led to the first enthusiastic trading in shares, and the emergence of a small group of professional stockbrokers to handle the business. First in the field was Edward Khull, a former Victorian Government Printer who found gold and share trading more rewarding than working for bureaucrats. Khull commenced publication of Melbourne's first advertised share quotations in the *Argus* on 18 October 1852. He listed shares of thirteen companies—five banks, three railway companies, and five other firms dealing in shipping, insurance, gas, water, and private gold escort operations.

The idea that company shares could be bought and sold for profit or loss spread among Melbourne's middle class. By 1853 the merchant J. B. Were had begun to offer stockbroking services to the public. Soon William Clark & Sons, J. R. Fraser, and a few others were handling share trading. The failure of some private railway companies in the mid-1850s dealt a severe blow to brokers and clients who had taken up their shares. J. B. Were went bankrupt in 1857, but had recovered by 1859, when what the *Age* described as a 'share buying mania' rocked Melbourne.

The share boom at the end of the gold decade was largely based on fundamental changes occurring on the diggings. Most easily-won gold had been scraped out of rivers and shallow holes by individual miners working on their own account. To get at gold lying deeper in the ground, mining companies using expensive machinery and employing wage labour had to be floated. Their results seemed so good that the shares became the talk of Ballarat, Bendigo and Melbourne.

'The city is in commotion about mining, sluicing, crushing and water-supplying companies', said the *Age* on 30 July 1859. The public had paid 'extravagant premiums' for their shares. But, warned the newspaper, in most cases 'the bubble bursts and leaves a host of dupes to lament its explosion'.

So it proved. When about fifty mining companies had floated, the banks suddenly announced in September 1859 that no further loans would be made with mining shares as collateral. Confidence collapsed overnight. One company, W. J. T. Clarke's Bolinda Quartz Mining Co., had seen its shares more than double in price to £4 10s before they dropped to nil. In the meantime, Clarke had sold hundreds of acres of alleged gold-bearing land to the company for £16,000, half of which he took in cash. He was laughing: other investors were weeping.

The first Temple Court was built on the north side of Collins Street, midway between Queen and William streets, in 1858-9. At first it was intended solely as lawyers' offices, but was gradually taken over by stockbrokers, insurance companies, and shipping agents. At left in this engraving is Lloyd's Rooms, ship brokers. The building on the right was occupied by George Walstab, estate agent; and Gordon & Gotch, newsagents' distributors.

Attempts to regulate share trading by forming a permanent stock exchange began in October 1859. Chief promoters were the broking partnership of W. G. Baillie and J. S. Butters, who proposed a management committee representing investors as well as stockbrokers. After many difficulties, a regular stock exchange with rules based on those of the London Stock Exchange finally emerged in 1861.

During these varied financial experiences, a £50,000 Melbourne Exchange Company had been floated to erect a stock exchange building. Its main promoters were William Nicholson, William Locke, Thomas Dickson, Walter Hammill, D. S. Campbell, John Goodman, D. H. Cleve, Edward Khull, A. R. Cruikshank, and James McCulloch.

The government allowed the company to lease part of the Custom

Many artists were attracted to paint the Melbourne Exhibition Building of 1854 in William Street, but none quite matched the exuberant atmosphere of S. T. Gill's lithograph. (La Trobe Collection).
The inset photograph shows John Brooke, a journalist who supervised construction of the leaky building.

The Melbourne Exhibition Bu
N. W. Angle. 185

House reserve, providing an allotment on the south side of Flinders Lane, between Market and William streets, directly between the Custom House and Western Market.

Young architect Lloyd Tayler designed a romantic structure for the site, its frontage heavily decorated with Grecian columns. The building was complete by 1858, but was never successful as a commercial centre. Most brokers preferred to operate in a more central part of town. The government resumed possession the following year, using the building for a Central Telegraph Office between 1859 and 1872.

After reading reports of the amazing Crystal Palace exhibition in London in 1851, the ambitious citizens of Melbourne decided they should erect a similar venue to publicise the colony's progress.

A Victoria Industrial Society had been formed in 1850 under the management of former Aboriginal Protector William Le Souef, but after one mediocre exhibition, the society became moribund during the early gold rush years. It revived in 1854, when the government commissioned Samuel Merrett to design Melbourne's own Crystal Palace.

The site chosen was an allotment of Crown land on the eastern side of William Street, between Little Lonsdale and La Trobe streets, where the Old Royal Mint building stands today. A 28-year-old radical journalist and politician, J. H. Brooke, was charged with supervision of the £21,000 project.

Samuel Merrett's design envisaged an elegant, airy framework of timber and iron, painted white, 257 feet long, 90 feet wide, and 50 feet high. Let into its walls were nearly 200 large windows, while the roof itself mainly comprised frames fitted with glass. The exhibition area contained nearly 20,000 cubic feet of space, well lit on even the dullest day, while 300 gas lights were added for evening events as soon as mains were laid. William Kelly took several newly-arrived friends to see the building, and was pleased by their 'ebullitions of astonishment'.

Governor Hotham opened the first twelve-week exhibition on 17 October 1854 to the sound of cannon firing on Flagstaff Hill, bands playing, and almost the entire population of Melbourne crowding around to view the wondrous addition to their city. Massed choirs burst into a Handel oratorio, while an Exhibition Ode written by *Age* journalist David Blair called on residents to 'mould a noble nation'. The *Age* scored another publicity scoop by installing its presses in the building, and running off the first copies of their new newspaper to hand out to spectators.

Most of the 400-odd exhibits were connected with agricultural and gold production. However, intimations of manufacturing skill appeared. William Kelly was impressed by fine leatherwork in racing, hunting and ladies' saddles. However, locally-made jewellery was 'of that massive, ponderous manufacture generally adapted to parvenus [social climbers]'; while the paintings, he thought, lacked an 'easy style of faultless finish'. In the machinery section, quartz crushers were the main item, while Reginald Scaife used a coining machine to punch out commemorative Exhibition medals.

Several further displays held in the building showed continual progress in local manufactures. But within three years the structure had deteriorated, while constant criticism was heard of unbearable light and heat streaming through the glass roof during summer. Some panes cracked, and the roof had to be covered with canvas to keep out the rain. In 1858 the panes were repaired and coated internally with white paint, reducing the glare.

A further major exhibition was held in 1861, featuring a vast pyramid, 10 feet square by nearly 45 feet high, representing the amount of gold officially exported during the 1850s. But by 1869 the building was in such poor shape that it had to be demolished.

Quite a number of secondary industries were set up in Melbourne and suburbs during the gold decade. The most significant using steam power in 1860 were:

	No. of firms	No. of employees
Agricultural machinery	6	31
Biscuit makers	2	19
Boiler making	1	20
Breweries	10	139
Brickyards	13	77
Coach factories	10	151
Cordial factories	5	57
Electroplaters	2	7
Fellmongers	3	41
Gas manufacture	2	75

	No. of firms	No. of employees
Ginger beer and soda water	2	14
Ice making	1	7
Iron rolling	2	24
Laundries	1	4
Machinists	2	106
Metal foundries	8	422
Millwrights	1	12
Organ and piano makers	2	4
Paper bag makers	2	9
Rail carriage factory	1	40
Sawmills	20	242
Soap and candle makers	6	59
Sugar refinery	1	100
Surgical instrument makers	3	7
Tanneries	4	85
	114	1,782

Of these 1,782 employees, only 13 were women, most being employed in soap and candle works, and three in the only steam laundry. Among the biggest employers of labour—iron, brass and copper foundries and sawmills—no women at all were employed.

Manufacturers of wearing apparel, who did not use steam power at that time, were bigger employers of women. Bourke Street draper Mars Buckley told a Legislative Assembly inquiry into tariffs in 1860 that while he relied mainly on English goods, his manufacturing section in Melbourne employed twenty women and ten men to make tailored suits, dresses, mantles, straw and silk bonnets, and even carpets.

Another clothing manufacturer, James Nesbitt of Henry & Co., said he employed up to 120 women during good times to make medium-grade clothing. They were paid from 20s to 30s a week, depending on output, and worked from 8.30 a.m. to 6 p.m., six days a week. However, imported clothing had cut employment to about thirty women. The remainder—mostly wives of men at the diggings—were suffering 'great distress' through lack of work.

A boot manufacturer, Henry Turnbull of Collingwood, told the inquiry that several shoe factories which had once employed up to fifty people each were now reduced to four or five, with perhaps one woman. He did not know of a single apprentice in the trade.

Melbourne's biggest employer of industrial labour was Scottish-born Thomas Fulton, who established the first foundry in 1842 and built Victoria's first stationery steam engine. Fulton worked in partnership with George Annand and Robert Smith until 1855, then continued the business as sole proprietor. By the end of the gold decade, Fulton was employing 150 men on a large allotment running from Flinders Street through to Flinders Lane, near the west side of King Street. He supplied every kind of metal manufacturing and repair work needed by the growing city, as well as crushing machines for the diggings.

Smaller metal-working enterprises were set up during the gold decade by hardworking tradesmen who seized opportunities to expand. John Buncle, born in Edinburgh, emigrated in 1852 and at first worked for Robert Langlands's well-established foundry alongside the Fulton works. Within a year Buncle was able to open his own foundry in Flemington Road, supplying ironwork for several Melbourne bridges before specialising in agricultural implements.

John McIlwraith, a Scottish-born plumber, emigrated in 1853, opened shops to sell lead and zinc pipes, and in 1861 established his own factory to manufacture lead products. Later he became prominent in the shipping industry.

Another lead pipe maker was James Coop, who arrived in 1855 and started business on the south side of Little Collins Street, between Elizabeth and Queen streets. Coop complained that rent, fuel and water was much more expensive in Melbourne than in England. He employed his five sons in the business, and told the 1860 inquiry that 'If I had wages to pay I could not compete [against imports]'.

John Danks, a Staffordshire man, emigrated in 1857, opening a hardware manufacturing establishment next door to the Britannia Inn, which occupied the south-east corner of Bourke and Queen streets. One of Danks's early contracts was to make pipe connections for the Yan Yean water scheme. The firm established many branches and grew to 200 employees by the end of the century.

Local stoneware was moulded and fired both at Batman's Swamp (below Batman's Hill) and in Flemington. Thomas Kelly, who emigrated from Glasgow, told the 1860 tariff inquiry that there were 'acres of best pipe clay' in Batman's Swamp, from which he made jars for preserves, ginger beer bottles, milk pans and drainage pipes. However, every ship that arrived carried tons of cheap imported stoneware as 'dead weight' in the hold.

E. B. Williamson, proprietor of Flemington Pottery, said he could make one mile of earthenware piping per week. He wanted to import an American machine which could mould eight ginger beer bottles per minute, but cheap imports put it out of the question.

The final sad story on import competition came from Joseph Wilkie, MLA, who made a living in Collins Street by selling pianos and sheet music. Plenty of skilled piano-makers had emigrated to Melbourne, said Wilkie, but every attempt to compete with imports on price had failed. He was backed by James Carnegie, an immigrant of 1856, who had been trained in London to make high-grade piano cabinets. Carnegie said that most piano-makers in Victoria were 'positively destitute', and were trying to scratch out a living on the goldfields. Complete pianos could not be made here for less than £45, whereas they could be imported for about £30. Carnegie himself had been forced to make coffins and act as undertaker in his small factory on the corner of Hoddle and Highett streets, Richmond.

The main surviving factory of the 1850s which can be seen today is the Swallow & Ariell biscuit works on the corner of Stokes and Rouse streets, Port Melbourne. This was built by Thomas Swallow, an Englishman who went to the California gold rush in 1849, and four years later married Scottish-born Isabella Fulton of Vermont, USA. Swallow took his wife and a consignment of the latest Colt revolvers to the Ballarat diggings in 1853. They prospered, although the couple's first child was born in a tent. Returning to Port Melbourne, Swallow went into partnership with Thomas Ariell, renting premises in Rouse Street from T. B. Payne to make ships' biscuits. Soon the partners were supplying the entire waterfront, and were able to begin building the three-storey rendered brick corner structure which still stands.

Swallow told the 1860 tariff inquiry that he was employing twenty men and boys to make up fifteen tons of ships' biscuits and two tons of fancy biscuits each week. (He brought samples with him to give to committee members). With a 10% tariff, said Swallow, he could supply the entire colony. After protection was granted, Swallow & Ariell's works expanded by the end of the century to cover three acres and employ 1,600 people. Today the factory is deserted.

Many of these manufacturers of the 1850s were able to survive because of the 'natural protection' given by Melbourne's remoteness from world production centres. In order to develop beyond that stage, artificial protection had to be given by means of high tariff barriers.

Throughout most of the gold decade, the British ideal of 'free trade' had been accepted by practically all Victorians. One of the few exceptions was James Harrison, editor of the *Geelong Advertiser*, who advocated a mild form of protectionism from 1851 onwards. His ideas received support in 1856, when the Tariff League of Victoria was formed with many manufacturers and artisans in support. During a temporary slump that year, a petition to Parliament from 'tradesmen, mechanics, artisans, laborers, &c.' claimed that unemployment was being 'mainly produced by the undue competition to which Victorian labor is exposed, owing to the unrestricted imports of all kinds of manufactured articles and produce'.

The petitioners forecast 'evil consequences that must inevitably ensue to thousands of the rising youth of the Colony, unless means be adopted to encourage native industry'. Apprenticeship had already been almost extinguished, 'debarring the younger portion of the community from becoming skilled in various trades and useful branches of mechanical labor that are generally fostered in civilised countries'.

Wholesale merchants, who controlled most channels of distribution, were not necessarily averse to handling local manufactures as well as imported goods. Even a long-established importer like G. W. Cole could write in the introduction to an 1860 book named *Protection* that tariffs should be levied on all manufactured imports, as this would 'induce people to settle in the colony, and embark in manufacturing industry'.

The story of how *Age* proprietor David Syme became converted from free trade to protectionist ideas, and used the columns of his newspaper to force politicians into adopting tariffs, belongs to a later period, and need not detain us here. It is sufficient to say that by 1865, the first moderate duties had been imposed on imports of many articles of wearing apparel and saddlery which could be manufactured locally. Under this steadily expanding system, Melbourne grew into one of the world's biggest manufacturing centres outside Europe and America. Today, under a renewal of free trade ideology, Victoria's manufacturing and employment capacity has been shattered, perhaps permanently.

Collins Street became the financial heart of Melbourne after the gold rush. This view by Francois Cogné looking east from Queen Street shows at extreme left the Bank of New South Wales, the facade of which can be still be seen at Melbourne University. The lower buildings include warehouses and James McEwan's first ironmongery. In the distance can be seen the spire of Scots Church and the Treasury. At extreme right is the Union Bank. To its left is the Hall of Commerce and Criterion Hotel. The National Bank is further down the same block. (La Trobe Collection).

12

A pleasant decade
for bankers

Four small banks were sufficient to handle Melbourne's financial affairs before the gold rush. But when wealth beyond dreams flooded into the city from the diggings, nine major banks began conducting business, their new buildings helping to convert Collins Street into an imposing boulevard. Edwin Booth observed at the time that 'Next to the churches, the banks are perhaps the most conspicuous objects in the city'. Each vied with the others in erecting magnificent business premises. 'Polished marble and granite, imported from Europe at immense cost, form the porticoes and pillars of nearly all of them, whilst the sculptor's art has been laid under contribution for an ornamentation sometimes more costly than correct', said Booth.

Banking in the 1850s seemed to prosper regardless of trade fluctuations. Deposits in the nine trading banks increased from less than £800,000 in 1851 to £7,225,000 ten years later—and on most of this huge amount they paid no interest at all. As major buyers and shippers of gold bullion, the banks possessed large reserves against which they could safely issue their own banknotes, discount bills, and lend money on mortgage at high interest rates. In 1860 the major banks were circulating £2 million in notes and bills, and another £2 million in gold and silver coins. They were holding nearly £10 million in secured loans, and already owned more than £500,000 in landed property. Yearly dividends ranged from 10% for the Colonial Bank to 15% for the local branch of the Bank of New South Wales. Heady days!

Melbourne's first bank was established by the Sydney-based Bank of Australasia. Samuel Ramsden built its two-storey stone headquarters in 1840 on the north side of Collins Street, near Queen Street. In 1852 a single-storey annexe was added at the corner of Bank Place to cope with extra gold-rush business. By 1860 the Melbourne bank was making profits at the rate of £56,000 a year.

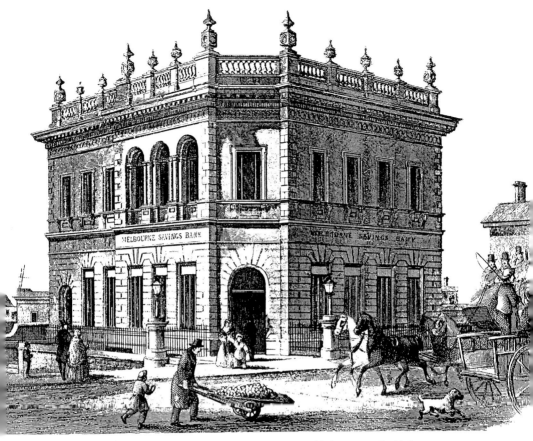

The Melbourne Savings Bank, which began in 1841, was able by 1858 to build this striking white stone head office on the south-west corner of Flinders Lane and Market Street. It remained head office until 1912, being sold to the Harbour Trust then demolished in 1929.

The Sydney-controlled Union Bank opened its first modest rented premises in Melbourne only a few weeks after the Bank of Australasia. In 1845 it erected an impressive two-storey freestone headquarters on the south-east corner of Collins and Queen streets, spacious enough to see it through the gold rush. By 1860, manager Frederick Cook was able to report happily that the Melbourne branch could pay a 14% dividend.

The highly successful Melbourne Savings Bank began with government assistance in 1841. Its aim was to provide the working classes with a safe place to deposit their humble shillings. By the time of the gold rush, it was conducting steady, cautious business on behalf of 700 depositors, and branches had been opened at several provincial centres.

With the huge increase in gold-rush population, the government decided (by Act 16 Vic. No. 37, 7 February 1853) to place all savings banks under a central group of five commissioners. The first appointed were three established merchants, Andrew Knight, MLC; Octavius Brown; and Andrew Russell, MLC; with Henry Smith as chairman, and retired squatter Charles Hutton as fifth member.

The Melbourne Savings Bank's founding part-time manager, magistrate James Smith, soon retired. English-born Charles Flaxman, 47, a former editor of the *South Australian Register*, was appointed in his place with the title of Comptroller; assisted by James Brock as Actuary.

At first the new bank continued business in its tiny rented premises in the Melbourne Fire & Marine Insurance Co. building in Collins Street. John Alsop, who started there as a 14-year-old counter clerk in 1854 and later became Actuary, recalled that the counter was doubled in width to prevent customers from assaulting officers. This made it almost impossible to open the cash drawer. A 'cedar box' about three feet square served as office lavatory.

Flaxman soon began planning spacious new premises. Land was granted by the government in 1854 on the north-west corner of the Customs reserve, at Flinders Lane and Market Street. Architects Charles Swyer and Albert Purchas designed a solid but decorative square building, faced in light-coloured stone from Kangaroo Point near Ararat. The building was erected by John and Alfred Craven of Collingwood for £10,800, and opened for business on 22 June 1858.

By June 1860 the commissioners were handling 11,400 savings accounts—6,700 of them in Melbourne—on which 4% interest was paid. Melbourne deposits alone totalled £350,000. The commissioners judged this to be 'gratifying and encouraging evidence of provident habits among the laboring classes'. During the 1850s the money was mostly loaned on property mortgages at high interest rates. In 1858 the commissioners abandoned mortgages for some years, and followed a more conservative line of investing in government debentures paying 6%. This policy enabled loans to be granted for completion of the Yan Yean water supply works, besides shielding the bank's depositors against economic fluctuations. If similar ideas had been followed in our own times, the State Bank would still belong to the people of Victoria.

Just before the major gold discoveries, Sydney's Bank of New South Wales (now Westpac) decided that its Melbourne business was extensive enough to replace an agency arrangement operated by accountant Archibald McLachlan. In January 1851 the bank rented as its first premises Cr H. W. Mortimer's three-storey stone butcher's shop and

H. W. Mortimer's substantial butcher's shop and residence on the north-east corner of Collins and William streets, altered to become the first Bank of New South Wales chamber in 1851. S. T. Gill's sketch shows the scene in 1855. (La Trobe Collection).

residence on the north-east corner of Collins and William streets. Charles Vallack, the first full-time manager, ordered a supply of £1 and £5 banknotes to be engraved in Melbourne by Thomas Ham.

With the discovery of gold later that year, the Bank of New South Wales was well placed for expansion. In 1852 it bought an allotment on the north side of Collins Street, between Elizabeth and Queen streets. The bank paid £5,700 for half the area which had been sold by the Crown in 1837 for only £28. Rush of business and difficulty of finding builders prevented immediate construction of a new bank. Then in 1854, manager Vallack resigned, leaving accountant John Badcock to carry on.

Not until the mid-1850s was there time to hold a design competition for a new bank building. The contest was won by a 28-year-old

Cornish-born architect, Joseph Reed, who had just finished designing the Melbourne Public Library. For the bank, Reed designed an elaborate two-storey Italianate facade, based on St Mark's Library in Venice. W. C. Cornish, Parliament House builder, erected the bank for £24,000; while sculptor Charles Summers carved intricate friezes for the Collins Street frontage. The bank opened its new quarters on 1 July 1858. Melbourne loved it so much that when demolition was necessary in 1933, the facade was transferred piece by piece to Melbourne University. There, with extraordinary lack of taste, it was stuck to the wall of a box-like brick School of Commerce, where it may be seen to this day.

Should all the dividends from Melbourne banking business go to Sydney and London? Melburnians didn't think so, and attempted to float their own banks. Unfortunately, a locally-financed institution, the Port Phillip Bank, had collapsed before the gold rush and was remembered with bitterness. But in 1852 the colony seemed so much wealthier that Melbourne investors again became confident of good returns.

One night towards the end of that marvellous gold-rush year, 1852, Dr Thomas Black was dining at his Richmond home with William Highett and other merchants. They determined then and there to float a local bank, and next morning approached Captain G. W. Cole to take up shares. He roared 'I'll have nothing to do with it!' Returning to Collins Street, the would-be entrepreneurs saw Henry Miller, MLC, plodding up the hill: he too refused. Then they went into Germain Nicholson's grocery, and he agreed to buy shares. Other prominent men like Hugh Glass and William Westgarth promised support. A public meeting was held at the Royal Hotel (soon to become the Criterion), where Henry Miller changed his mind and took up shares. After that the bank's success was assured.

The enthusiasts called their institution the Bank of Victoria. Their first chamber was established in three adjoining two-storey houses on the east side of Swanston Street, between Flinders Lane and Collins Street, belonging to Dr Black. Openings were knocked through the walls to give access, and trading began on 3 January 1853. Arrangements for floating the company were ratified by Legislative Council Act 17 Vic. No. 17, dated 1 March 1854. First directors were Henry Miller (chairman), William Highett, William Nicholson, W. F. Splatt, W. H. Tuckett and Alexander Wilson. The manager was 32-year-old John Matheson, self-educated son of penniless Scottish tenant farmers, who had worked for several branches of the Union Bank. Matheson held his position for nearly thirty years, building 'St Leonard's' at St Kilda and retiring wealthy.

Under Matheson the bank did extremely well, showing £25,000 profit and paying 10% dividend in 1860. The following year it bought a large allotment on the south side of Collins Street, between Elizabeth and Swanston streets, for £22,000. Architects Alfred Smith and Arthur Johnson designed a substantial new building, attractively faced in freestone, erected at a cost of £40,000.

The London-based Oriental Bank began business in 1854 in a tall red-brick building on the eastern side of Queen Street, between Flinders Lane and Collins Street. In 1858 it leased that structure to promoters of the National Bank, and moved across Queen Street to a new building designed by architects James Robertson and Thomas Hale to look more

By 1857 the Oriental Bank had made enough profits from the gold rush to build this Grecian-inspired banking temple on the south-west corner of Queen Street and Flinders Lane. In this engraving, the Ship Inn which can be seen further along Flinders Lane still stands.

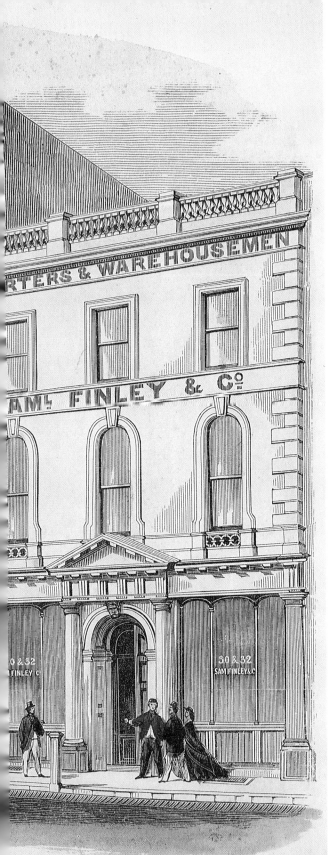

The locally-financed Bank of Victoria built this solid head office on the south side of Collins Street, between Elizabeth and Swanston streets, in 1861. (Engraving by Sam Calvert, La Trobe Collection).

Dr Thomas Black, who invented the Bank of Victoria at a good dinner.

The support of Henry Miller, MLC, renowned as a financial wizard, was vital to the bank's success.

John Matheson, 32-year-old son of a Scottish crofter, was first manager of the Bank of Victoria.

like a Greek temple than a financial institution. Manager Francis Cargill retired soon afterwards in favour of Adam Burnes. By 1860 the Oriental Bank was making a profit of £88,000 a year in Melbourne and paying 14% dividend. London headquarters collapsed in 1884 after making large advances to sugar and coffee planters, dragging the Melbourne operation down with it.

Another English institution, the London Chartered Bank, was sufficiently impressed by Melbourne's prospects to establish a branch under manager John Bramwell in 1854. This bank set up modest offices on the south side of Collins Street, between Queen and Market streets. By 1860 it was showing an annual profit of £25,000 and paying 7% dividend to shareholders.

The English, Scottish & Australian Bank began trading in Melbourne at about the same time as the London Chartered Bank. Manager F. A. Walsh established the E. S. & A's first offices on the north-west corner of Flinders Lane and Elizabeth Street. Although profitable, this bank adopted a cautious policy, paying only 5% dividend in 1860, and spending most of its assets on setting up suburban branches in George Street, Collingwood, and Thompson Street, Williamstown.

The Bank of Victoria consumed all locally-available banking capital for nearly three years after its formation. In July 1855, however, other Melbourne entrepreneurs decided there could be a place for a bank concentrating on small investors and borrowers. This was the brainchild of Alexander Gibb, a St Kilda investor ambitious to run his own bank.

Gibb enlisted the aid of John O'Shanassy, MLC, persuading him in October 1855 to accept the position of chairman of the Colonial Bank of Australasia. O'Shanassy sent dozens of agents around Melbourne and the diggings, offering the bank's shares on easy terms. The prospectus promised to pay good interest on deposits while arranging overdrafts on the strength of personal guarantees. Conservative bankers were horrified, but soon the bank was on its feet, with £30,000 subscribed. Incorporation was approved by Legislative Council Act on 19 March 1856. The new institution was popularly known as the 'Diggers' Bank' or the 'Catholic Bank'.

For its immediate needs, the Colonial Bank bought the freehold of the Imperial Hotel on the north-east corner of Elizabeth and Little Collins streets. The premises were quickly converted and opened for business on 14 April 1856.

As manager the directors had enticed from the Union Bank the experienced T. E. Boyd, paying him the unprecedented salary of £1,500 a year. Boyd was admiringly described by other bankers as 'strict and severe'; while to 'Garryowen' he was 'a thorough "pincher".' It was probably due to Boyd's tight control as much as to O'Shanassy's popularity that the bank survived. By 1860 it was showing £15,000 a year profit on paid-up capital of £312,000.

For reasons not on record, O'Shanassy refused to appoint Alexander Gibb to an executive position with the Colonial Bank. Angrily, Gibb determined to float yet another local institution, to be called the National Bank. At public meetings during October and November 1857, he persuaded a number of Melbourne merchants that the decision by

Extraordinary events, satirised in this Melbourne Punch *cartoon of 1858, surrounded the opening of the new National Bank. A wealthy squatter named Andrew Cruikshank (standing, below) decided to back the bank, but appointed his 'lapdog' Daniel Hughes (below, right) as manager. This antagonised Alexander Gibb, who refused to hand over the books and keys. Hughes arranged for the safe to be cracked, and opened for business on 4 October 1858. (National Bank Archives).*

The National Bank established its head office in 1859 in this unpretentious stone building on the south side of Collins Street, between Elizabeth and Queen streets. Alfred Bliss, next door, was an auctioneer whose building was shared by J. M. Grant, solicitor and radical politician. On the other side was James Wade's little warehouse.

established banks to back railway construction would severely limit the funds available for normal mercantile operations. Thus a new bank was needed: one which would use the miners' gold to help finance merchants.

The National Bank's first prospectus was printed, and Gibb, accompanied by a professional spruiker known as James 'Orator' McEachern, took off by coach for the diggings to approach miners. Their best efforts failed: less than £1,000 worth of shares were sold. Gibb was ready to give up, when he met Andrew Cruikshank, MLC, a wealthy 37-year-old squatter and merchant who had just resigned from the Union Bank board after disagreements with other directors, and wanted to start his own bank.

By this stroke of fate, the National Bank was saved. With Cruik-shank's name and wealth behind it, nearly 70,000 shares were rapidly subscribed by 1,300 shareholders. The original premises of the Oriental Bank in Queen Street were leased and made ready for opening.

Now Cruikshank too turned against Alexander Gibb. As general manager he appointed Daniel Hughes, a 38-year-old Irish banker and P. & O. agent. Osmond Gilles of Hobart was named as manager. Once again Alexander Gibb had been refused an executive post. In a fury, he refused to hand over the account books or keys to the strongroom.* Hughes arranged to have the strongroom broken open, and was able to begin business on 4 October 1858.

Extraordinary meetings of shareholders who supported Gibb tried to prevent Cruikshank and Hughes from continuing operations. The *Age* called the pair 'discreditable and audacious schemers', who were trying to run the bank for their own benefit. After directors' meetings at which physical violence was threatened, Cruikshank resigned in disgust, and died only a few weeks later, on 10 February 1859. A new board was elected, dominated by F. B. Franklyn, proprietor of the *Herald*.

As the bank began to settle down from its early turmoil, it leased from shipping agents Mackay, Baines & Co. a new head office. This was a modest two-storey stone building on the south side of Collins Street, between Elizabeth and Queen streets, which remained headquarters from 1859 to 1870.

However, when independent auditors Thomas Loader and Moritz Michaelis examined the books in 1860, they found that most of the new directors had loaned themselves large amounts. In Melbourne's first major banking scandal, nearly £70,000 of the bank's £200,000 paid-up capital had been lost forever. Five directors—Thomas Lempriere, John Hastie, F. B. Franklyn, Thomas Brown and John Houston—were forced to resign. Manager Osmond Gilles was dismissed and replaced by an experienced banker, Alexander Cunningham.

A year later the bank was able to pay its first dividend, and begin its long struggle to become Melbourne's leading private bank, the only survivor of the gold-rush decade to continue trading today under its original name.

---

* Gibb later received £1,000 in damages from the bank, but lost it all by investing in the unsuccessful Melbourne & Essendon Railway Co.

13

Expansion of
communications

Gold-rush immigrants desperately needed a means of keeping in touch with families, friends and associates left behind in Europe. Striving for success on the farthest edge of the world, the newcomers felt isolated from all they had known, and dependent on erratic sea-mail services for news, money, documents, and reassurance.

These were common feelings among families already established in Melbourne in 1851, but the pioneers had developed a fairly self-sufficient way of life which recognised that letters to Britain and orders for goods might take six months to yield results. With gold immigration, this leisurely attitude was swamped by a rush of many times the number of urgent overseas letters, newspapers and business transactions.

During the first few months of the gold rush there was little increase in postal business, some half-million letters and 650,000 newspapers being handled in Melbourne for both 1850 and 1851. In 1852, however, a marked increase occurred, to 970,000 letters and 710,000 newspapers. These figures were dwarfed in 1853, when more than 2,000,000 letters and 1,600,000 newspapers went through Melbourne's GPO. The flood continued, with a further increase of 60,000 letters during 1854.

A post office considered large enough for Melbourne's needs had been erected in 1841 and extended eight years later, on the south-east corner of Elizabeth and Little Bourke streets. During 1853, corrugated iron extensions were hastily built to accommodate the huge bulk of mail. The adjoining Detective Office in Little Bourke Street was moved, its quarters being used to unload horse drays packed with mailbags from ships just arrived. Even with the extra space, reported Postmaster Alexander McCrae, it was 'a matter of surprise how the work was carried on at all'.

To share the load, McCrae appointed William Grover as Chief Clerk in charge of the mail, letter and newspaper branches. Grover was evidently unhappy with his previous occupation as a squatter, watching sheep graze on the area now known as Bulleen. When he started work at the post office early in 1853, there was never time to be bored. He told a Legislative Council inquiry four years later that he had been forced to work 16-hour days, six days a week, to try to keep the mails up to date. Most of his forty clerks had to work nine to twelve hours every day except Sunday.

In order to keep Grover on the premises all day and night, he was lodged in a small cottage in Mail Road which then ran behind the GPO. He complained to the inquiry that 'it is not a fit place for a family to live in; it is shut in, and within eight yards of my back door there is a range of seven privies and water-closets, the stench from which is insufferable, night and day'. Even when he was at work, said Grover, 'The heat of the building [the GPO] is excessive; there is a difference of fifteen degrees in the iron buildings compared with the brick ones'.

One customer, the author Robert Martin, described how the public had to queue for at least two hours, often in the rain, to get to a mail delivery window. Inside, the post office was 'a disgrace to the British character'. Martin observed that 'clerks might be seen walking over floors a foot deep with letters and newspapers'. Thousands of postal articles, he claimed, never reached their destination.

Adolphus Sievwright, a clerk appointed by La Trobe in 1850 to handle foreign mails, told the 1857 inquiry that 'When the gold mania broke out, clerks were expected to sign an agreement to remain three months'. As mail poured in, he had often stayed at work until 'one or two o'clock in the morning', before walking home to Richmond. Then he had to rise at 4.30 a.m., to be back at work by six. 'I was so completely overdone that I fainted twice in one day', said Sievwright. In addition, 'the heat of the iron building during the day is so great, that not a day passes but somebody is ill through it and the stench', throwing extra work on to others. No overtime was paid.

Such evidence, combined with still-increasing postal business, led the Legislative Council to recommend erection of a much larger GPO on the corner of Elizabeth and Bourke streets, where it stands today. The new building was designed in 1857 by architect Arthur Johnson, with an estimated total cost of £96,000. The initial contract was awarded to W. C. Cornish, who built the first stage in 1859-60 for

Gold-rush expansion swamped postal facilities. By 1853, when Edmund Thomas drew the scene at the corner of Elizabeth and Bourke streets, the GPO had become a motley collection of extensions and verandahs. The adjoining building was Schultz & Reid's warehouse, followed by the Herald *office, Buckley & Nunn's drapery, and the Albion*

£27,000. Upper storeys and clock tower were added in the 1860s, completing the magnificent glass-roofed postal hall which may still be seen today in its restored form.

Alexander McCrae retired as Postmaster in 1857. The government took advantage of this to remove the Posts and Telegraphs Office from direct control of the Treasury Department. Former Police Commissioner William Mitchell, MLC, was appointed Victoria's first Postmaster-General. William Turner became first permanent head of postal operations.

Creation as a separate department gave new life to the post office. The first cast-iron pillarboxes were installed in Melbourne streets in 1858. Letter-carriers began delivering to city and inner suburbs three times a day (including Saturday), and clearing pillarboxes six times a

Hotel. The corner building at right, by the oil street lamp and stone gutter, was occupied by Ellis's drapery in 1853 and Benjamin Lawrence's shoe shop in 1857. A trooper, bullock team and water cart add to the heavy traffic in Bourke Street. (La Trobe Collection).

day. This meant that letters posted within the area before lunch could be delivered the same afternoon, a customer service far superior to that offered today. Sometimes Melbourne's fourteen letter-carriers did not finish work until 11 p.m., but now they were paid overtime.

Another great public benefit was the first Money Order service, which began in July 1858. This enabled people to transmit amounts below £10 easily from one place to another. In urgent cases, the funds could even be transferred by the amazing new electric telegraph.

New post offices were constantly opened in suburbs and country towns. By the end of 1860 Victoria had a total of 312 post offices. Twenty-nine of these were full-time government establishments: the remainder were set up in trustworthy stores.

Local printing of postage stamps became difficult after Thomas

Arrival of mail from the diggings always caused a stir in Bourke Street. This sketch by an unknown artist shows the American wagon driver smoking a cigarrito, stout merchants, and bearded diggers. At right is a soldier with woebegone wife and daughter. (La Trobe Collection).

Ham retired from the commercial engraving and lithographic trade in 1855. Other printers were tried, but problems of quality and security arose. Some orders even had to be sent to England.

In March 1859 a section of the GPO was set aside, and 'the whole process of electrotyping and mounting the dies, printing, gumming, and perforating stamps' was carried out under security arrangements. From that date to the end of September 1862, 11,109,000 penny stamps were printed here for newspaper mail; 1,440,000 twopenny stamps for use on local letters; 480,000 threepenny and 12,320,000 fourpenny stamps for country and interstate letters; and 1,524,000 sixpenny stamps for overseas mail.

While all this was going on, Melbourne authorities were trying to improve the means by which mails were transported from Britain. They met with little encouragement, until the gold rush brought vastly increased population and massive increase in overseas postal business. Several shipping companies now competed for the profitable contracts.

The first English mail which came direct to Melbourne without calls at other Australian ports was carried on the Peninsular & Orient Company's 80 h.p. steam paddlewheeler *Chusan*, arriving in Melbourne on 28 July 1852. Over the years the legend has arisen that the *Chusan* came direct from Southampton. In fact she picked up the mail bags from what was known as the 'Overland Route'. Under this system, passengers and mail went by ship or train to Marseilles or Brindisi, by ship to Alexandria, then by riverboat up the Nile to Cairo. There the company employed 3,000 camels to transport each ship's complete contents overland to the Gulf of Suez, where they were put on board another ship to India, Ceylon, Singapore and Australia. Peculiar though this route may seem, it often cut several weeks off the long sea voyage around the Cape of Good Hope.

In the same year, 1852, governments paid the Australian Royal Mail Steam Navigation Co. £26,000 a year to bring English mail every second month via the Cape to all major Australian ports including Melbourne. The company's four mail steamers, named *Australian*, *Sydney*, *Melbourne* and *Adelaide*, could not keep up the contracted speed of 8.5 knots per hour, and the service lapsed. The P. & O. Company again picked up the contract, continuing to use the Overland Route until 1854, when its vessels were withdrawn to help transport troops to and from the Crimean War.

A new mail contract was written in 1854 with the General Screw Steam Shipping Co. This line's propellor-driven steamers greatly reduced the time for a direct service from England to Melbourne. *Croesus* took 89 days, *Bosphorus* 86 days, *Queen of the South* 78 days, *Calcutta* 72 days, *Lady Jocelyn* 67 days, and *Argo* 63 days. Then these vessels too were withdrawn for use in the Crimea. Mails now depended utterly on clipper ships of the Black Ball and White Star lines, sailing the dangerous 'Great Circle' route through Antarctic regions to reach Melbourne.

Dissatisfied with the result, the Australian colonies got together in 1856 and began paying the European & Australian Royal Mail Co. £185,000 a year to deliver mails by steamship to Albany, Melbourne and Sydney.

This company employed four steamers to connect with the Overland Route, under a government edict that fines of £50 a day would be

*The first English mail direct to Melbourne was brought from Suez by the P. & O.
Company's* Chusan, *which arrived on 28 July 1852. The 700-ton barque-rigged
paddlewheeler was fitted with an 80-h.p. steam engine to assist her sails. This painting by
C. D. Gregory shows* Chusan *cruising outside the Heads, past Queenscliff on the left.
(La Trobe Collection).*

imposed on any vessel taking more than fifty-one days to reach
Melbourne. The best results were achieved by the s.s. *European*, which
was only a day or two late. The *Columbian* usually managed to arrive a
week or two behind schedule. The *Emeu* sailed only once during 1857,
and was eight days late. The *Simla* had the worst record, often being five
to seven weeks late. A year later, the company went into liquidation.

The mail contract returned in 1858 to the P. & O. Company, which
was able to charge £135,000 a year for a regular monthly service using
its greatly improved screw steamships in conjunction with the Overland
Route. For some years yet, Melburnians' letters would jog on the backs
of camels from one heat-drenched seaport to another. This arrangement
satisfied the colonists' demands for dependable overseas mails until
1869, when a direct continuous sea route became available with the
opening of the Suez Canal.

Invention of the electric telegraph was second only to steam power in
bringing a technological revolution to gold-rush Victoria. Before the

telegraph, transmission of messages was limited to line-of-sight helio-graph, flag and semaphore signals. But when American inventor Samuel Morse developed a practical system of using electromagnetic impulses to send messages along wire, it became possible to connect cities, suburbs, country towns and even overseas countries to an ever-growing network of almost-instantaneous relays. News, business affairs and personal messages could be transmitted and answered within hours instead of weeks or months.

An Irish-Canadian, 24-year-old Samuel McGowan, introduced the revolution to Victoria in 1853. Trained by Samuel Morse himself, McGowan brought the first telegraph equipment to Melbourne in the *Glance*, intending to set up a private company. But the government decided (by the Electric Telegraph Act, 17 Vic. No. 22, 11 April 1854) that the Victorian telegraph service, unlike that of the Americas, should be operated by a public monopoly. McGowan was appointed super-intendent of a new Electric Telegraph Department, and charged with building the first line from the Harbour Master's Office at Williamstown to a Central Telegraph Office established on the north-east corner of William and Little Bourke streets, Melbourne.

McGowan had stringy-bark poles erected about seventy feet apart between Melbourne and Williamstown, following the northern bank of the Yarra. Galvanised iron wire was strung on insulators, batteries and instruments tested, and the service inaugurated by La Trobe on 3 March 1854. This was the first electric telegraph route in the southern hemisphere, superseding the erratic visual signalling system between Williamstown and Flagstaff Hill.

After this success, telegraph poles were quickly erected to connect

Samuel McGowan, the young Irish-Canadian who brought the first electric telegraph equipment to Melbourne in 1853. (Georg von Neumayer Polararchiv).

[245]

the service to Geelong on 5 December 1854, Queenscliff on 30 January 1855, and Port Melbourne on 1 July 1855. This enabled a simultaneous system of time-signalling to be adopted for all maritime centres, time balls being dropped at exactly 1 p.m. each day. Ballarat, Castlemaine and Bendigo were connected to the network in December 1856, and most other provincial centres during 1857. Lines were completed to Adelaide in July 1858, and to Sydney the following October. The magic wire was beginning to link the colony to the nation.

The Central Telegraph Office in Melbourne became ever more busy, even with charges starting at 1s 6d for the first ten words and 1d for each additional word. Dates, addresses, signatures and delivery were free. All telegraph offices stayed open from 8.30 a.m. to 8 p.m. The Melbourne office was managed by Thomas James, assisted by a staff of eleven operators and trainees.

By 1857 the original Melbourne office was so overloaded that a branch had to be set up in four rented rooms in the Hall of Commerce, Collins Street. This move again increased business, with the result that more than 130,000 telegrams were sent in Victoria during 1858; nearly 18,000 being government despatches relayed free of charge. Although £70,000 had been spent to this time on erecting lines, trading profits were running at about £5,000 a year. To help overcome transmission delays, lines between Melbourne and many outlying stations were duplicated during 1859-60.

By 1859 the rooms in the Hall of Commerce had also become inadequate. The Melbourne Exchange Company, finding it difficult to let all of its rather extravagant building in Flinders Lane, offered space to the government. Much of the building was occupied in August as a new Central Telegraph Office, which later took over the entire structure.

Eight hundred miles of telegraph line had been erected in Victoria by 1860, covering all settled areas through thirty-three main offices. During that year 167,000 telegrams were sent. Frederick Standish, Chief Commissioner of Police, wrote to McGowan congratulating him on the 'invaluable assistance' given by telegraph offices in tracing absconding criminals. The Railways Department was also making extensive use of special telegraph lines built along its routes to Geelong and Woodend.

Although triumphant on land, Sam McGowan failed in his first efforts to join Tasmania to the Victorian telegraph network by means of a cable under Bass Strait. In this he was not alone: attempts to lay a trans-Atlantic cable in 1857 and 1858 were unsuccessful, and South Australian authorities failed in an 1858 trial at transmitting through a cable laid towards Victoria under Guichen Bay. Undeterred, the Victorian Parliament voted £23,000 to McGowan to make the Bass Strait attempt.

McGowan sought tenders for the difficult work, accepting one from Joseph Oppenheimer, Melbourne manager of Menken Meyer & Co. However, Meyer's London principals were uneasy about the Atlantic failure, and abandoned the contract, forfeiting their £1,000 security.

The contract went instead to the Tasmanian firm of Brown & McNaughton. This partnership succeeded in 1859 in laying a 196-mile British Henley insulated cable from Cape Otway, via King Island, Three Hummock Island and Circular Head, to Low Head on the Tasmanian coast near Georgetown. The Melbourne firm of McMeckan, Blackwood & Co. built the cable-layer s.s. *Omeo* specially for the job. Navigation and depth-sounding were in the hands of Captain W. H. Norman, commander of the colony's warship, HMCSS *Victoria*. Many quarrels occurred between him and the *Omeo*'s Captain Hugh McMeikan before the cable was completed.

At first the project seemed successful, the first messages being transmitted from Melbourne to Launceston on 2 October 1859. Next day the *Age* rhapsodised on 'this lightning girdle about the globe . . . one of the most marvellous performances of the current day of marvels'. The journal forecast that very soon London and Melbourne would exchange share prices every day, Flinders Lane merchants would chat with Liverpool on trade matters, and political events in both hemispheres would be published in next day's newspapers. To the isolated colonists, that appeared an almost-unbelievable forecast.

With their initial success, Victoria and Tasmania together had beaten the first trans-Atlantic transmissions by nearly nine years. Unfortunately, in April 1860 the Bass Strait cable failed between King Island and Circular Head, and all attempts to repair it were unsuccessful. Total cost of the doomed enterprise was £53,000.

In 1869, using improved methods, the Telegraph Construction & Maintenance Co. laid a new cable from Flinders at the end of the Mornington Peninsula to Georgetown in Tasmania. This operated successfully for many years, was duplicated in 1909, and replaced by a telephone cable from Apollo Bay in 1935. Few recalled then that this age of technological wonders had begun with the gold rush.

Arrival of ship mail led to indescribable confusion in Elizabeth Street. This vivid scene outside the old post office, painted by Russian-born Nicholas Chevalier, can be dated at

about 1860 because of progress made on the new GPO (at right), which still stands at the corner of Bourke Street. (La Trobe Collection).

14

Suburban development
intensifies

At the beginning of the gold rush, urban settlement was practically limited to the city area, with slender fingers of development reaching out to Port Melbourne, St Kilda, East Melbourne, Collingwood, Fitzroy, and North Melbourne. Most of the remaining land was still timbered, or was used for minor agricultural and grazing purposes.

During the gold decade, however, the suburbs expanded greatly, making those almost empty acres extremely valuable for subdivision into housing and shopping blocks. Better roads and the first railways accelerated the suburban boom. By the end of the 1850s, Melbourne had grown beyond the wildest dreams of those who founded it only a quarter-century earlier.

In the frenzy of the first gold rushes, the government was able to continue auctions of Crown land around Melbourne in order to raise extra funds. However, it failed to supervise what happened once the land was sold. The result in 1853-4, wrote Patrick Just, was that 'Every suburb was speedily covered over with dwellings; and tracts of land, which a few months before were either waste or swampy flats, began to exhibit all the busy activity of town or village life'.

William Kelly attended several government land sales in 1853. He described how allotments on the 'naked hill' of North Melbourne and Carlton fetched up to £1,800 an acre, and double that amount in East Melbourne. In Bay Street, Port Melbourne, the owner of the Sandridge Inn euphorically paid a record price of £4,200 for his quarter-acre site.

Andrew Clarke, 29-year-old former captain of Royal Engineers, replaced the ageing Robert Hoddle as Surveyor-General in May 1853. Clarke continued the government's policy of surveying main roads through the suburbs so that profitable land sales could continue apace. As a government representative in the Legislative Council, Clarke played an important role in reorganising municipal government. His worst failing was to abandon Hoddle's and La Trobe's vision of great boulevards leading out of Melbourne in every direction, causing difficulties for future generations trying to cope with narrow highways.

Along these narrow roads the land was subdivided again and again, almost without control. When Louisa Meredith visited Melbourne in the mid-1850s, she was not at all impressed with the burgeoning suburbs. Every way she looked she found an 'extraordinary number of small, mean habitations' and shops 'of the meanest grade', interspersed with a few 'good, spacious, comfortable houses'.

Melbourne's inner suburbs at that time were still supposed to be controlled by the City Council, but it had enough problems trying to remake its central streets and collect rubbish. A Legislative Council committee chaired by J. L. F. Foster recommended in March 1854 that every locality containing more than 200 franchised male householders should be permitted to form its own municipal borough, able to levy local rates and apply for government subsidies to carry out major works. Melbourne Council fought against this great diminution in its powers and duties, but by December 1854 the government had passed the enabling Act, 18 Vic. No. 15. Within a year, three of Melbourne's inner suburbs—Richmond, South Melbourne and Collingwood—had broken away from the central city and set up their own local councils.

East Melbourne remained under the control of Melbourne City Council, even after population swelled as a result of Crown land sales there in 1852-4 and 1858. As soon as Spring Street was confirmed as the site for Parliament and most government offices, East Melbourne became a favoured suburb for politicians, officials, merchants, judges and other professional men to build their two-storey town houses, mostly in permanent brick or stone. This preponderance of upper bourgeoisie gave the suburb five early churches, six schools, and no hotels. By 1861 East Melbourne had more than 260 rateable buildings: many still stand today.

The first suburb to form itself into a separate municipality was Richmond, a large area east of Melbourne bounded by Punt Road, Victoria Street, and the Yarra River. In 1855 most of the suburb was still quite heavily timbered, with gentlemen's residences on large blocks fronting the Yarra, but a fair amount of hotel and tenement development reaching out along Bridge Road and Church Street.

This picture shows the Yarra Park area in 1854, when most of riverside Richmond was still being used as farming and grazing land. It was painted by 34-year-old George Strafford or Stratford, who was later committed to Yarra Bend Asylum. The house at left was possibly 'Jasmine Cottage', built about 1840 by newspaper editor George Arden. On the right can be seen a group of Aborigines, beside a dead tree from which a shield has been cut. Behind them is a footbridge over the Yarra, and in the distance the hilly area where the Botanic Gardens were established. (La Trobe Collection).

Bridge Road alone had about thirty hotels catering for passing traffic on this main route to Hawthorn. In his pharmacy near Church Street, young Joseph Bosisto was distilling large quantities of 'Parrot Brand' eucalyptus oil, still being marketed today, but for household rather than medicinal use.

During the gold decade, Richmond residents were not at all unanimous about the desirability of local government. A series of excited meetings held over several nights in May 1855 were dominated by small householders who wanted the suburb developed rapidly and heavy rates imposed to pay for street improvement. However, two large landowners, Henry Miller, MLC, and William Burnley, MLC, were able to persuade a majority of residents to vote for a 'No taxation' ticket. In this way, the day of municipal intervention was put off for a

time, with, according to one resident, 'the population condemned to live in dirt and filth'. Not until extensive further subdivision took place did the suburb's affairs cease to be dominated by a few wealthy residents seeking to preserve their riverside idylls. In 1862 the mayor (chairman), Phillip Johnson, pleaded for government assistance in building roads and drains. He added a then-radical idea that property-owners should be forced to pay for construction of roads along their boundary lines.

By this time, Richmond had grown to more than 11,000 population, 3,000 of whom were ratepayers entitled to vote. Yet its annual income from rates was less than £3,500. Total paid staff was four, assisted by an honorary health officer. Some seventeen miles of road had been metalled, and eleven miles of footpaths made, but much more was

James Service, later Premier, refused to pay rates even when Melbourne City Council sent bailiffs to his home.

Joseph Bosisto, prominent Richmond resident, began manufacturing eucalyptus oil in his Bridge Road pharmacy. (*VPL*).

needed before gravel replaced mud outside the doors of most house-holders.

The second municipal council to be authorised was at Emerald Hill, today called South Melbourne. With the opening of Princes Bridge in 1850, South Melbourne was so handy to the city that it soon became a popular suburb. The scandals of crime-ridden 'Canvas Town' held it back only temporarily.

At the first sales of Crown land in August 1852, sixty-eight one-acre allotments were sold in the vicinity of Clarendon and Coventry streets for prices ranging up to £780. Flinders Lane merchant John Orr was the biggest purchaser: the first substantial house in South Melbourne was built for him in 1853. Two years later the area could boast of more than 1,100 rateable houses and shops.

Corrugated iron houses were popular in early South Melbourne, and some survive even today. William Howitt wrote in 1853 that 'These houses seem to have a vast demand, because they are rapidly put together; but they should send out iron constitutions with them'. He thought the structures would prove 'admirable houses—for the doctors'.

A radical young Scottish-born merchant, James Service, led the South Melbourne push for local government by refusing early in 1855 to pay rates to Melbourne City Council, which had done little for the area. The MCC sent bailiffs to seize Service's furniture from his home in Dorcas Street: a fellow Scot named John Nimmo rang the fire bell to summon a crowd which refused to allow the bailiffs in.

A few weeks later South Melbourne was declared a municipal district, holding its first election on 29 June in 'The Great Iron Store' which stood in Cecil Street until recent decades. James Service was elected as first mayor. His friend John Nimmo was appointed rate collector, with a staff of five men to put down nuisances.

By 1862 South Melbourne had developed into a thriving suburb with a population of nearly 9,000. Rates yielded £3,000 a year. Six miles of road were metalled, and another twelve miles formed. Shopkeepers helped to flagstone main footpaths. Clarendon Street was extended southwards to give access to St Kilda through Albert Park; and formed northwards as far as the Yarra River, where a bridge crossing to Spencer Street was urgently needed. Mains water from Yan Yean was supplied to every house.

Collingwood was the third municipality to begin operations in 1855. Called 'East Collingwood' at the time to distinguish it from Fitzroy Ward, it ran eastwards from Smith Street to the Yarra River, also encompassing today's Clifton Hill and Abbotsford.

Collingwood's cheap low-lying 'flats' near the river encouraged the erection of jerry-built housing on leasehold land during the gold rush. At the city end were some 'imposing houses', wrote Edwin Booth, but to the east the dwellings dwindled away into 'squalid blocks of weatherboard cottages and ill-smelling tenements'. William Howitt measured the joists as some cottages were being built, discovering they were 'about two inches by three': and 'evidently not intended for eternity'. In the whole eastern area, added Howitt, 'There is not the trace even of the idea of a garden'. Many of these slums were occupied by mothers trying to raise young families while husbands were absent at the diggings.

Sections of Collingwood along the Yarra were preserved from the blight, only because wealthy merchant John Orr held the original farm 'Abbotsford', named after its Scottish original; while Edward Curr's family continued to own the farm 'St Heliers' (now largely occupied by the Abbotsford campus of La Trobe University). During the gold rush, wrote William Howitt, both of these farms had 'one-storey houses, surrounded by their green enclosures and large gardens and vineyards, with cattle and horses grazing, and children at play'.

John Orr's Emerald Hotel on the corner of Market and Cecil streets became the social centre of early South Melbourne. Liardet's painting shows a cricket match in progress, with men in the background throwing horseshoes at a peg in the ground. William Kelly wrote that the hotel was frequented by 'the more respectable and quietly-disposed class of diggers'. (La Trobe Collection).

Below: Prefabricated iron buildings helped to overcome Melbourne's accommodation problems during the gold rush. This rare survivor at 399 Coventry Street, South Melbourne, was erected in 1853.

Despite its sometimes sombre appearance, bluestone was favoured during the gold rush for solid buildings. This delightful pair of houses still standing at 13–15 James Street, Richmond, was built about 1857 for Eneas MacKenzie, a civil servant.

By 1862, Collingwood housed 12,600 people, more than any other suburb. About 3,700 were ratepayers. Rates were supposed to raise £3,800 a year, but much remained unpaid. Fourteen miles of roads had been metalled, and ten miles of streets kerbed.

Mayor Isaac Reeves complained that when the government spent £10,000 in building a main drain along Reilly Street (today Alexandra Parade) towards the river, most of Fitzroy's pollution finished up on the Collingwood flats. The resultant diseases, mainly typhoid, caused 'very great distress' among single mothers and families living there. With so many rates unpaid, the council needed government help to reconstruct Simpson's Road (today Victoria Street), which was in an 'absolutely dangerous state to passengers'.

Two new suburban councils, Williamstown and Prahran, were formed in 1856. Williamstown has already been dealt with in chapter 2. Prahran in the 1850s covered the area east of Punt Road and south of the Yarra, reaching as far as the hills of Toorak on the east and Dandenong Road on the south. Most of it was used as market gardens and grazing land, but a long line of shops, hotels, chapels and dwellings stretched southwards along Chapel Street, on allotments subdivided from the original Crown land sales in 1849-50.

The artist William Strutt bought a house block in Prahran in 1852, paying a carpenter £1 a day to 'put up a little dwelling', just in time to beat the tidal wave of gold-rush immigration. Claud Farie, Sheriff of Melbourne, lived nearby. So did Henry Chapman, defender of the Eureka rebels. Chapman's son Frederick, later a judge, recalled how as a schoolboy he was served in the 'tuck shop' by 'a man with long arms, who worked in his shirt sleeves'. This was Graham Berry, later Premier of Victoria, who built South Yarra's first shop on the corner of Toorak Road and Chapel Street.

By the end of the gold decade, Prahran Council had formed and metalled Chapel Street from the Yarra to Dandenong Road, as well as twenty miles of subsidiary roads. The main cross roads, Toorak and Dandenong roads, were constructed and maintained by the government. Punt Road, which still came under Melbourne City Council, remained a constant problem.

In 1862 the entire Prahran municipality contained just on 10,000 people, of whom 2,400 were ratepayers. Rates raised £5,000 a year. The area could boast of seven churches, nine schools, and twenty-three

'Avoca', the South Yarra residence of George and Elizabeth Kirk, owners of the Victoria Tannery in Richmond.

hotels. Prahran was unusual at this time in possessing its own substantial stuccoed brick town hall, built in Chapel Street by Benjamin James in 1860 for £6,700. This building incorporated Melbourne's first municipal library, where the librarian (who doubled as hall-keeper) was paid £70 a year, about one-third of the rate collector's salary.

Although South Yarra was part of Prahran municipality, it developed along different lines. Ever since Aboriginal tribes were evicted from their traditional grounds on the south bank of the Yarra, much of the land sold for 'suburban farms', and the Botanic Gardens established, wealthy families had tended to monopolise the area. William Kelly noted in the mid-1850s that 'the *bon ton* of the metropolis' were 'enabled to build fine dwellings and surround themselves with gardens and pleasure-grounds'. Their villas were 'of a superior order, with grounds scrupulously neat and trim'.

Among these desirable homes was 'Fairlie', a large timber dwelling modelled on Government House at Norfolk Island, where its owner, Lieutenant-Colonel Joseph Anderson, had once been commandant. Merchant Archibald MacLaughlin, who had bought land at the first

Henry de Gruchy and Stephen Leigh, Flinders Lane engravers, produced this superb aerial view of Melbourne from the north in 1868. At left, the development of East Melbourne can be seen, with Fitzroy Gardens, St Patrick's Cathedral, Parliament House, Government Printing Office, and Treasury. Further south can be seen the Richmond train, Melbourne Cricket Ground, the Yarra,

Botanic Gardens, South Yarra, St Kilda, and the swampy land which became Middle Park and Albert Park. Prominent features at lower right are Melbourne Gaol, Public Library, and Melbourne Hospital; with the original Melbourne Cemetery and Flagstaff Hill at far right. South of these features can be seen Spencer Street station, Melbourne Gas Co., Yarra shipping. (La Trobe Collection).

South Yarra sales, took Anderson there to view the adjoining acres. 'The situation we at once thought beautiful, though then rough and without any house near, with exquisite views of the bay on one side, and distant hills on the other', Anderson recalled.

La Trobe at first refused to grant a special auction to Anderson, but when he produced a letter from NSW Colonial Secretary Deas Thomson extolling his military service, La Trobe changed his mind and had the land auctioned for the Lieutenant-Colonel's benefit. Anderson imported materials from England and built the house in 1855. Later he sold the property to town clerk Edmund FitzGibbon, who erected a conventional two-storey Georgian mansion, also named 'Fairlie'. Today it is remembered by Fairlie Court, off Anderson Street, opposite the Botanic Gardens.

Another charming colonial establishment in early South Yarra was 'Avoca', owned by George Kirk and his wife Elizabeth. In 1860, the grounds of 'Avoca' ran from Gordon Grove to the river front road. It almost faced the Kirks' noisome Victoria Tannery, but that was safely across the river in Richmond, and only proved a nuisance on north wind days. The Kirks' daughter Eliza later married Walter Hall and established a famed £1-million philanthropic trust with their inheritances.

A few memorable South Yarra houses and mansions of the late 1850s were built on spacious allotments on the eastern side of Chapel Street. Generally their carriageways opened on to Toorak Road (then called Gardiner's Creek Road), which had been macadamised by the government in 1854 in preparation for Sir Charles Hotham's occupancy of Government House in St Georges Road, Toorak.

Frederick Chapman, who lived in the area as a boy from 1854, recalled the properties clearly. The first house east of Chapel Street was 'Trivolia', later known as 'Tivoli', remembered by today's Tivoli Road. This 11-roomed stone mansion was built by Chief Aboriginal Protector G. A. Robinson, who employed blacks to carry blocks of stone up from the river bank. In 1855 the house was bought by Melbourne merchant W. M. Bell, whose daughter Jessie recalled the family being rowed along the Yarra each Sunday to attend John Knox Free Presbyterian Church in Swanston Street.

After 'Trivolia' came 'Rockley' (today's Rockley Road), owned in 1860 by R. H. Bland, director of the Port Phillip & Colonial Gold Mining Company.

Occupying the entire corner of Toorak and Williams roads, including today's Como Park, was the glorious two-storey mansion 'Como', largely built by wine merchant John Brown in 1854-5, and today preserved by the National Trust. Beyond 'Como' there were only a couple of houses, a smithy and a hotel, before Government House was reached. Today the area is among the most expensive real estate in Australia.

Residents and shopkeepers in the more populous parts of South Yarra complained long and bitterly about the concentration of council expenditure in the southerly portions of Chapel Street. From 1857 Graham Berry and others tried to have South Yarra made into a separate municipality, on the grounds that few of their roads had been metalled, rubbish remained uncollected, and pigs and goats roamed freely around the neighborhood. Eventually they accepted their fate, managing to win control of the council by 1863 and ensuring that funds were spread more evenly.

A further two councils, St Kilda and Brunswick, were formed in 1857.

St Kilda was already well established as a resort in the 1840s, following Crown land sales of building allotments and a rush by Melbourne merchants to build imposing seaside villas.

The suburb's popularity increased further during the early years of the gold rush. William Kelly attended an auction there during the 'mania for land speculation' which he said 'even infected sober, thoughtful, and calculating citizens with a morbid craving' for ruinous purchases. Kelly went down St Kilda Road, where 'crowded vehicles rattled along, and horsemen at mad speed darted past in great numbers'.

The auction itself was accompanied by band music and a champagne luncheon, attended by all kinds of people including 'ladies and good-looking nursemaids, in quite as gay attire as their mistresses, and assuming airs of sauciness meant for colonial independence'. When bidders for land were half-intoxicated, they agreed to 'outrageously extravagant' prices far beyond the cost of choice allotments in central London.

Once mansions were built along the beach front, St Kilda became a focus of social life. Henry Brown, who had done well from a store at the diggings, returned to experience 'a complete change of existence', with 'balls, parties and picnics following each other in rapid succession'. Even during temporary slumps, he wrote, 'money seemed plentiful, and every description of elegant and comfortable luxury was freely enjoyed'.

Wilbraham Liardet painted this picture of the St Kilda coastline southwards in 1862. At lower left, Aborigines can be seen frolicking on the beach. Above them, on what became today's Jacka Boulevard and Fitzroy Street, are the mansions and hotels of white civilisation. The fishermen in the centre are pulling a seine net into shore with the day's catch. Above them, a flag shows the entrance to St Kilda Pier, with its sea bathing establishments. In the distance at right is Point Ormond, where a beacon guided yachtsmen. Directly inland are the Elwood swamps, with cattle grazing on their banks. In the far distance can be seen some of the buildings of early Brighton. (La Trobe Collection).

By 1862 St Kilda had 6,400 residents, of whom 1,400 were rate-payers. So powerful was the influence of these residents that Melbourne City Council spent part of the Gabrielli loan on making its roads. When the money was repaid, Melbourne agreed to let the suburb go, and the first St Kilda Council was elected in March 1857.

Within five years the council had spent £2,000 on building its own town hall, the second suburban one in the metropolis. Main drains were formed, water laid on, municipal gardens planted, and a cemetery established. Twenty-four miles of roadway were built, of which eighteen miles were macadamised. Six miles of streets had been kerbed with hardwood, later replaced by bluestone pitchers.

Brunswick, on the other side of Melbourne to St Kilda, presented a telling contrast to the wealthier suburb. Occupying a large area on both sides of Sydney Road beyond Carlton, Brunswick had long been a refuge for the poorer classes. Most residents did not want a local council with the accompanying liability to pay higher rates. However, when government grants became available, they took heed of one of the district's main land speculators, Thomas Wilkinson. After an election held late in 1857, Wilkinson became first mayor. The result was the subdivision of allotments into even meaner areas, with narrow streets which still choke the suburb today.

By 1862 Brunswick could levy only £900 in rates—less than a quarter of St Kilda's—and even then most of Brunswick's rates could not be collected from its 3,000 population.

'There is a considerable amount of distress among the working classes', said mayor Ebenezer Rosser. Many husbands had left to seek work elsewhere, 'and their families are brought into great distress . . . sometimes quite trying to witness'. The council could afford to give only £30 to the local Ladies Benevolent Society to help buy food and clothing for those in desperate need. Less than a mile of roads had been formed and metalled.

Fitzroy was the only suburb to become a municipality during 1858. Although it joined Collingwood at Smith Street, the higher ground of Fitzroy always attracted a wealthier class of resident. According to Edwin Booth, 'Fitzroy is just as conservative and quiet as Collingwood is radical and riotous. The houses have a look of staid respectability, and the people a gravity of manner, that Collingwood wonders and sneers at'.

As soon as building labour was available after the first gold rushes, successful people began erecting solid houses and terraces in Fitzroy's best streets. Often these were impressive two-storey bluestone constructions. The best-known surviving example is Royal Terrace in Nicholson Street. A glance at directories of the period shows that many politicians, lawyers, doctors, artists, musicians and builders were moving into the area; besides a multitude of small tradesmen wanting a central location. Hotels, churches and schools were rapidly increasing in number.

After several public meetings, the prosperous suburb was able to wrench itself free from Melbourne City Council. The first Fitzroy council was elected in September 1858. By 1862 the suburb had nearly 12,000 population, including more than 3,000 ratepayers. Mayor Charles Vaughan, MLC, told an 1862 parliamentary inquiry that the council's £6,000 annual rates were almost fully paid up. Nineteen miles of roads had been metalled and another nineteen miles kerbed; while nearly thirty miles of footpaths had been formed and gravelled. The suburb was obviously in good shape, with the council itself dispensing aid to the few poor residents who applied.

Three more local councils—Brighton, Footscray and North Melbourne—were elected during 1859.

The first represented the rising seaside suburb of Brighton, founded by Surrey farmer Henry Dendy in 1841. Dendy went bankrupt, and few good houses were built in Brighton before the gold rush. When William Strutt moved there in 1853 and put up 'a little dwelling' on several acres, he enjoyed on one side a glorious view of Port Phillip Bay 'seen through a thicket of trees'; while on the other side was 'a grand stretch of virgin forest' reaching to the Dandenong Ranges. Strutt thought he might have made 'a serious mistake' by moving so far from his art pupils in South Yarra. However, as horse 'bus and steam train services began later in the decade, Brighton grew rapidly in popularity.

Resident J. B. Were began advocating a municipal council in 1856, hoping that its activities would increase land values. Most other locals at first resisted the idea, preferring to struggle through boggy patches of roadway rather than pay high rates. By 1859, however, majority opinion had changed, and in February a seven-man council was elected, with 'Yankee solicitor' Thomas Warner as mayor.

By this time the government had spent about £13,000 on macadamising the main road link between St Kilda and Brighton, making it much easier for market gardeners and other Brighton residents to reach the city. Within three years the Brighton council macadamised six miles of lesser roadways and formed seventeen miles of roads and footpaths.

The suburb's 2,500 population could now move about with comparative ease. Many fine homes were built between New Street and the beach, and occupied by Melbourne professional men and their families. As the railway extended through Brighton at the end of the gold decade, hundreds of substantial brick and timber villas began appearing around the stations.

Again, on the other side of Melbourne, a poor suburb was struggling in 1859 to form itself. Footscray known mainly as a stopping place on the road to Geelong, and a site of quarries for basalt used on Melbourne's roads and buildings, began to develop when the railway went through from Williamstown to Sunbury in 1858-9. Hundreds of navvies working on the line occupied cottages hastily built at Footscray and Yarraville.

City speculators moved in and subdivided land along the railway into building allotments, but even by 1860 Footscray could muster barely a thousand population. One visitor that year, Phillip Rayson, described the area as 'a jumble of wooden huts', with only two or three two-storeyed buildings or hotels. Nevertheless a local council had been elected in July 1859, with retired mariner Captain Alexander Dove as first mayor. Rates were supposed to raise £700 a year, but nearly half of this was left unpaid.

As the railway boom collapsed, many residents quit Footscray, leaving houses vacant. By 1862 only half a mile of roadway had been metalled. The council could not afford its own offices: business was conducted in a rented police office. Footscray had to wait for a later surge of industrialisation to become a vigorous suburb.

The third local council formed in 1859 was at North Melbourne, in those days called Hotham. The land had been subdivided in the 1840s,

The scene at Pentridge, painted from Sydney Road, Coburg, by an unknown artist about 1851, shows its early days as a prison. The rough timber stockade at right surrounds some of the first gaol buildings. (La Trobe Collection).

but was dominated by a large Benevolent Asylum for aged and incurable paupers, located across the western end of Victoria Street.

Hundreds more quarter-acre blocks were sold at a Crown land auction in September 1852 to help house Melbourne's new population. At that time, wrote gold-rush immigrant Albert Mattingley, the land had 'a beautiful park-like appearance', being 'richly carpeted with grass and studded with noble redgum trees', where Aboriginal tribes still occasionally camped.

But the Melbourne Building Act was not extended to the new suburb. It soon became covered with tents, cheap housing, stables, corrugated-iron sheds of small manufacturers, and thirty hotels. Most of the red gum was chopped down for firewood. The population grew rapidly to more than 6,000 by the end of the gold decade. Tradesmen's

families occupied the 1,700 dwellings, filling the suburb's eight schools and seven churches. Gas was laid on in 1859, but the Yan Yean water supply did not reach the area until the mid-1860s.

North Melbourne's first council was elected in October 1859, with John Davis as mayor. By 1862 the area was raising £2,400 from its 1,500 ratepayers. That year the current mayor, solicitor Francis Gell, complained that the suburb's eight miles of roadway were 'in a very unfinished state, little kerbing or channelling being done except in leading thoroughfares'. This caused 'accumulation of filth', while drainage from piles of nightsoil dumped near the University passed through the northern end of the suburb, giving rise to 'injurious exhalations'.

When the noted educationist James Bonwick bought two acres at Kew in 1854, Aborigines were still living on the subdivision. Bonwick's wife Esther tried to stop one tribal elder from beating his wife's head with a waddy: she refused help, crying 'I him lubra, good he beat me'. The Bonwick family camped in a tent beside this tribe, while cutting timber

*Writer and historian
James Bonwick, one
of the first settlers at
Kew. (VPL).*

to build a small cottage. Bonwick walked more than a mile to the Yarra each day to bring buckets of water back to the tent. After the cottage was built, Bonwick started the district's first school, and helped to found Kew chapel.

From such humble beginnings, multiplied by the efforts of hundreds of other pioneer settlers and squatters, grew the Boroondara Road District, covering today's suburbs of Kew, Hawthorn and Camberwell.

Kew and Hawthorn, being closer to Melbourne and punts and bridges across the Yarra, developed soonest into recognisable communities. They elected their first local councils in 1860. Since the main easterly outlet from Melbourne ran along Bridge Road to Burwood Road, Hawthorn became a leading commercial suburb, its population increasing to nearly 2,500 by 1862. Kew remained more residential, with a population of 1,500 at the same date. It was noted for a small number of ratepayers living on comparatively large blocks of land.

The result of all these breakaway councils was to reduce greatly the area, population and power of the City of Melbourne. When the 1862 parliamentary inquiry met, suburban councils represented 86,000 residents. The City of Melbourne, which continued to include Carlton and East Melbourne, now represented only 37,000 people.

Responsibility for local affairs in the more distant suburbs had been placed where it belonged—on local residents. Although the results were occasionally unfortunate, this was grass-roots democracy in action. Henceforth, much of Melbourne's economic creativity would show itself in the suburbs as well as in the central city.

15

Melbourne's ring of parks
and gardens

One of Melbourne's proudest boasts is that it possesses an incomparable circle of public parks and gardens surrounding the city and extending into the suburbs. These green areas were saved with difficulty from the jaws of those who wished to monopolise them, often with the best of intentions, for specialised purposes.

The battle began in the 1840s, became passionate during the gold decade, and continues even today. One only has to glance at a modern map to see, for instance, how the original Police Paddock between the city and Punt Road has been nearly consumed by railways and sports grounds. The public is effectually locked out of these precincts for leisure activities during most of the week. Yet in the 1850s, the entire 240-acre segment was supposed to have been reserved as a magnificent Yarra Park, open seven days a week to equestrians, picnic parties, and pedestrians.

The attempt to form an inalienable green belt around the city is generally credited to Charles La Trobe, Superintendent of Port Phillip in the 1840s and Lieutenant-Governor of Victoria up to 1854. However, La Trobe does not appear to have issued broad policy instructions on the matter. He proceeded case by case, preserving open land where possible, giving way to commercial and political imperatives only where there was no alternative.

One reason for this was La Trobe's intense distrust of Melbourne City Council, riddled with jobbery and corruption, and dominated for much of the period by his outspoken enemy, town clerk and journalist William Kerr. La Trobe constantly rebuffed the council's attempts in the late 1840s to take control of public parkland at Batman's Hill and the newly-established Botanic Gardens in South Yarra. Early in 1851 he reluctantly agreed to allow the council supervision of a new 34-acre

Ferdinand von Mueller, a brilliant young naturalist, put the Botanic Gardens on a scientific basis in the 1850s. It remained the most popular leisure attraction in Melbourne, easily reached by several bridges across the Yarra. The footbridge shown near the site of today's Swan Street bridge was built in 1858. Francois Cogné's careful drawing of about 1863 also shows, at left, the modest tower of Melbourne's first Town Hall, and on the horizon, the spires of Scots and Wesley churches. To the right can be seen the narrow southern facades of the Treasury and Parliament House. Swampy land below the Botanic Gardens had not yet been fully converted into today's ornamental lakes. (La Trobe Collection).

park to be established on the north-east side of Princes Bridge (today's Batman Avenue). But Governor FitzRoy wrote sternly from Sydney on 16 April 1851 that even this small area must be vested in trustees appointed by the government, not the City Council.

The coming of railways after La Trobe's departure shattered all preconceptions about public parklands along the north bank of the Yarra. Much of the Batman's Hill parkland was given over to railway companies laying their lines to the west and north, becoming Spencer Street terminus. The proposed park between Batman Avenue and Flinders Street became Princes Bridge station. As train services grew, more public land was taken over by Jolimont railway yards. The east-bound lines neatly chopped Yarra Park in half. Other solutions had to be found to provide extensive public breathing areas so much desired by the majority of Melbourne residents.

The Botanic Gardens, occupying 115 acres of prime land in South Yarra, was reserved from sale by La Trobe in 1845. By the start of the gold decade, Scottish-born curator John Dallachy had fenced a considerable portion, started growing many kinds of exotic plants, and begun excavating the lake still a major attraction today.

William Kelly visited the gardens on his arrival in 1854, as part of a 'gay and happy throng' enjoying themselves on slopes and valleys. Kelly praised the 'exquisite taste and skill' of those who had preserved the best original trees, while adding 'all the rare evergreens and beauteous flowering shrubs of the entire Polynesian archipelago that could be acclimatised'.

Kelly's words were echoed by William Howitt, who attended the annual flower and vegetable show in 1855. Thousands of visitors were present, including 'many beautiful and truly elegant women'. Howitt found the four miles of walks now completed to be 'a real delight'. Many cultivated beds were in flower, which 'loaded the breeze with a delicious fragrance'.

That was the public face of Melbourne's favourite resort. Behind the scenes, La Trobe had appointed a brilliant young German scientist, Ferdinand von Mueller, to the position of Government Botanist. Together with Dallachy, Mueller visited remote regions and returned with hundreds of plant specimens not previously known to exist in Victoria. Many were placed in a herbarium built in 1857, when Mueller was appointed first director of the Botanic Gardens.

Within a year, other public gardens being established in Victoria were supplied annually with more than 7,000 plants and 20,000 packets of seeds. Mueller also reported that 'a copious supply of seeds of our heat-resisting trees and grasses were transmitted to the British Consul at Jerusalem, for aiding in his endeavours to restore forests in some now timberless wastes of the Holy Land'.

During 1858, Mueller decorated the barren west side of the lagoon with rows of Norfolk Island and Aleppo pines, and Moreton Bay fig trees. Lines of blue gums were planted along the Yarra bank. By the end of the decade, something like 300,000 visitors were patronising the gardens each year, with especially large crowds on Sunday afternoons, when the 40th Regimental Band under Sergeant Johnson played for their entertainment. By this time, old paling fences around the perimeter had been replaced by high iron fences which still stand today.

One of Mueller's innovations of the 1850s was an attempt to acclimatise foreign birds and animals which might be useful to local residents. In 1858 he established an aviary in the northern area of the gardens, near today's Birdwood Avenue. The aviary, intended to promote the 'general distribution of foreign song birds over Australia', contained many pairs of thrushes, blackbirds, starlings, skylarks, goldfinches, and pheasants. These were liberated as they bred, and soon were seen in many parts of Victoria, sometimes to the distress of crop-growers.

By 1861 a two-storeyed stone house which still stands in Dallas Brooks drive had been erected for Mueller. From here he supervised the daily routine of the gardens, conducted scientific experiments intended to benefit farmers and graziers, kept up an enormous correspondence, and began compiling his classic seven-volume *Flora Australiensis*.

The large area east of St Kilda Road known today as Alexandra Gardens, Queen Victoria Gardens, and Kings Domain was reserved as public parkland by La Trobe just before he left Melbourne in 1854. It seemed to him the ideal site for a future Government House, but this was not to be built until years later.

The river bank now occupied by boat sheds was the site of Melbourne's original brickfields, and often subject to flooding. An immigrants' home was erected on slightly higher ground in 1853, converted to a military barracks, then reverted to the equivalent of a paupers' workhouse.

Henry Burn's beautiful painting, now sadly deteriorated, shows the track which became *Wellington Parade*, leading from Richmond to Melbourne. At left are government paddocks which became today's *Yarra Park* and railway yards. At right are the *Fitzroy* and *Treasury Gardens*, already benefiting from fencing, draining and replanting begun by James Sinclair in the late 1850s. Some of the city's church steeples can be seen in the distance, probably dating the painting to the late 1860s. (*La Trobe Collection*).

When Mueller became director of the Botanic Gardens, he undertook to improve what he described as this 'desolate locality'. In 1860 he was able to report that 'levelling of the drive marked out last year has been completed, the old roads and tracks have been obliterated, and the bare spots have been sown with grass and clover seeds'. Since grazing had been halted, young native trees were flourishing again. On higher ground, said Mueller, 'a circular enclosure of iron fencing has been erected surrounding a number of elms'.

The following year Dr James Harcourt, superintendent of the Immigrants' Home, set the inmates to work on building a road from Princes Bridge to the Botanic Gardens. Today it forms part of Alexandra Avenue. The pauper-labourers also trenched the ground and planted 'several hundred good-sized weeping willows' by the river. When the tumbledown Immigrants' Home was finally demolished and today's Government House built on the upper slopes in the 1870s, its aristocratic occupants could look out over a glorious stretch of gardens, towards a bustling city getting ready for its next economic boom.

Yarra Park had originally been intended by La Trobe to stretch along the river all the way from Swanston Street to Punt Road, an open area of about 240 acres. On 30 September 1850 he wrote to the City Council that he was 'quite disposed to see the reserve made subservient to the recreation and amusement of the inhabitants of the city', but that the huge park must remain 'under the sole control, and in the hands of Government'.

The first bites out of this area were taken in 1853, when Melbourne Cricket Club was granted permissive occupancy of nine acres, and Richmond Cricket Club of six acres, for their playing ovals. At the time this did not seem serious, for there were no encircling grandstands and fences, and the public still had open access. Bit by bit, however, much of the remaining area was taken over by enclosed sporting arenas, railways, army depots, and a police station site which became Yarra Park primary school, now deserted.

Mueller, director of the Botanic Gardens, was given thirty-three acres of Yarra Park in 1858 to be fenced and used as Melbourne's first zoo. Although intended mainly for scientific breeding and acclimatisation of foreign species, the zoo became enormously popular with visitors.

To stock his menagerie, Mueller imported English fallow deer, monkeys, llamas, angora goats, alpacas, Cashmere goats, Chinese sheep, North American beavers, and even twenty-four camels and dromedaries from India. A pair of ostriches sent from Capetown died on the voyage. In return for gifts from overseas zoologists, Mueller shipped out black swans, kangaroos, platypus, and other Australian novelties.

A Zoological Society was formed in 1858 with Governor Barkly as patron and Justice Redmond Barry as president. In 1861 the society persuaded the government to transfer Mueller's animals to Royal Park and establish today's Zoological Gardens. The original zoo in Yarra

Park then became the Friendly Societies' Gardens, but today is Olympic
Park, with stadiums blocked off from everyday public use.

Royal Park, north-west of the city, was originally a 2,500-acre reserve
occupying a huge triangle between Flemington and Sydney roads.
Sheep were allowed to graze there in the early 1850s, the lessee paying
the government £400 a year for the privilege.

Just before he retired in 1854, La Trobe gazetted 680 acres on the
western side of this area for permanent use as Royal Park. Nearly
£4,000 was spent on fencing, and construction of a carriage drive
around the perimeter. Residents of northern suburbs were able to
gather there to ride horses and ponies on grassed areas, and hold picnics
in the thick scrub.

After La Trobe's departure, Royal Park began to suffer the same
kind of excisions which practically ruined Yarra Park. In 1858 a 145-acre
'experimental farm' was fenced off in the north-western corner, where
government establishments like Turana Boys' Home and Royal Park
Psychiatric Hospital are now located.

Organisation of the experimental farm was entrusted to Thomas
Skilling, a practised farmer with advanced views, who held a diploma
in agriculture from Queen's University, Ireland. Under Skilling, the
farm carried out research into the best methods of sowing, fertilising
and reaping crops; and developing new varieties. Skilling ordered a
Fowler's steam plough from England, the first to be seen in Victoria,
and analysed the results of deep and shallow ploughing in various soils.
He also experimented with the use of Melbourne's sewage as fertiliser,
but concluded that guano and horse manure gave better results. Skilling
pointed farmers towards growing unfamiliar crops like sorghum and
maize, and strongly recommended rotation of crops. Forty tons of
mangel-wurzels grown on the farm were fed to camels being gathered
at Royal Park for use in the Burke and Wills expedition.

Unfortunately, ignorant politicians and bureaucrats took a short-
term view of Skilling's research, and decided in 1860 that 'the farm
ought to be self-supporting'. A management committee was formed
under elderly squatter J. M. Matson, acting for a new Board of
Agriculture. According to Skilling, 'the experiments on cropping,
draining, and sub-soiling were condemned in unmeasured terms, and
peremptorily suspended'.

Matson instructed Skilling to concentrate on growing mulberries,

On his last day in Melbourne in 1854, Governor La Trobe reserved a large area north-west of the city for permanent use as Royal Park. An experimental farm was established in the north-western corner in 1858. Two years later the Burke and Wills exploring party gathered there for its official departure, painted here by William Strutt. 'A most picturesque sight, full of life and colour', wrote the artist, not knowing of the tragedy to follow. (Victorian Parliamentary Library).

olives, tea and coffee—ridiculous in Melbourne's temperate climate—and at the same time reduced Skilling's salary to that of an artisan. Skilling resigned, whereupon the Board closed down the farm. The former director managed to win a Legislative Assembly inquiry, which censured the Board and allowed Skilling almost a year's severance pay. But his expertise was lost forever.

Meanwhile the Zoological Society had been allowed to transfer its animals from Yarra Park to a 50-acre enclosure in Royal Park, forming the foundation of today's zoo. Seven years later an impecunious government decided to auction the opposite corner of Royal Park, forming today's wealthy suburb of Parkville. Other pieces of the park were hived off at various times to build the Children's Hospital, a golf course, and various sports ovals, so that today less than 450 acres remain of La Trobe's original scheme.

Royal Park originally continued over the eastern side of Sydney Road (today Royal Parade), taking in all the area up to Lygon Street now occupied by Melbourne General Cemetery and Melbourne University. The Collingwood town herd grazed peacefully over this large area in the early 1850s, providing milk for that suburb's growing population. However, when burials began in the new cemetery in 1853, and the university commenced in 1855, the parkland east of Sydney Road was reduced to 150 acres, becoming known by today's name of Princes Park.

Further south in Carlton, a 63-acre area bounded by Victoria, Nicholson, Carlton and Rathdowne streets had been reserved for Carlton Gardens. In the mid-1850s, goat herders illegally allowed their animals to graze there, stripping the reserve of young trees and grass. The government of the day passed responsibility to Melbourne City Council, which in 1857 commissioned Edward La Trobe Bateman, a cousin of C. J. La Trobe, to design a miniature botanical garden for the bare clay site. By 1870 Bateman had succeeded in creating fenced paths, fountains and luxuriant growth, providing pleasant walks for Fitzroy residents. Much of his work was destroyed in 1878 when the huge Exhibition Building was erected across the centre of the gardens.

Fitzroy Gardens and the adjacent Treasury Gardens, originally covered with large redgum trees, escaped subdivision and development as building blocks by the merest chance. Surveyor Robert Hoddle had originally planned the subdivision in the late 1830s, soon after Melbourne was founded. Fortunately the depression of the 1840s halted sales for private purposes.

When La Trobe decided in 1849 that the east side of Spring Street should be reserved for future parliamentary and governmental buildings, he instructed Hoddle to abandon the subdivisional plan, and reserve Fitzroy and Treasury Gardens as public parks.

For some years the 64-acre Fitzroy Gardens remained a series of quarries, and a dumping ground for the city's nightsoil, intersected by a small polluted stream. Georgiana McCrae recounted that when she strolled back to East Melbourne one night in 1855, she 'had to "walk-the-plank" across the gully . . . the boys formed a line to help me over'. Treasury Gardens, meanwhile, remained a turgid swamp into which drainage from the Eastern Hill found its way.

Since East Melbourne was still part of the area covered by Melbourne City Council, the government agreed in 1855 to the corporation taking over responsibility for Fitzroy Gardens, on condition that the space should 'forever remain open and free for the use of the public'. The following year, dumping of thousands of tons of rubble and soil began, to fill up the dangerous quarries and creek edges.

Edward La Trobe Bateman was engaged to design an attractive park. His rather formal plan was abandoned in 1857, when a renowned 48-year-old Scottish-born landscape gardener, James Sinclair, took over as curator. Sinclair designed today's walks shaded with elms, poplars and plane trees, broken up by shrubberies, flower beds and lawns. A low fence was built around the park in 1860 to protect the new plants from wandering stock. Yan Yean water arrived in 1860, when Sinclair began living in a cottage in the park so that he could irrigate the plants at night.

The Treasury Gardens, west of Lansdowne Street, were suggested in 1853 as a possible site for Melbourne University. However, the lower section along Wellington Parade was still very swampy, and little space was available for the university to expand. Eventually, in 1859, the government decided to build a row of public offices on the dry upper section (today Treasury Place), and convert the remainder into a small park. By 1861 the gardens had been fenced, and an ornamental lake formed to help drain the area.

Amidst all this activity by government and corporation, one privately-owned pleasure garden was attempted along the Yarra River. It was the brainchild of James Ellis, who had operated Cremorne Gardens in London and thought he could see a similar opportunity in Melbourne.

Ellis made money at the height of the gold rush by taking over the decrepit Salle de Valentino dance hall at the top of Bourke Street in 1853. With the profits, he bought ten acres of Henry Ginn's riverside land in Richmond, between today's Cremorne Street and the railway line. Ellis had the soggy land drained into an artificial lake near the Yarra, and built pavilions, grottoes, and ornamental bridges. His opening of Cremorne Gardens in December 1853 featured band music, singing, dancing, and fireworks. It attracted wide support, for profits from the one-shilling tickets went to a Melbourne Hospital appeal for funds to build a new wing in Lonsdale Street.

After a successful first season, the gardens closed for the winter. When they reopened in October 1854, Melbourne found to its delight that Ellis had added a huge covered rotunda capable of holding 2,000 dancers. Occasionally it was cleared so that 'a ballet company composed of French artists' could perform.

Fitzroy Gardens, east of the Treasury Gardens, were formally designed by Edward La Trobe Bateman in 1857 to replace the area's use as a city rubbish dump. Bateman's plan was considerably modified by curator James Sinclair, a renowned Scottish landscape gardener. This 1863 painting by Francois Cogné shows at left a fountain designed by surveyor Clement Hodgkinson and sculpted by Charles Summers. In the background can be seen bay shipping and the chimney of the steam water pump at the end of Spring Street. In the middle are houses in Spring Street; and at right, a rear view of the Treasury. (La Trobe Collection).

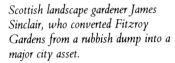

Scottish landscape gardener James Sinclair, who converted Fitzroy Gardens from a rubbish dump into a major city asset.

George Coppin, the well-known actor and entrepreneur, bought Cremorne Gardens from the creditors in 1856 for £11,000, spending another £30,000 over the next few years on improvements. He added a theatre called the Pantheon, a shooting gallery, a bowling saloon, and a large panorama showing a volcano with glowing 'lava' pouring down its sides. These sensations were unveiled before a select audience of Melbourne society on 1 November 1856, and for a time seemed successful.

The following year, Ellis introduced a 250-ft painted panorama of the siege of Sebastopol, behind which live rockets and fireworks exploded, while gunners of the 40th Regiment fired blank shells with their field guns. Visitors could also wander around a maze, look at sparkling fountains and illuminated grottoes, or watch a 'sagacious elephant' performing tricks in a small menagerie. So successful were the gardens that a separate company was formed to operate a colorful

This S. T. Gill sketch of 1854, made from 'Fairlie', Lieutenant-Colonel Joseph Anderson's residence in Punt Road, South Yarra, gives a rare southern view of Cremorne Gardens across the river in Richmond. In the left foreground, off Punt Road, is part of solicitor David Ogilvie's property. In the right foreground is the lower paddock of 'Avoca', owned by tanner George Kirk. (La Trobe Collection).

paddle-steamer, the *Gondola*, bringing hundreds of passengers at a time from the city to Richmond.

But an increasingly respectable Melbourne frowned on the easy availability of liquor. Bars in the gardens were licensed, until several disagreeable incidents allowed what William Kelly called 'owl-looking evangelicals' to have a law passed forbidding the promoters to sell alcoholic drinks on Sundays. Since this was the most popular day for visitors, profits vanished and Ellis was forced into bankruptcy.

During a visit to England, Coppin purchased a large gas balloon, which he named *Australasian*. He persuaded two aeronauts, Charles Brown and Joseph Dean, to come to Melbourne to make Australia's first balloon ascent. On 1 February 1858, the great canopy was partly filled at the Melbourne gasworks, then lifted by dray and thirty men to Cremorne, where inflation to 35,000 cubic feet was completed at Coppin's private gas retort.

Huge crowds gathered to watch Dean take off in the balloon just before 6 p.m. Dr James Neild, who paid the five-shilling admission fee, wrote: 'I do not know when I have seen people so much excited'. Soon the balloon was just a 'little speck which reflected the sun like a transparent water-drop', heading for Heidelberg where it landed success-

The locally-built 60-ft paddle-steamer Gondola began hourly services in 1854 to take 200 pleasure-seekers at a time from Princes Bridge up-river to Cremorne Gardens in Richmond. After a few years, the expansion of suburban railways and cheap fares doomed such river enterprises. (Artist unknown; La Trobe Collection).

George Coppin's 'Australasian' balloon made Australia's first flight from Cremorne Gardens on 1 February 1858. This medallion was struck for the occasion.

fully. Dean and Brown made many more flights in Melbourne and Sydney, some not so successful. But Brown, who settled in Melbourne, forecast accurately that 'a time will come when "Aeronautics" will be reduced to a practical science'.

Such sensations could not save Cremorne Gardens. In 1862 George Coppin over-reached himself by building the expensive Haymarket Theatre next to the Eastern Market in Bourke Street. He was forced to close the gardens in January 1863, while Cremorne railway station closed at the same time, never to reopen. The gardens area was sold for only £4,500 to Dr James Harcourt, who used it to establish a private asylum for incurably insane and inebriate patients. The land was sold again in the 1880s and subdivided into small lots to build factories and workers' cottages.

16

Sports and other amusements

Horses were such an important means of transport in the gold decade that their care and breeding remained a primary concern to city as well as country dwellers. One sure way to test breeding was to hold regular race meetings. Almost from the birth of Melbourne, these contests between enthusiastic owners became major sporting events, as well as satisfying needs for social contact, gambling and drinking.

Melbourne's first races were held in 1838 on a flat grassy plain west of Batman's Hill. Scottish-born Andrew Russell used to ride over the area, but recorded that he 'found the ground rather swampy'. As a result, the venue for races was shifted north-westerly to another level area along the Maribyrnong River, where Flemington Racecourse is located today. In December 1840 the Port Phillip Turf Club (later Victoria Turf Club) was formed 'with a view to the improvement of the breed of horses in the colony generally'.

La Trobe granted the club a ten-year lease of the 360-acre area (sections 23 to 28 in Doutta Galla Parish) in 1848, on condition that it was used for no other purposes than horse-racing, and that 'when the time of surrender arrives, to interpose no obstacles of any description whatsoever in the way of resumption of the land' by the government. Annual rental was one farthing.

To ensure that the land was used only for the public benefit, six trustees were appointed from among Melbourne's most respectable citizens: James Simpson, F. A. Powlett, Robert Hoddle, J. C. Riddell, Dalmahoy Campbell and W. F. Stawell. Soon crowds of several thousand spectators were attending each spring and autumn meeting. The Victoria Derby, introduced in 1856, was first won by H. N. Simson's 'Flying Doe'.

By 1859 the trustees had fenced and greatly improved the race track.

J. B. Henderson's delightful watercolour of 1855 shows the primitive clubhouse of the Melbourne Cricket Club at Richmond. The family in left foreground was that of NSW Commissary-General Coxworthy, visiting because the match was between Sydney and Melbourne. In the centre background played a British regimental band stationed in Melbourne. (Mitchell Library).

George Cavenagh, founder of the Melbourne Herald, was a renowned cricketer and nine times president of the Melbourne Cricket Club.

This grandstand on the hill at Flemington Racecourse was completed in time for Etienne de Mestre's five-year-old 'Archer' to win the first Melbourne Cup in 1861. In the background, Edwin Hooper of the Globe Hotel in Swanston Street provided drink. Food was supplied by Felix Spiers and Christopher Pond, owners of the Cafe de Paris in Bourke Street, who also sponsored the first visiting English cricket team later the same year. (Newsletter of Australasia, *November 1860*).

That year, squatter W. C. Yuille's 'Flying Buck' won the first Australian Champion Sweepstakes, for which entries were received from all over Australia. A large partly-roofed grandstand was erected the following year to replace the early primitive stand, while Melbourne caterers set up booths to provide food and drink.

Eighteen horses started in the first two-mile Melbourne Cup handicap race in November 1861, the winner being Etienne de Mestre's five-year-old 'Archer', carrying the heavy weight of 9 stone 7 lbs. Since that time the Melbourne Cup has become Australia's most famous race, bringing the nation to a halt on the first Tuesday in every November.

Other race meetings were held in southern suburbs. The Brighton races which began in 1845 developed into another 'fashionable' occasion partly aimed at bringing marriageable females and males together in a fairly exclusive but emotional setting. Coaches left Melbourne early each race day, and steamers were hired, to transport Melbourne ladies invited to take luncheon before the races. Only males had to pay for admission: 'Gentlemen had better be in time!' warned one newspaper.

The desire of British immigrants to re-create customs they had known 'at home' was nowhere more evident than in the formation of hunt clubs. Foxes were released in rural areas in the 1840s, and the first formal hunting forays with packs of imported hounds began at Ballan and on the Leigh River.

The Melbourne Hunt Club was formed in 1854 by George Watson,

lessee of Kirk's Horse Bazaar in Bourke Street. At first its members hunted kangaroos, foxes and red deer released on the Chirnside brothers' properties at Werribee. Sometimes they tried the other side of Melbourne, hunting game on the broad acres of Cheltenham and Hawthorn. When they met for the traditional stirrup cup at Robert Knox's property along Gardiner's Creek in June 1857, *Bell's Life*, sporting bible of the day, enthused: 'We are glad to see this style of hospitality commencing, for what can be a more lovely sight than hounds and pink-coated horsemen assembled on a grassy lawn, and the eyes of beauty looking on to inspire the daring lovers of the chase?'

Cricket was even more important to lovers of English sporting pastimes. The first organised cricket matches began in Melbourne in November 1838 near the gentle northern slope of Batman's Hill, described by squatter W. L. Morton as 'a beautiful rising grassy knoll, openly covered with handsome casuarina, or so-called sheoak trees'. Daniel McArthur, who was grazing sheep at Point Ormond, brought along the first bats and wickets to enable soldiers and civilians to compete.

Matches became so popular that in 1848 La Trobe granted the Melbourne Cricket Club permissive occupancy of ten acres near the Yarra in South Melbourne, originally part of J. P. Fawkner's cultivation paddock where the settlement's first crops had been grown. One of the club's best batsmen, and nine times its president, was George Cavenagh, founder of the Melbourne *Herald*.

By 1858, when Henry Glover drew this detailed scene, many buildings and booths had sprung up around the Melbourne Cricket Ground playing area. The occasion was the

'third grand intercolonial cricket match', played between Victoria and New South Wales in January 1858. Victoria won by 171 runs. (La Trobe Collection).

With massive immigration during the gold rush, the club quickly outgrew its South Melbourne home. In 1854 it was given permission to fence nine acres of Yarra Park, on the site of today's Melbourne Cricket Ground. J. B. Henderson's watercolour of 1855 shows the original roughly-built clubhouse, which contained a large dining-room, a bar and two dressing rooms.

Regular intercolonial matches, forerunners of today's annual Sheffield Shield contest, began on the new ground in 1856. Crowds flocked to each match. Richard Horne wrote that 'The mania for bats and balls in the broiling sun during the last summer exceeded all rational excitements. The newspapers caught this flying epidemic, and . . . devoted column after column to minute accounts of the matches played incessantly by upwards of a hundred different cricket clubs!'

The MCG was redesigned in 1861 by R. C. Bagot, a 33-year-old Irish-born civil engineer. Bagot laid new turf on the playing area and built inner and outer fences, between which he planted 400 saplings donated by the Botanic Gardens.

That summer Melbourne was thrown into a new cricketing mania when Messrs Spiers & Pond of the Cafe de Paris brought out the first English cricket team ever to play against a Melbourne side. Nearly 20,000 people crammed the ground on the opening day, many being 'elegantly dressed ladies whose charming toilets and bright eyes added greatly to the beauty of the scene'. Over the four days of the match, inevitably won by England, Spiers & Pond made £11,000 profit from ticket sales and catering. The long tradition of England v. Australia matches had begun.

Football attracted comparatively little interest during the gold decade, although a few small suburban clubs played under widely varying rules. Organised games began in 1856 when a wealthy squatter's son, Thomas Wills, returned from boarding at Rugby school in England.

Wills advised his 20-year-old cousin Henry Harrison not to play rugby, saying it was 'unsuitable for grown men engaged in making a living'. That is, the risk of serious injury was too great. But Harrison, a Customs tide-waiter at Williamstown, wanted to develop a vigorous winter game. With Wills's help, he evolved a variant of rugby involving less body contact and faster play. Wills wrote to Bell's Life in July 1858: 'I say, form a football club, and form a committee to draw up a code of laws'.

The suggestion was taken up the following month by Melbourne Grammar School and Scotch College, who played one of the first so-called 'Australian Rules' matches on 7 August 1858 at Yarra Park. The teams were huge: forty boys on each side. It is not certain exactly how the rules of rugby were modified on that historic day. After several hours play, each team had scored one goal each, and in fading light the match was declared a draw. The rules kept on evolving through experience, being finally codified by Harrison in 1866 to win him the title 'Father of Australian Rules football'.

A number of minor sports engaged the attention of gold-rush residents wanting an outlet for their surplus energy.

Prize-fighting with bare fists, although supposedly illegal, remained a favourite entertainment of the working class. One bout recorded by *Bell's Life* in 1857 took place among a nest of grog shanties in the bush. Two young men belted each other mercilessly for more than an hour, remaining on their feet after forty-two rounds.

When a similar bout took place 'within a very short distance' of Melbourne police headquarters in 1859, the *Age* roared that nothing was 'more repulsive in its inhuman and depraved character' than such 'disgraceful exhibitions'. Rules for compulsory wearing of gloves and attendance of doctors did not evolve until the 1880s.

Rowing contests, which had been popular in Sydney since 1818, took some time to reach Melbourne. A great sculling match took place in June 1857 between Alfred Holland and William Jewiss, who raced five miles from Hawthorn Bridge to Church Street, Richmond, in 32-foot cedar boats fitted with outriggers. Holland won by two lengths, but after a protest the race was declared a draw. Intercolonial races began six years later when a Melbourne crew visited Parramatta.

Melbourne pioneers made such a fearful mess of their main river, the Yarra, that by the early 1850s swimming, a favourite summer sport, had to be abandoned there. Keen swimmers began travelling to suburban beaches instead.

The first person to organise beach bathing appears to be Mrs Mary Ford, who owned a small house on St Kilda Esplanade. In 1853 she began letting rooms on an hourly basis, so that swimmers could change before and after bathing. The following year Mrs Ford sold up to Essex-born

The western fences of Captain William Kenney's sea baths are prominent in this 1863 view of St Kilda by J. B. Philp. At left, behind the yacht mast, is St Kilda railway station, today derelict. Across Fitzroy Street is the 1858 Wesleyan Church, which still stands at the south-west corner of Princes Street, but lacking the pinnacles seen in this sketch. Flying a flag is Bennett's 1857 three-storey Terminus Hotel, then one of Melbourne's leading resorts. It changed into the George then Seaview Hotel, but still stands. Along today's Jacka Boulevard can be seen John Yewers's New Bath Hotel, Miss Matthieu's Ladies School, William Kesterton's Prince of Wales Hotel, and John Mooney's Royal Hotel. (La Trobe Collection).

Captain William Kenney, who had arrived in Melbourne in charge of a shipload of gold immigrants. Kenney purchased a condemned 200-ton brig named *Nancy*, scuttled it at St Kilda, and used it as a solid base to fence in a large area of shallow water north of today's pier.

The baths made little profit for the first two seasons, but in 1857 Kenney added large numbers of changing cubicles on the landward side, separated for males and females. These buildings also helped to screen

bathers from passers-by. Charges were 6d for men, including a towel, or 50s for the season. Women were charged 1s per session, but this included use of a voluminous bathing costume.

Sea bathing now became enormously popular, especially after the railway reached the area. Clara Aspinall wrote that 'The bathing at St Kilda is excellent—much better, I think, than at many English watering-places'.

Amateur sports held at St Kilda in 1860 were described by the *Argus* as 'capital'; while Richard Horne 'performed some curious evolutions in the water' to demonstrate 'the buoyancy of the human frame' as an encouragement to beginners. Captain Kenney continued to operate the baths for many years, not dying until 1907 at the age of eighty.

Meanwhile, a few advanced Melbourne doctors began recommending regular bathing instead of medicine for their patients. Dr J. W. Mackenna, who established a Lying-in Hospital in Dublin before emigrating to Melbourne in 1854, advocated the 'tonic powers' of cold baths and sea bathing.

Dr Thomas Embling, a radical Fitzroy physician, persuaded the Legislative Assembly in 1856 to inquire into the provision of public baths. His committee urged that 'every municipal district should be provided with an ample site' for the installation of facilities, with particular attention to the needs of women and children.

This led the government to grant Melbourne City Council a triangular site bordered by Swanston, Franklin and Victoria streets. Here the first City Baths (not the present building) were designed by James Balmain in 1858 and opened in January 1860. Hot baths, soap and towels were available so that residents could cleanse themselves before entering the swimming area.

South Melbourne council erected 'Female Bathing Houses' on the beach side of Beaconsfield Parade in 1858, charging 2d for women and 1d for children. Men were forced to bathe behind canvas screens some distance away.

Brighton council divided its sea frontage into male and female areas in 1859. Captain Kenney was licensed to build Brighton Baths in 1863, charging 3d per session. He flew a red flag when naked men were bathing, and a white flag during the hours allotted to costumed women.

Organised open-air gymnastics began on Flemington Racecourse in August 1850, attracting nearly as many spectators as horse-racing carnivals. Events included foot races (known then as 'pedestrianism'), high and long jumps, weight putting and hammer throwing.

The following year Edward Schlobach, styling himself a professor of gymnastics from Saxony, opened the Victoria Gymnastic Yard on the corner of Victoria Parade and Fitzroy Street, Fitzroy. Here he taught fencing and 'German gymnastics' to young gentlemen aged between eight and thirteen years, who needed 'development of the youthful frame'.

Apart from swimming, practically the only sport in which women were invited to participate in the 1850s was archery, sometimes called 'toxophily', a medieval term meaning 'addiction to the bow'.

Wilbraham Liardet had attempted to introduce archery at his Port Melbourne hotel in 1840, but the movement faded out. It was revived in 1856, when Sir Henry Barkly organised the first major contest at 'Toorak House'. The following year John Hodgson formed the Victorian Archery Club, and soon every well-to-do suburb had a thriving band of members.

Archery became a favourite sport for men and women in Melbourne in the late 1850s. According to this Punch *cartoon of 1857, each lady should provide herself with a 'beau'.*

Clara Aspinall wrote at the end of the decade that the sport had become 'decidedly the rage', with archery parties 'conspicuous among the gay gatherings of Melbourne'. She reported that 'the "fair Toxopholites" always returned in higher spirits than even from more ambitious gatherings'. In fact the contests were a thinly-disguised way of meeting eligible marriage partners.

Dancing was the favourite evening amusement of all social groups, but soon became separated into functions intended only for the 'respectable' class on the one hand and the working class on the other.

For upper-class men and women seeking excitement or marriage partners, the annual Squatters' Ball remained the highlight of the summer season. The event had begun in January 1845 at Cowell's Ballroom off Collins Street, but with thousands of people wishing to attend, constantly moved as larger venues became available. Lasting until dawn, each ball was said to be 'a magnificent assembly of beauty and fashion'.

The distance Melbourne had come in less than thirty years was shown when Governor

Darling staged this dazzling vice-regal ball in the Exhibition Building in 1864.

Another favourite annual dance was the mayor's Fancy Dress Ball, inaugurated by J. T. Smith in 1853 at the Queen's Theatre. In this early gold-rush year, social classes mingled in a way rarely seen again. The merchant George Train, who went dressed as a barbarian chief, wrote that 'many were no doubt admitted to the grand *soirée* who, a short time since, judging from the way they murdered the king's English, were washing dishes at ten shillings a week'. Nevertheless, thought Train, 'some of the dresses were truly magnificent', and the guests reasonably well behaved.

On his arrival in mid-1854, Governor Hotham and his wife agreed to attend a tradesmen's ball at the new Criterion Hotel in Collins Street. On arrival, wrote William Kelly, they found 'an assemblage of hard-brushed, shiny-haired operatives, publicans, corporations, and small shopkeepers, with their wives and daughters, girthed in silk or satin, and moist with mock eau-de-Cologne and Macassar [oil]'.

One alderman rushed the Hothams to the bar, thumped the counter, and asked 'Now thin, what'll yer Excell-lencies have—stiff or limber?' The councillor's wife chipped in, 'Try a brandy cocktail, it's mate [meat], drink, washin' an' lodgin' all in one'. After this episode, said Kelly, the vice-regal party watched 'the grotesque gymnastics of the dance', which resembled 'the awkward bobbing and jostling of empty bottles in a water-butt: polking with an Irish jog step, performing the schottische in the style of the Highland fling, and waltzing like so many Westmoreland wrestlers'.

During Sir Henry Barkly's time as Governor, a greater separation of classes occurred. The annual Queen's Birthday Ball at 'Toorak House' became a formal occasion for presentation of debutantes, when only 'respectable' people were invited. Society matrons also organised an annual series of six private 'subscription assemblies', held in a large ballroom in William Hockin's three-storey Commercial Hotel (formerly Passmore's Family Hotel), built on the north-west corner of Elizabeth and Lonsdale streets, opposite St Francis Church. Richard Horne complimented the organisers of these balls for the 'moral courage' with which they had refused 'the claims for admission of some of the wealthy unwashed, and other unsuitables'. Horne added that 'Money is not quite everything, even in Melbourne'.

Dancing was equally a preferred working-class relaxation. At the height of the gold rush, many miners visiting Melbourne patronised the 'Salle de Valentino', a timber and canvas marquee on the north-west corner of Bourke and Spring streets, where popular concerts and dance nights were held. James Armour, who arrived in 1852, wrote that 'though the assembled company might not be strictly select, the music was'. James Smith recalled the 'often costly and generally gaudy attire of the "ladies" with whom the miners waltzed'.

With the end of the wildest gold-rush days, and demolition of the Salle de Valentino in 1856, public dancing took place mostly at Cremorne Gardens, hotels, or 'shilling balls'. Louisa Meredith attended one Saturday-night shilling ball, conducted in a large well-lit room with an excellent band. The young men wore their 'mud-bespattered' work clothes, kept their hats on, and smoked pipes while dancing. Not one drunken person could be seen. The women wore 'dowdy common gowns', said Louisa, but danced quadrilles, polkas and waltzes 'with great precision and evident enjoyment'.

Outdoor dancing was just as popular. When the railway line to Sunbury opened in 1859, Messrs Spiers & Pond organised a 'Monster Pic-nic' and 'Bal al Fresco' at Jackson's Creek, not far from the station. Nearly 1,000 'lovers of Terpsichore' travelled there with a German band, to be entertained in a 'monster marquee' measuring 50 ft by 200 ft, with food, drink, band music, and waltzes and polkas danced on the bare ground.

Theatres and music-halls attached to hotels were popular evening entertainments for prosperous gold-diggers, but they were not usually places in which well-bred ladies or serious devotees of the drama could safely hope to escape from reality.

The only regular theatre which survived from the 1840s into the early gold-rush years was the Queen's Theatre in Queen Street, owned by J. T. Smith and leased to a popular English-born comedian named Charles Young.

Young made several efforts to improve theatrical tastes, but during the early 1850s was defeated by the overwhelming demand of diggers for rowdy, sensational entertainment. William Kelly attended one performance early in 1854, describing the interior as 'overcast by a dark cloud of tobacco smoke' from the pipes of both male and female spectators. The pit was filled with 'pert gents, fast tradesmen, and mechanics, some few with their colonial wives'. The dress circle, wrote Kelly, was crammed with 'florid-looking women in too low satin dresses'. Some were crowned with tiaras, and others 'all hung round

Melbourne's main theatre of the 1840s, the Queen's Theatre near the south-west corner of Queen and Little Bourke streets, was rebuilt after the gold rush. Attempts were made to stage better-class plays, but the proprietors were forced to change to music-hall farces played for half-drunken audiences. S. T. Gill captured this scene between dress circle and stalls in 1853. (La Trobe Collection).

with chains, watches, collars, and bracelets'. The men wore either tartan jumpers or red worsted shirts, and indulged in 'indelicate attentions'. The gods were filled with youngsters: 'shrieking Bedouins of the streets', and sailors escorting women wearing greasy 'cast-off satins'.

On the night Kelly was there, an American couple named Stark were trying to play 'Hamlet', but were greeted with yells of 'Give us

"Black-eyed Susan", old gal!' Meanwhile brandy bottles were let down and hoisted from one tier to another by ropes made of handkerchiefs, 'amidst a tempest of toasts'. At the end of the performance, the players were rewarded with 'a pelting shower of nuggets' from drunken miners.

Late in 1854 the Queen's Theatre was refurbished for the visit of the great Irish soprano Catherine Hayes, who had already caused a sensation in Sydney with selections from opera and ballads of the British Isles. In Melbourne she was received with similar rapture: according to James Smith, she 'transmuted her silvery notes into gold', with tickets selling at up to one guinea. Tears rolled down the faces of recent immigrants as she sang 'Home Sweet Home'.

Exhibitions of human freaks, wild animals and other novelties attracted gold-rush audiences to temporary venues along Bourke Street. A Mrs Williams set up an 'Australian Wax-Work Exhibition' on the north side of Bourke Street, between William and King streets, where she showed likenesses of the Royal Family and notable local murderers. Further east, on the same side of Bourke Street, was 'Wombwell's Exhibition of Wild Beasts', charging one shilling to view four lions and a Bengal tiger. The manager put his head into the lion's mouth twice daily.

At a 'medical museum' nearby, Messrs Baume & Kreitmeyer admitted adults only, with men and women separated, to view their

Irish soprano Catherine Hayes, first great world artist to visit Melbourne, made a fortune when she sang at the Queen's Theatre in 1854.

Charles Young, lessee of the Queen's Theatre in the early 1850s, found it was difficult to improve the tastes of gold-rush audiences.

display of foetuses, skeletons, wax models of female generative organs, sperm (2,000 magnification), and a life-size 'Anatomical Venus' which could be taken to pieces to show the effects of syphilis.

As the main city population moved eastwards, the focus of theatrical activity moved too. Large areas of city land suitable for theatres were preserved for some years by the popularity of circuses near the top of Bourke Street. In 1853, for instance, James Mooney built what he called 'Astley's Ampitheatre' next to Dr William Turnbull's surgery in Spring Street, naming it after a popular combination of circus, music-hall and melodrama based in Westminster Bridge Road, London. George Lewis leased the Melbourne Astley's, using it successfully for equestrian and burlesque shows for some years. With timber walls and canvas roof, it could accommodate 2,000 spectators.

The structure was demolished late in 1856, and the land bought by a wealthy goldfields carrier, John Black, who financed erection of the first Princess Theatre on the site in 1857. As shown in Henry Gritten's painting on page 93, this was a huge two-storey structure running to Little Bourke Street, a site still occupied by today's Princess Theatre built during the 1880s land boom. The original Princess could hold 2,500 people, and according to the *Argus* was 'unrivalled in beauty, elegance and comfort by any other theatre in the Australian colonies'.

John Black leased the building to Alexander Henderson, who began operations with an opera season in April 1857. Season tickets sold at six guineas for dress circle and four guineas for orchestra stalls. One of the theatre's leading attractions in 1860 was 18-year-old London-born Julia Matthews, who had proved herself as a child actress in Sydney and on the diggings. Irish-born police superintendent Robert O'Hara Burke fell in love with her and proposed marriage just before leaving on his ill-fated exploration across the continent. Julia rejected Burke and married her manager, later becoming the first Australian-trained singer to appear at Covent Garden.

In a transformation similar to the Princess Theatre, Fawcett Rowe's American Circus on the south-east corner of Lonsdale and Exhibition streets was replaced in 1855 by George Coppin's new Olympic Theatre and Thomas Nunn's adjoining Olympic Tavern.

The iron framework of theatre and tavern was prefabricated by Bellhouse & Co. in Manchester, shipped to Melbourne, and erected in only six weeks. The 40 ft by 88 ft cast iron walls were encased in a

George Coppin's Olympic ('Iron Pot') prefabricated theatre, imported in sections in 1855 and erected in Exhibition Street on the present site of the Comedy Theatre.

brick facade, and a huge iron and glass frontage installed. The theatre, with interior decoration by William Pitt, could hold 1,150 people. It quickly won the name 'Iron Pot'.

Noted 37-year-old Dublin-born actor G. V. Brooke opened the Olympic Theatre on 30 July 1855 with a prologue written for the event by amateur poet and Supreme Court Chief Justice Sir William à Beckett. This unusual beginning was followed by a number of popular romantic tragedies and Shakesperian plays, in a successful season lasting nine months. According to one memory of the time, 'Old playgoers felt their hearts swell with emotion at witnessing such scenes as they never dreamt they could witness again after leaving the shores of Old England'. Coppin was supposed to pay Brooke £10,000 salary for the season, but went into partnership with him instead, besides marrying his sister-in-law in August 1855.

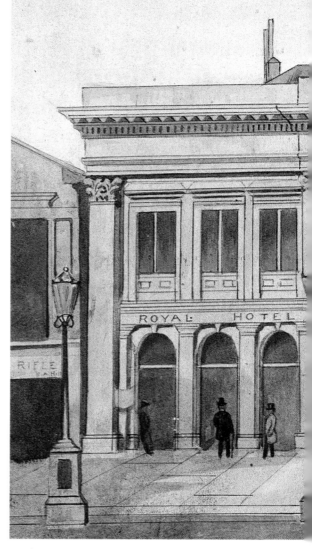

This anonymous painting shows John Black's Theatre Royal and associated buildings of 1855 on the north side of Bourke Street, between Swanston and Russell streets. The Vestibule and Royal Hotel became notorious as the haunt of prostitutes. George Coppin staged a grand opera season at the theatre in 1856, followed by many dramatic productions. (La Trobe Collection).

The Olympic Theatre was later converted to house gymnasiums and Turkish baths, but burned to the ground in 1866. Today the site is occupied by the Comedy Theatre.

Coppin's Olympic Theatre met with strong competition when the former goldfields carrier John Black opened the Theatre Royal in Bourke Street in 1855. This was centrally located on the north side of that popular thoroughfare, between Swanston and Russell streets, today occupied by a Coles-Myer store.

Black set out to eclipse all other Melbourne venues, hoping to pay for expensive overseas artists by building 'a magnificent theatre' which

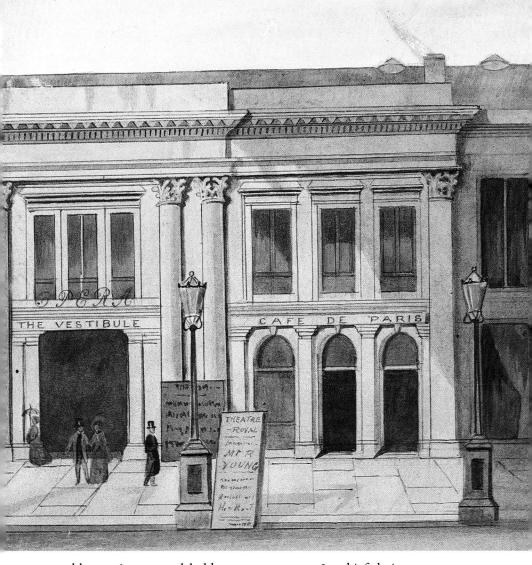

would cost £95,000 and hold 3,300 spectators. Its chief designer was
Samuel Merrett, architect of the original Exhibition Building. Merrett
included a 7,000 cubic feet gasworks at the rear to light 600 burners
inside the auditorium. These gave brilliant illumination, in contrast to
the 'lugubrious dimness' of other theatres.

The Theatre Royal opened on 6 July 1855 with G. H. Rogers starring
in 'The School for Scandal'. Then Black made the mistake of engaging
the notorious 37-year-old courtesan Lola Montes, who had arrived in
Victoria to make her fortune by entertaining gold-diggers. In September
1855 Lola performed her erotic spider dance at the Theatre Royal,
raising her skirts so high that the audience could see she wore no

underclothing at all. Next day the *Argus* thundered that her performance was 'utterly subversive to all ideas of public morality'. Respectable families ceased to attend the theatre, which began to show heavy losses.

The appearance of Lola also gave the signal to Melbourne prostitutes to emerge from their back-alley haunts. The Theatre Royal's central vestibule, said William Kelly, became 'the great focus of attraction for the most depraved characters', who assembled in 'beastly, abominable crowds'. The west side of the vestibule had several entrances to the adjoining Royal Hotel, where patrons were served at a 150-foot bar by girls wearing tights. This area became known as 'the Saddling Paddock', from where prostitutes carried off their drunken clients to nearby dens.

English journalist Frank Fowler, visiting Melbourne at the time, looked at such haunts in Durand's Alley behind the theatre. Most of the houses there had earth floors, and were 'utterly destitute of windows, chimneys, and doors', with 'brazen women, hulking bullies, and grimy children' lolling about. Fowler claimed that 'scenes of riot and debauchery — sin in its bizarre and most lurid aspects — are daily and nightly enacted in these localities'.

With heavy losses on both the theatre and his horse repository in Lonsdale Street, John Black was forced into bankruptcy. The Theatre Royal was taken over by the ever-ambitious George Coppin and his partner Gustavus Brooke in 1856. The two men now practically monopolised the leading Melbourne theatres. They transferred the magnificent English soprano Anna Bishop from singing ballads at the Olympic Theatre to a season of lyrical drama at the Theatre Royal, introducing such operas as Bellini's 'La Sonnambula'. Melbourne, said the *Argus*, was rapidly becoming 'the Athens of the South'.

Another opera season at the Theatre Royal in 1859 included the first Australian performances of 'La Traviata' and 'Il Trovatore'. These highlights were interspersed with popular spectacles such as 'Lewis's highly talented equestrian company', who galloped horses around the stage while performing difficult acrobatic feats.

Coppin and Brooke also attempted to remove the stigma of prostitution from the Theatre Royal. They got rid of Henry Gregory, licensee of the adjoining Royal Hotel, and installed the partnership of Felix Spiers and George Hennelle. In 1858 Hennelle was replaced as partner by Christopher Pond, a more experienced hotelier. Spiers & Pond then converted the eastern side of the Theatre Royal into a lavish upstairs restaurant, with spacious billiard, coffee and newspaper reading rooms attached. Governor Barkly opened this 'Cafe de Paris' in June 1858. Its

Notorious courtesan Lola Montes shocked Melbourne with her erotic 'Spider Dance' at the Theatre Royal in 1855.

George Coppin entertained gold-rush Melbourne with many different enterprises.

'Royal Dining Hall' was described as 'a large and elegant apartment, with an elegant dome roof fitted with stained glass'. At one end was an enormous gridiron, on which patrons could watch their meat grilling.

On his election to the Legislative Council in October 1858, Coppin sold his share in the Theatre Royal to Brooke. Although a fine actor, Brooke proved to be a poor manager. He turned to drink, and was sometimes incapable of appearing on stage. The result was bankruptcy after his final appearance in May 1861. He returned to London, always meaning to come back in triumph to Melbourne, but was drowned when his ship sank in 1866.

The Theatre Royal meanwhile had fallen under the management of Shakesperian actor Thomas Sullivan, who popularised the idea of cheap admission to the pit. Sullivan's most notable success was the engagement of an American opera company formed by Irish-born entrepreneur W. S. Lyster, which played at the Theatre Royal throughout 1861. The theatre burned down in 1872 and had to be completely rebuilt.

George Coppin's first wife Harriet died in childbirth in 1859. Seventeen months later, in a scene reminiscent of one of his own melodramas, Coppin married his step-daughter, the 18-year-old Lucy Hilsden. Their first child was born seven months later.

The following year, 1862, Coppin returned to the theatrical scene by erecting the Haymarket Theatre adjacent to the Eastern Market in Bourke Street. The building cost far more than he expected, and bankruptcy loomed again. Coppin was saved temporarily by engaging Charles Kean, Queen Victoria's director of private theatricals, and his actress wife Ellen, to tour Melbourne and the diggings in 1863. The resulting profits enabled Coppin to pay his creditors in full. But the Haymarket Theatre had to be converted into the Haymarket Hotel, which burned down in 1871. In all of gold-rush Melbourne's theatrical glories, fire or bankruptcy seemed to be the common end.

The first St Paul's Church at right faced two hotels across the intersection of Flinders and Swanston streets: Cornelius Hayes's Bridge Hotel (later Young & Jackson's), and William Perrett's Freemasons' Hotel. In this Edward Gilks lithograph of 1864, a telegraph messenger rides past gossiping citizens. (La Trobe Collection). Dennis Keogh, MLC (top), a wine and spirit merchant, bought the Bridge Hotel freehold in 1856, later leasing it to Messrs Young and Jackson.

17

Hotels and their
antagonists

Rapidly expanding societies need large amounts of temporary accommodation and food supply. Public houses provided these valuable services from Melbourne's earliest years, but had to expand almost overnight when the gold rush began. The result, as soon as builders could be found, was a boom in hotel building. At one stage it seemed that Melbourne would finish up with a pub on every corner.

At the height of gold immigration in 1853, almost any structure could be licensed as a hotel or lodging house. Edwin Booth noted that any building 'formed of weatherboards, measuring ten feet by twelve, with a recess at the back large enough to contain an American cooking-stove, and frontage sufficiently long to display a signboard is, in a "colonial sense", a hotel'.

Henry Brown, landing in Melbourne in 1853, had the misfortune to stay at an inn where every room was crammed with drinkers. At 11 p.m. the landlord and 'a blowsy Irish woman' cleared out the drinkers and deposited dingy bundles of blankets on the floor 'as close as they could pack'. Brown was bitten so badly by vermin during the night that he had to move to the woodshed. Next morning, the publican offered him a breakfast of warmed-over hash, stew and steak.

Arriving in Melbourne the following year, William Kelly found that 'the bars were always full, the tap-rooms always crowded'. He observed that 'women were as numerous as the men', and asserted their equality with 'as deep potations, and as blasphemous and obscene vociferations'.

As long as the gold boom lasted, publicans could make huge fortunes. R. M. Thomas spoke to one licensee who claimed he had made £20,000 profit in 1853. William Westgarth, looking back on those wild days, wrote that 'A public-house had become a sort of unfathomable

Successful diggers returning to Melbourne often spent their hard-earned profits on grog. Lavish new hotels sprang up in every main city block to meet the extraordinary demand depicted here by S. T. Gill. (La Trobe Collection).

abyss of fortune, alike for landlord and tenant'. Rents of £5,000 a year would be 'freely tendered' for any city pub.

Governments shared in the plunder, increasing publicans' licence fees from £30 to £100 a year, and imposing heavy fines for unlicensed or after-hours trading. Even more profitable was the import duty on spirits, which increased from a total of £30,000 in 1851 to nearly £600,000 in 1854.

The number of breweries also multiplied. By 1860 there were sixteen independent brewers of beer, including three in the city, four at Collingwood, three at Richmond, two at Abbotsford, two at Prahran, and one each at North Melbourne and Port Melbourne. The most important was probably Robert McCracken's City Brewery, situated

The Criterion Hotel in Collins Street became a centre of business entertainment life after the gold rush. At left were the Criterion Sale Rooms, later taken over by J. Simmons & Son. To the right of the hotel, F. Cooper had his pharmacy, with surgeon Richard Heath operating on the floor above. James Blundell conducted a bookselling, stationery and

lithographing firm next door. He allowed S. T. Gill, who drew this sketch, space for a studio on the first floor, where some of the illustrations in this book were prepared. (La Trobe Collection).

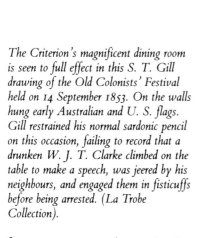

The Criterion's magnificent dining room is seen to full effect in this S. T. Gill drawing of the Old Colonists' Festival held on 14 September 1853. On the walls hung early Australian and U. S. flags. Gill restrained his normal sardonic pencil on this occasion, failing to record that a drunken W. J. T. Clarke climbed on the table to make a speech, was jeered by his neighbours, and engaged them in fisticuffs before being arrested. (La Trobe Collection).

for many years on the north side of Collins Street between William and King streets—almost next door to St James Church. Perhaps the leading suburban brewer was Thomas Aitken, who in 1854 established the famed Victoria Brewery in Victoria Parade, East Melbourne.

The temporary slump of 1854 wiped out a number of publicans who had over-reached themselves financially. At the same time, the building of larger hotels had commenced. These were generally completed, often with different licensees.

At the then-popular west end of the city rose Sir Charles Hotham Hotel, built on the eastern corner of Flinders and Spencer streets in 1854-5 to commemorate the new Governor's arrival, and leased by

James Orkney. At the time, this was a three-storey brick construction, later rebuilt to make the structure of the same name which remains today.

Much of the Flinders Street frontage between Spencer and William streets was occupied by gold-rush hotels. One was the Yarra Family Hotel, built on the western corner of William Street in 1853-4 by Eugene McLaughlan and leased to John Jones. Its three stone and brick storeys contained twenty-six rooms plus a large cellar.

One of the most interesting west-end hotels is the former Ship Inn at today's 383 Flinders Lane. This survives almost intact from the gold-rush years. Designed by Samuel Marlow, it was built in 1850-2 as hotel and adjoining offices for John and Mary Tighe. The art-nouveau

On the south side of Bourke Street, between Elizabeth and Swanston streets, only the
Bull & Mouth Hotel survived the retail shakeout after the gold rush. The remainder of
these businesses did not commence until the mid-1860s, when Sam Calvert engraved the

scene. From left can be identified James Blair's pharmacy, then the Bull & Mouth, then
A. Maclean's pastry shop, above which were Ladies' Refreshment Rooms, Hosie's Scotch
Pie House, and 'Gentlemen's Dining Rooms'. (La Trobe Collection).

[325]

decorations still in good condition were added in 1906 when the building became Tavistock House.

Further east along Flinders Street, between Elizabeth and Swanston streets, another favourite hostelry was the 26-roomed Port Phillip Club Hotel, converted from John Hodgson's private house and first licensed in 1850. When William Kelly arrived early in 1854 and tried to get a bed for the night, licensee Edward Scott told him that 'every hearth-rug in the establishment' was engaged. Kelly finally managed to find space in the newly-opened Duke of Wellington Hotel nearby, but was offered 'no softer bed than the dining-room table'.

A few doors along from the Port Phillip Club, on the north-west corner of Swanston Street, was the historic Bridge Hotel, better known today as Young & Jackson's. This was a three-storey bluestone building erected in 1853 on a half-acre corner block for which John Batman paid £100 at the first Melbourne land sale in June 1837. During the Batman family's financial difficulties, the freehold fell into the hands of city solicitor Henry Jennings. Jennings allowed a 21-year lease to Thomas James, a St Kilda investor. James demolished the old Batman buildings and erected the existing bluestone block for use as warehouses and butcher's shop. Then in 1856 Jennings sold the land to 30-year-old Irish-born wine and spirit merchant Dennis Keogh, MLC, a successful gold-rush immigrant. Keogh leased the corner shop to John Toohey, who on 1 July 1861 opened it as the Bridge Hotel, later Princes Bridge Hotel. Several changes of licence occurred before Henry Young and Thomas Jackson took over in 1875 and created the famous 'Young & Jackson's' name.

The Duke of Wellington Hotel, which still stands on the north-eastern corner of Flinders and Russell streets, was originally erected by builder Timothy Lane as a 14-roomed town house for himself and family. Mrs Rebeccca Smith conducted it as a high-grade boarding house from 1850 to early 1853, when Richard Dalton was granted a licence to convert it into a hotel. L. J. Michel, wealthy gold discoverer, added the property to his chain of hotels in 1861. Today the Duke of Wellington is the oldest licensed house still operating in the city area.

Melbourne's most famous gold-rush hotel was undoubtedly the Criterion. This was converted in 1853 from J. W. Cowell's original Royal Exchange Hotel, located on the south side of Collins Street between

Elizabeth and Queen streets. The new owners were two American gold immigrants, Samuel Moss and Charles Wedel, who built a new three-storey frontage to Collins Street with twenty-eight bedrooms. One was a bridal chamber decorated in amber satin. The older part at the rear was converted into a series of bars, dining-rooms, billiard saloon, bath-house, hairdresser, bowling saloon, and even 'a pretty ornate little vaudeville theatre' holding 500 people. William Kelly admired the main bar, with its 'grand mirrors, imposing decanters, marble counter, monster claret-cup bowl', and American waiters who dazzled customers with their dexterity in mixing cocktails.

On Independence Day in 1853, the American owners of the Criterion shocked loyal Britons by 'thrusting a jurymast through a skylight in the roof, to sustain the broad American flag, and the projection of horizontal yards from the front windows to display miniature editions of the star-spangled banner'.

The main event of 1853 was an Old Colonists' Festival in the giant dining-room on the evening of 14 September, to honour 300 pioneers who had been in the colony for more than ten years. La Trobe was naturally the guest of honour. As usual he left early, after eight of the nineteen toasts had been drunk. Soon afterwards, an inebriated W. J. T. Clarke rose to announce that the colonists had made 'a great mistake' by not putting him in the chair. His equally-drunken neighbours cried 'Turn him out!' and tried to pull him down. According to the *Herald* report, Clarke defied them, shouting 'Come one, come all!' The 'choice old colonists pitched into the aforesaid inebriated butcher, who fought at great odds like a Hercules', said the newspaper. After 'wine bottles, wine glasses, punch bowls and their fragrant contents were summarily kicked down', Moss called in the police, who arrested Clarke and had him fined for drunkenness. After this riot, no further old colonists' dinner was held for sixteen years.

As the eastern half of Bourke Street developed into a popular enter-tainment area, dozens of large and small hotels began to line each side of the road from Queen Street through to Spring Street. In the lowest-lying area now dominated by the GPO and large department stores, John Watson's 60-bedroom Albion Hotel formed a general meeting-place, for it was here that Cobb & Co. and other coach lines had their offices.

Across the road was the high-grade Union Hotel, started in 1853 by

Bourke Street was a favoured location for hotels and entertainments. This Francois Cogné lithograph of 1863 shows (from left): William Bignell's New Hotel on the north-eastern corner of Swanston Street, just converted from Hickinbotham's drapery. In the same block of Bourke Street were Spiers & Pond's Royal Hotel and the Theatre Royal. Parliament

House can be seen at the far end of Bourke Street. On the right side, corner of Russell Street, was Thomas Nunn's hotel, then Gosling's Royal George Hotel, and the Victoria Temperance Brewery. At extreme right was William Finley's Royal Mail Hotel. (La Trobe Collection).

an American hotelier and, according to William Kelly, 'conducted with a degree of care and sumptuousness which rendered it justly famous'. Apart from French cuisine, it offered orchestral evenings in a great room which 'filled every night with musical devotees'. This entrepreneur aimed too high and went bankrupt. The new licensee, Edward Jenkins, converted the music room into a billiard room and prospered.

Further along Bourke Street towards Swanston Street was James Bartholomew's famed three-storey Bull and Mouth Hotel, described by William Kelly as 'the great popular central tap [bar] of the day'. Drinks were served to milling crowds all day and evening, at a uniform price of a shilling a glass. On the ground floor, said Kelly, the atmosphere 'was one of spirituous essences, as dense as a Scotch mist'; while waiters flew up to the first floor tables, 'the stairs positively dripping alcohol'. Neighbouring businesses such as the Melbourne Cigar Divan and Eureka Bowling Saloon did not survive the extensive rebuilding of this section of Bourke Street after the 1850s.

The next section of Bourke Street, between Swanston and Russell streets, was dominated on the north side by the Royal Hotel, described in chapter 16. The other side of Bourke Street contained several large hotels, some later converted to theatres and small shops.

On the north-east corner of Bourke and Russell streets, the Australia Felix Hotel made large profits during the gold rush from its upstairs 'Alhambra' dance-hall and associated bars. William Balch rebuilt it in 1860-1 as a solid two-storey 'family hotel': the building still stands although delicensed many years ago. At the extreme eastern end of Bourke Street, the Imperial Hotel of the early 1860s still trades on the site left vacant when the 'Salle de Valentino' was demolished.

Numerous small hotels sprang up during the gold rush in the infamous Little Bourke and Little Lonsdale streets area on the city's northern edge. A few have been preserved in current redevelopment plans for the locality, as a reminder of Melbourne's frontier days.

The most noteworthy northern building still standing and trading more or less as in gold-rush days is Mac's Hotel on the north side of Franklin Street, between Swanston and Elizabeth streets. Mac's was built late in 1853 for publican John McMillan, to a design by James and Charles Webb. Builder of the two-storey 22-roomed complex was James Lawrence, who later erected part of the Treasury in Spring Street. By 1857 McMillan had transferred the Mac's licence to Matthew Muir, and five years later Henry 'Money' Miller bought the freehold, valued then at only £180. The extensive stabling which once existed at the rear has long since been built over.

S. T. Gill's merry cartoon entitled 'Spirits in Bond' shows a well-dressed squatter being arrested in Melbourne. The police, in uniforms adopted after the gold-rush era, carry the man's cabbage-tree hat and riding crop.

Huge consumption of alcohol in Melbourne during the gold rush led to many outcries against excesses. 'It is in the grog-shop that you find nine-tenths of the population of Victoria; that is their school, their haunt, and their home!' cried William Howitt, with little exaggeration. He castigated the 'monstrous and all but universal drunkenness' which was 'destroying the lives and substance of the bulk of the laboring class'. Expenditure on grog was particularly distressing to thrifty elements of an emerging middle class seeking to build urban retreats away from the wicked city.

Abraham Howgate's delightful Galloway Arms Hotel in Johnston Street, Collingwood, was a favourite suburban resort in the 1850s. Watercolour by Henry Gritten. (La Trobe Collection).

Melbourne's Total Abstinence Society, begun with high hopes in the 1840s, was overwhelmed by the early gold rushes. The society's chief activist, a coach-builder named Richard Heales, sailed to England in 1852, leaving meetings to be organised by Mrs Isabella Dalgarno, wife of Captain Joseph Dalgarno of Williamstown. Being childless, Mrs

Dalgarno had leisure to address many rallies. She advised seamen that they should 'look upon a public house as a ship with the yellow flag hoisted, signifying that disease was on board, and put it under quarantine at once'. By and large, her words convinced only the converted.

So bad was the problem of public drunkenness that the Legislative Council appointed a select committee in 1853 to investigate whether the Maine (USA) experiment of total liquor prohibition should be adopted in Victoria. Chairman of the committee was Edward Parker, a former Protector of Aborigines and now a nominee MLC.

City Coroner Dr W. B. Wilmot told the committee he had 'seen misery in its most appalling shape brought on by habitual drunkenness'. He felt that 'the desire to drink ardent spirits amounts to a perfect disease'. Before the gold rush, only one or two deaths a year had been directly traceable to alcoholism. In 1852, however, out of 200 inquests conducted by Wilmot, forty deaths were directly due to intemperance, and another fifty-six indirectly. Dr Wilmot felt that alcoholics should be compulsorily 'incarcerated for a time and separated from the cause of evil'.

Rev. John Milton, MD, who had charge of the Female Reformatory and City Court Mission House, went further. 'I would let drunkards be exposed in the public streets', he said. 'I am convinced it would have a very salutary effect to put drunkards to work in the public streets, and cause them to be marked as drunkards'. Dr Milton cross-examined nearly 600 prisoners who had come under his care, and found their losses through robberies and expenditure on alcohol to be 'utterly astounding', amounting to nearly £150,000 in twelve months. He denounced the whole public-house system as 'fearfully demoralizing, and extensively injurious to the many, while it enriches the few'.

Then came the evidence of the oddly-named John Tankard, who operated Melbourne's first Temperance Hotel on the south side of Lonsdale Street, between Queen and William streets. Tankard claimed that most lodging-houses were in fact sly-grog outlets, making alcohol available seven days and nights a week. A Benevolent Asylum committee member, Tankard claimed that 'of late nearly every case has been brought there directly or indirectly through intemperance'. The asylum also held thirty children 'deserted by their parents through drunkenness'. Tankard supported the establishment of more coffee shops in the city with popular libraries attached, to help keep people out of hotels during their leisure hours.

John Tankard, who built this Temperance Hotel in Lonsdale Street, claimed that other lodging-places sold sly grog at all hours. (Illustrated Melbourne Post, *18 July 1863*).

The Legislative Council committee decided that total prohibition would be impractical unless it won 'the approval and support of the community generally'. However, to help overcome the 'frightful results' of alcoholism, more temperance hotels should be set up. Existing publicans should forfeit their licences if they knowingly supplied habitual drunkards with liquor. But in the end, the government of the day could only be persuaded to increase the fine for selling sly grog from £30 to £100 (Act 17 Vic. No. 24, 11 April 1854).

Few more powerful images of dissipation have ever been painted than this picture of two addicts chained to 'The King of Terror' as they pass the devil posing as a pawnbroker. The artist, S. T. Gill, himself suffered from alcoholism and syphilis. William Henry's Blue Bell Tavern was on the north side of Little Collins Street between Exhibition and Spring streets, a red light area after the gold rush. (Dixson Galleries).

Richard Heales returned to Melbourne in 1855, setting up business with Edmund Ashley on the corner of Swanston and Therry streets as coach importers. In his spare time, Heales began reorganising anti-liquor forces. Recognising that total prohibition was a lost cause, he formed the Temperance League of Victoria in 1857 and called mass rallies in the William Street Exhibition Building. The movement spread rapidly to the newly-respectable cities of Bendigo and Ballarat, where large temperance halls were built. The associated 'Band of Hope' movement also grew, attracting all age groups with musical entertainment interspersed with anti-liquor speeches and slogans.

Riding the wave of popular support, Heales was elected continuously to the Legislative Assembly from 1857 on a radical policy of temperance, education and land reform. By January 1860 he was prominent enough to become chairman of a new select committee on the licensing laws. This produced much telling evidence from police officials charged with enforcing the regulations.

Captain E. P. S. Sturt, Melbourne police magistrate, and brother of the famous explorer, considered that hotels should be forbidden to operate dance halls, concert rooms and casinos in conjunction with their liquor trade. The practice, he said, was 'very pernicious', and led to 'lowering the morals of the people'. Many Bourke Street hotels were 'very badly conducted; prostitutes assembling there, and disturbances occurring and robberies'. Sturt agreed that 'all those houses of bad fame in Little Bourke Street and Exhibition Street, in fact several hundreds of them, are all sly-grog shops'.

Sturt's most sensational evidence concerned honorary magistrates responsible for granting and renewing liquor licences. Usually only one or two such magistrates bothered to sit alongside him on the Melbourne bench, but on licensing days, said Sturt, 'twenty or thirty' magistrates turned up. This was because 'the majority were interested in public-house property' and were 'apt to be biassed'. Since they had wide latitude to fine or even imprison other liquor-sellers, Sturt thought they should be disqualified from judging such cases.

Police Inspector Brannigan told the inquiry that drunkenness was still increasing in Melbourne, partly because there were 'a great deal too many licensed houses'. In one stretch of Little Bourke Street, half a dozen low-class houses traded within 200 yards: 'I have never seen but very bad characters in those houses'. Drunken men and women were present in 'nearly equal proportions'.

*Melbourne police were notorious for turning a blind eye to sly-grog trading. In this
Melbourne* Punch *cartoon, a constable blithely tells a temperance worker that the
publican is holding his regular Sunday prayer meeting.*

Inspector Brannigan added that sly-grog selling presented serious
health problems. 'I know that deleterious liquor is sold; tobacco is put in
it, I have found figs of tobacco myself in grog that I have seized', he
said. 'That maddens them and makes them commit crimes'. Brannigan
was supported by the new *Australian Medical Journal*, which revealed that
a favourite trick of Melbourne brewers was to mix a compound of
burnt sugar and sulphuric acid with the beer to give it 'a deep colour
and appearance of strength'.

Superintendent Charles Nicholson, head of the Melbourne detective
force, observed that people who patronised sly-grog sellers 'keep
tippling there in bad company, and often get robbed'. He believed that
'If sly-grog selling were put down, that would decrease crime very
much'.

Lesley Moody, Chief Inspector of Distilleries, told the inquiry that
'every third lodging-house' in Melbourne was a sly-grog shop. Moody's
assistant, John Exshaw, said he had visited 190 grog-shops in Melbourne:
'All the dining-rooms and boarding-houses sell grog, and in most of the
grocers' shops you can get nobblers', especially in Swanston and
Elizabeth streets. Melbourne's north-eastern brothel area alone had 100

sly-grog sellers. 'Most of those houses are served by Jews, who buy liquor at auction rooms and hawk it around', said Exshaw. The main supplier was the pawnbroking establishment of Allan & Cohen in Exhibition Street.

Exshaw said he visited sly-grog shops 'in all sorts of disguises'. They were frequented by 'the vilest characters', who drank 'fearful stuff' and spent most of their time gambling. Often young children were present. Exshaw claimed that every licensed hotel sold liquor on Sundays: 'The back door of the bar is always open'. In Collingwood he knew of 220 grog-shops: 'All the grocers sell it there with impunity, especially in Smith Street and on the Flat, that is down about the brickyards'. Richmond was not so bad, except around Cremorne Gardens. In Port Melbourne 'almost every house' sold liquor. In St Kilda the illicit trade was 'not carried on so largely, but there are a good many on the beach'.

Frederick Standish, Chief Commissioner of Police since 1858, and himself addicted to a life of pleasure which finally caused his death from cirrhosis of the liver, admitted to the inquiry that he had instructed police not to prosecute sly-grog cases. His reason was that evidence could only be gained by 'a system of espionage' which caused police to 'lose the confidence of the people', and placed constables' lives in danger. Even when certain cases were brought to court, most were dismissed by the magistrates on some pretext. Standish felt that all retailers should be allowed to sell bottled liquor: 'If everybody were allowed to sell, there would be less drunkenness. People would not congregate as they do now in the bars of licensed houses'.

With all this evidence before it, Richard Heales's committee reached the conclusion that police were not the proper agency to enforce the liquor laws. A separate 'Excise Police' such as existed in Britain should be formed. Magistrates should be prohibited from hearing cases in which they had a personal interest. No new liquor licences should be granted in localities where one-third of the house-holders lodged an objection.

Nothing changed much at this time, but Heales had laid the foundation for a much more powerful attack on liquor interests during the later Victorian era. Aged only forty-two, Heales died of tuberculosis in 1864, leaving a large family which had to be rescued from destitution by a special parliamentary grant of £3,000. Temperance as well as intemperance had its martyrs.

18

Religion and education
in a new land

Life seemed simple to God-fearing people in pioneering times. One either believed in the bible, obeyed its commandments, and ascended to heaven after death; or joined the godless throng leading hedonistic lives, but doomed to suffer an eternity of torment in hell.

Each brand of religion developed variations on these themes, but the basic lesson remained the same: that a joyous immortality could only be assured by obeying God's laws, as interpreted by earthly ministers. Many men (no women) found satisfaction in gaining the necessary qualifications to be called 'Reverend' and spending their lives telling the remainder of the people how they should behave.

This process did not suit large elements of the Australian population, whether they were convicts with a much harsher experience of life, or gold-rush adventurers to whom material wealth was the beginning and end of their desires. In a situation where chance played such a major role in the fate of individuals, it was difficult to discern a realistic basis for God-given moral imperatives. Large numbers of immigrants retained little faith in organised religion.

This change was at first disguised by the sheer numbers of gold immigrants who flooded into Melbourne. The fifty or so churches and chapels built in city and suburbs by 1851 were overwhelmed by those newcomers who desired religious solace for themselves and education for their children.

As soon as the first rush settled down, a vigorous construction programme of churches and associated buildings began throughout Victoria. Under a revised Church Act of 1853 (16 Vic. No. 28, 18 January 1853), congregations had to raise only £200 towards building a church, or £50 towards building a minister's residence, for the government to step in and contribute double the existing donations, up to a maximum of £2,400 per parish.

The first church spire built in Melbourne was that of the Wesley Church, still standing on the north side of Lonsdale Street between Russell and Exhibition streets. R. Shepherd lithograph, 1858. (La Trobe Collection).

North Melbourne rapidly filled after the gold rush with a large population of artisans and labourers. J. E. Butler sketched the Church of England facilities on the north-west corner of Howard and Queensberry streets: schoolhouse at left, Rev. William Byrnes's parsonage in the middle, and St Mary's Church at right. (La Trobe Collection).

In addition, government stipends of up to £400 a year were paid to any authorised minister. Free grants of one-half to two acres of Crown land were made throughout city, suburbs and country. All this, thought the Legislative Council, would assist 'the advancement of the Christian Religion and the promotion of good morals in the Colony of Victoria'.

The result was a perfect explosion of church building. By the end of 1860, Victorian congregations had erected no fewer than 874 churches, chapels, schoolhouses and ministers' houses. By far the busiest were the Wesleyan Methodists, with 217 buildings capable of holding nearly 35,000 worshippers. Next came the Church of England, with 190 buildings; then Roman Catholics with 119; then Presbyterians with 113.*
If all church buildings were fully occupied at one time, they would hold just on 150,000 of Victoria's 540,000 population.

Wesleyan Methodists became the most populous religious group in Melbourne, largely because of the number of noncomformist tradesmen and shopkeepers who came to the city during the gold rush. Wesleyan beliefs appealed to those who desired a less hierarchical method of church control, with less pomp and ceremony, while retaining basic Protestant ideals.

*Further details are in Appendix B, page 448.

The main Methodist chapel in Melbourne had been built during the 1840s on the north-west corner of Collins and Queen streets. With the huge increase in urban land values during the gold rush, D. C. McArthur, manager of the neighbouring Bank of Australasia, suggested to leading Methodists that they should sell their half-acre allotment and build a larger church elsewhere.

Rev. Daniel Draper, son of an English carpenter, now superintendent of the Victoria Wesleyan District, liked the idea, and persuaded his fellows in 1857 to sell the property for £40,000. The purchaser was James Webb, a prominent Brighton architect and builder. Webb lost heavily by speculating in railway shares, and was unable to meet the final £5,000 payment. The property fell into the bank's hands. The historic chapel was demolished, giving way to a Provident Institute of Victoria building in 1860, and later a much enlarged Bank of Australasia.

Meanwhile, the Methodists had used Webb's initial payments to develop a cheaper allotment on the north side of Lonsdale Street, between Russell and Exhibition streets. They invited competitive designs for a group of buildings to include a substantial church, school, bookroom and minister's residence. The winner was the noted Cornish-born architect Joseph Reed, a gold immigrant who had just finished designing the Melbourne Public Library nearby.

By 1856, Melbourne gentlefolk were interested in 'Christianising' South Sea natives. When the Wesleyan missionary ship John Williams docked just before Christmas, 3,000 adults and children paid the railway company 1s each to visit Port Melbourne. Merchant F. J. Sargood, MLA for St Kilda, stood in an open rail carriage to lead hymn singing; while Rev. Daniel Draper led prayers. A reformed cannibal chief on board 'offered a few observations in his own language', after which the children were 'regaled with lemonade and buns' and caught the train home, 'having spent a most agreeable afternoon'. Watercolour by William Strutt (Dixson Library).

Reed designed a church to be built in random bluestone courses, lightened with freestone dressing. It featured the first church spire built in Melbourne, rising 175 feet, and was described as the Wesleyan world's 'finest ecclesiastical edifice', attracting some criticism for that very reason. The contractor was William Forsyth, who was paid £26,000 for the four buildings, all erected in stone or brick. Governor Barkly laid the church's foundation stone on 2 December 1857. Construction was far enough advanced for the first service to be held on 26 August 1858. Pew rents were fixed at five shillings per quarter, a high figure reduced during hard economic times.

For nearly 130 years the Wesleyan Church remained the most striking feature of Lonsdale Street. Due to the expense of maintaining the old buildings, church authorities applied during the property boom of the 1980s for a permit to demolish all structures and redevelop the site. The Minister for Planning, Tom Roper, used the powers given to him by the Historic Buildings Act to reject the application. That is how the complex survives today as one of modern Melbourne's most notable reminders of the gold decade.

Wesleyan influence during the 1850s also reached deeply into suburban and provincial centres. Spare money from the Collins Street land deal was used to build new chapels and manses in North Melbourne, South Melbourne, East Melbourne, St Kilda and Fitzroy.

In the late 1850s a religious revival swept through Victorian Methodism, tranforming complacent churchgoers into 'eager soul-winners'. According to the church's historian, Rev. Irving Benson, 'The first glow burst into living flame at Brighton at a love-feast on 22nd May, 1859'. From there the 'contagion of grace' spread to other circuits, 'tears of penitence began to fall', and many 'seekers effectively found Christ'. By 1860 Victorian Wesleyans had built 179 churches, four chapels, ten schoolhouses and twenty-four manses.

Two breakaway Methodist groups which believed in direct communion with God also thrived. One was the Primitive Methodist Church, which had fifty-two small chapels and 7,000 adherents in Victoria. The second was the United Methodist Free Church, with sixteen chapels and 3,000 believers.

The Church of England, which today prefers to call itself the Anglican Church, had been favoured by Melbourne's 'Establishment' since the first days of white settlement. Because it was so conservative, and so allied to the English social and governmental systems, the church was not as popular with immigrants as other major denominations. Before the gold rush, Anglicans had succeeded in building only St James Church at the western end of Melbourne, St Peter's at the eastern end, and part of St John's in between. The first two churches still stand: St John's in La Trobe Street was demolished in the 1950s.

When Bishop Charles Perry arrived in 1848, he attempted to have the first St Paul's Church (designed by Charles Webb) built on the site of today's St Paul's Cathedral, diagonally opposite Flinders Street railway station. The gold rush disrupted construction, and this attractive bluestone church, seating 2,000 people, could not be opened until the end of 1852. George Train attended a service there in mid-1853, later writing that 'Never in my life was I so wearied with a morning service . . . over two hours in length!' As a good American, he was particularly repelled by constant allusion to her 'Most Gracious Majesty', and Prince Albert, and the Royal Family, and 'the nobility and great powers of England'.

Shortage of labour during the early gold rushes also delayed completion of Charles and Frances Perry's residence 'Bishopscourt', which still stands on the corner of Gipps and Clarendon streets, East Melbourne. Designed in 1849 by the architectural partnership of Arthur Newsom and James Blackburn, the bluestone portion of today's building could not be completed until 1853, by which time it had cost double the original estimate of £2,500. 'Bishopscourt' was renovated in the 1970s at a cost of $220,000, and is today the oldest surviving residence in East Melbourne. Bishop Perry had also planned an adjoining cathedral on the south side, but this site is occupied today by Holy Trinity parish church.

Anglicans enjoyed considerable success in building suburban churches and schools, especially in 'respectable' suburbs. By 1860 they had erected fifty-six churches, ninety-nine schoolhouses, and thirty-three parsonages throughout Victoria. Newsom & Blackburn designed the solid bluestone St Stephen's Church of 1851 which still dominates Church Street hill in Richmond. They also designed the classic Gothic St Mark's Church in George Street, Fitzroy, where the foundation stone was laid in 1853. The church still stands, but needs restoration.

Christ Church, which still occupies the south-west corner of Punt and Toorak roads, South Yarra, was largely built between 1856 and 1859, with tower and spire added in the 1880s. It became popular when Governors' families began using it as their parish church. St John's in Toorak, designed by William Wardell, was built in stages from 1860, and remains the venue for Melbourne's most fashionable weddings.

'Bishopscourt', still standing on the corner of Gipps and Clarendon streets, East Melbourne, was completed in 1853 as the home of Charles Perry (right), first Anglican Bishop of Melbourne, and his wife Frances.

Roman Catholic Bishop of Melbourne James Goold (left) insisted on building the huge St Patrick's Cathedral in East Melbourne. The lower section shown, built in the 1860s, is still in constant use today.

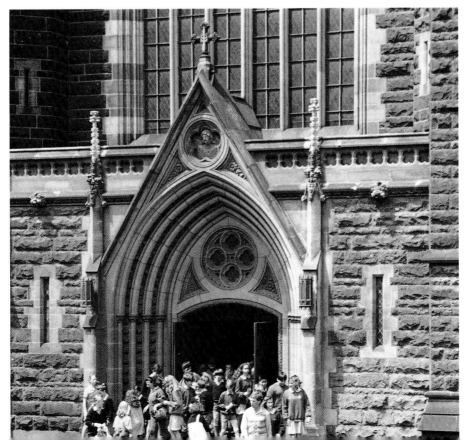

The Roman Catholic Church held an important place in early Melbourne, catering mainly for the needs of thousands of Irish working-class immigrants before and after the gold rush. The Catholic Church's great appeal to these hard-living people was its unchanging dogma, the emotional attraction of its ceremonies, the ready forgiveness of 'sins' through confession, and the willingness of most priests and nuns to assist destitute adherents.

Catholics built Melbourne's oldest existing church, St Francis, on the north-east corner of Elizabeth and Lonsdale streets, in 1845. It became extremely crowded during the gold decade, and a Lady Chapel designed by David Ross was added in 1857.

The first Catholic Bishop of Melbourne, Irish-born James Alipius Goold, arrived in 1848. He began searching for suitable land to erect a larger church, and in 1849 was granted a five-acre allotment in Gisborne and Albert streets, East Melbourne, where St Patrick's Cathedral now stands.

A substantial bluestone St Patrick's Church was begun on the site in the early 1850s, with James George and Joseph Schneider as architects. After £9,000 had been spent, Bishop Goold discovered that Schneider was often drunk, absent from the job, and responsible for 'many mistakes in his plans and specifications'.

Goold decided to demolish the almost-completed church, explaining that it was too small for Melbourne's rapidly-growing Catholic population. As new architect he appointed William Wardell, a 35-year-old London-born convert to Catholicism, who emigrated to Melbourne in 1858. Wardell was given the task of designing Victoria's largest church, which when completed would be acclaimed as one of the world's finest Gothic Revival buildings.

To help stem criticism from donors who had already seen so much money spent in vain, Wardell decided to keep the south aisle of St Patrick's Church already built, and to salvage other bluestone for use in new walls. Construction of the cathedral began in December 1858, under the daily supervision of Dublin-born Vicar-General, Dr John Fitzpatrick, who 'haunted the building like its ghost', and was largely responsible for raising the £150,000 required.

The Catholic Church continued to expand rapidly throughout Victoria. By the end of 1860 it had built twelve churches, twenty-three chapels, sixty-three schoolhouses, and twenty-one residences for priests, able to hold about 27,500 people when full.

The Free Presbyterian Church remained strong in Melbourne during the 1850s, accepting a government land grant on Eastern Hill: the area bordered today by Cathedral Place, Lansdowne Street, St Andrew's Place, and Parliament Place (now partly occupied by St Andrew's Hospital). Here the fiery preacher Dr Adam Cairns (left) built Chalmers Free Church. Alongside, the first purpose-built Scotch College (at right) was opened in 1854 under headmaster Alexander Morrison.

As working-class adherents obtained the vote, the church gained considerable political power. In one extraordinary act of religious discrimination, the Victorian Labor government in 1992 donated $2 million towards the cost of repairing the exterior and stained glass windows of St Patrick's Cathedral. The Anglican St Paul's Cathedral, equally in need of restoration, received only $5,000.

The Presbyterian Church had once given promise of being the most vigorous organisation in Melbourne, but was torn to pieces by a fierce schism in the mid-1840s over the question of whether governments should be allowed to interfere in church affairs. The Presbyterians split into three main groups, which at the end of the gold decade controlled the following land and buildings:

- *Presbyterian Church of Victoria*, the official body, which reluctantly accepted government intervention and assistance. It owned twenty-three churches, four chapels, twenty-nine schoolhouses, and fifty-seven manses throughout Victoria, with space for 11,300 persons.
- *Free Presbyterian Church*, which refused any government aid. It controlled seven churches and six schoolhouses, mainly in Melbourne, with space for 4,200 persons.
- *United Presbyterian Church*, which attempted to unite the warring parties. It controlled five churches with space for 2,000 people.

The main official place of worship remained Scots Church, on the north-west corner of Collins and Russell streets. This was built in 1841, and taken over by Scottish-born Rev. Irving Hetherington in 1847 after the great split. Hetherington slowly built up the congregation again, and in 1852 was able to erect a new two-storey manse in Collins Street. In 1857 he engaged architect David Ross to add a tower and spire to the original humble church at a cost of £5,000. The church was completely rebuilt by David Mitchell in 1873-4 to a design by Reed & Barnes, and extensively repaired in the early 1990s.

Few parents sent their daughters to the Scots Church school. To remedy this, Rev. Hetherington applied to the Irish National Society for an experienced female teacher. The result was the arrival in 1850 of Sarah Corrigan, first-class teacher from Dublin National School.

Headquarters of the breakaway Free Presbyterian Church remained John Knox Church, built in 1847-8 on privately-donated land at the north-west corner of Swanston and Little Lonsdale streets. Free Church

St Enoch's 'United Presbyterian' Church, probably named after the eldest son of Cain, graced the south side of Collins Street, between Swanston and Russell streets, until the schism in the Presbyterian Church was fully healed in 1870. Henry Gritten's watercolour shows Newsom & Blackburn's bluestone design, built in 1851. On the left side of the picture were small tradesmen and architects' offices; on the right side were Dr J. W. Mackenna's consulting rooms and residence. (La Trobe Collection).

membership diminished after the death of its founder, Rev. James Forbes, in 1851. A new influence arrived two years later with 51-year-old Rev. Dr Adam Cairns, who had set up Free Churches in Scotland and Gibraltar. Although a dynamic evangelist, Cairns was willing to compromise with governments by accepting land grants to build churches and schools, as long as politicians and bureaucrats did not try to interfere in their operation and teachings.

Cairns began preaching in 1853 in a temporary wooden building erected on a 1.5-acre site granted by the government in Lansdowne Street, East Melbourne. He immediately launched a campaign for funds to build a permanent church, and to the disgust of many Free Presbyterians accepted a government subsidy of £3,000. By 1854 enough money had been raised to commence building a simple rectangular stone church. Architect David Ross later added a modest tower and steeple. The building was named Chalmers Church after the eminent Scottish preacher Thomas Chalmers.

Dr Cairns's rousing sermons attracted many patriarchal characters among Melbourne's wealthy Scots. He believed in literal interpretation of the bible, and fulminated against those who would breach the rectitude of Melbourne Sundays. In particular, Dr Cairns was anguished by the 'wild passion' of Melbourne theatres, where, he thought, the 'witchery of female loveliness' was displayed with 'voluptuous elegance'. Stirred by sermons like that, 350 communicants were attracted to Chalmers Church by the mid-1850s.

Dr Cairns worked closely with the more restrained Rev. Hetherington during the 1850s to heal the schism in the Presbyterian Church. In 1859 they persuaded the government to pass an Act (No. 82, 24 February 1859) which transferred all government grants and other privileges to a new body called 'The Presbyterian Church of Victoria'. Forty out of fifty-five Presbyterian ministers attended celebrations at Scots Church on 7 April 1859, and the remainder slowly transferred their allegiance in following years.

The Independent or Congregational Church suited many worshippers who disliked any control by a church hierarchy, believing that every congregation should be completely independent and make its own decisions on matters of faith.

The first Congregational Church, built in 1839-40 on the north-east corner of Collins and Russell streets, became overcrowded by the early

1850s. Enough money was raised to build a second church on the north side of Lonsdale Street, between William and King streets. Architect Robert Rogers designed a tall stone building, which opened on 13 July 1851. By 1855 a manse and schoolroom had been added, at a cost for all buildings of £7,600. The church still stands, although drastically altered for use as office space. By 1860 the Congregational faith had a total of forty-two churches throughout Victoria, attracting 11,000 adherents.

Congregationalists opened their first schools in Collins Street on 2 April 1849, under the direction of J. R. Fraser. An infants' school gave elementary lessons to both sexes; a girls' school with separate entrance and playground taught 'useful subjects'; and a boys' school taught 'Sacred geography and mathematics'. The school separated from the church at the end of 1849, reopening on 7 January 1850 under the title of Victoria Grammar School. J. R. Fraser remained the principal; fees were fixed at £35 a year; and instruction continued in classics, mathematics, writing, French, drawing, and gymnastics.

The Baptist faith in Melbourne was originally based solely on the impressive Baptist Church built in 1845, which still stands on the northern side of Collins Street between Swanston and Russell streets.

Splits occurred in the late 1840s over various religious questions. One section known as Particular Baptists (a Calvinist breed) broke away to build a remarkable 'Zion Particular Baptist Church' on the north-west corner of Lonsdale and Exhibition streets. Another section who believed in infant baptism built their own chapel in 1853 at today's 486 Albert Street, East Melbourne. When that burned down, they rebuilt it in 1855 as a much larger church seating 700 people. The structure, designed by Thomas Watts, still stands, although today used for commercial purposes.

No statistics are available for separate Baptist congregations during the gold decade, but in 1860 the Baptist faith in Victoria comprised three churches and thirty-two chapels, able to hold 8,500 people.

Members of the Jewish faith, concentrated in Melbourne financial and retail enterprises, always seemed more prominent in religious affairs than their numbers justified. They built their first synagogue on the north side of Bourke Street, between Queen and William streets, in 1847, when only ninety-two people in Melbourne described themselves as Jews.

This spacious synagogue was built in Bourke Street between 1853–8. Watercolour by an unknown artist, painted in 1880, shows the new Supreme Court dome in background. (La Trobe Collection).

This tiny building was supplanted during the gold decade by a lavish new synagogue designed by Charles Webb, costing £14,000 to build and equip. Only males were admitted for worship to the richly-decorated 40 ft by 70 ft ground floor, where the five Books of the Law were screened by a gold-embroidered satin curtain. Women, as mere spectators of ceremonies, were shepherded through a separate entrance into a raised gallery running around three sides of the interior. On the northern wall, under a perpetual lamp, were inscribed in Hebrew the words 'Know before Whom thou standest'.

The synagogue's reader and schoolteacher, 34-year-old Moses Rintel, came into serious conflict with conservative members of the congregation in 1857 when he supported gentiles (especially potential wives) who wished to convert to Judaism. Rintel resigned, managed to obtain a small land grant from the government, and established the Michveh Yisrael ('Hope of Israel') synagogue and school on the south-west corner of Exhibition and Little Lonsdale streets. About thirty members of the Bourke Street synagogue followed him. Their attractive single-storey orange-brick building was consecrated on 28 December 1859, and still stands, although converted to other uses.

By 1860, assisted by considerable amounts of State aid, Victorian Jews had built five synagogues capable of holding 2,150 people. Rintel's congregation soon outgrew its Exhibition Street home, and bought land at today's 488 Albert Street, East Melbourne, where its new synagogue of the 1870s also survives.

This building which survives on the south-west corner of Exhibition and Little Lonsdale streets served as the Michveh Yisrael synagogue and school from 1859–77. After the 1877 opening of a new synagogue, which still stands in Albert Street, East Melbourne, this building became State School No. 2030. During the 1890s depression it was used as a labour bureau and women's refuge. In the 20th century it served as a free kindergarten then a creche until 1990. This photograph shows it being converted to current use as a Chinese restaurant.

Development of church schools

Education before the gold rush had been largely left to private teachers, who charged fees, and to small schools associated with churches, who took whatever fees and donations they could get from parents.

The government began to change this unsatisfactory system in 1848, when it appointed the first Denominational Schools Board in Melbourne with London-born barrister R. W. Pohlman as part-time chairman. During the first year of operation, the board distributed £500 to nine Anglican schools, £330 to five Wesleyan schools, £250 to four Roman Catholic schools, £160 to three Presbyterian schools, and £140 to three Congregational schools. Most of these establishments were located in Melbourne and suburbs.

The grants barely paid teachers' salaries. The board assisted further with boxes of books sent from London, and distributed to every school a copy of Sir Thomas Mitchell's new map of Australia.

Thousands of children still went without any education at all. The 1851 census showed that only 10% of school-age children attended any school. Of 34,000 people under twenty-one, half were illiterate.

Gold-rush immigration completely swamped an already unsatisfactory system. Pohlman reported in July 1852 that many teachers had left for the diggings: some schools had been forced to close altogether. The remainder were trying to cope with a huge increase in pupil numbers, and discipline had been 'injuriously affected'.

Most teachers were paid only about £60 a year, and often had to find their own accommodation. With huge increases in Melbourne rents, said Pohlman, 'the actual receipts of many intelligent schoolmasters are reduced below those of day laborers'. Unfortunately, among those who stayed in teaching, 'a large proportion are deficient in skill and general intelligence'.

Asked for his suggestions, Pohlman told the government in September 1852 that more money could solve most educational problems. He asked for £6,000 to import twenty prefabricated schoolhouses; and £4,000 to import twenty houses for teachers, who were often living 'in huts of the roughest description'. Another £7,000 a year would be needed to secure the services of 120 'really efficient teachers'.

The Legislative Council of 1853, backed by La Trobe, met all of Pohlman's requests and even went further. It also allotted £20,000 to assist denominational grammar schools, leading to a huge expansion of

Barrister R. W. Pohlman, first chairman of the Denominational Schools Board, was responsible for allotting State aid to church schools.

Richard Hale Budd, first headmaster of Melbourne Diocesan Grammar School, became secretary of the Denominational Schools Board.

church-based secondary education and the emergence of Victoria's 'Great Public Schools'.

The Denominational Schools Board was reconstituted with a full-time secretary and inspector, 38-year-old Londoner Richard Hale Budd, who had been associated with Pohlman in squatting ventures before becoming headmaster of the Anglican school linked with St Peter's Church. As a full-time government official from 1854, Budd was able to appoint several notable school inspectors, including James Bonwick and Edward Parker.

The first secondary school to take advantage of the government's munificence was Scotch College, which had already opened in Spring Street in 1851 under Scottish-born principal Robert Lawson. The college was granted a new site on the corner of Grey and Lansdowne streets, East Melbourne, alongside Chalmers Church, and here a large new school was built in 1853-4 at a cost of £10,000, including a government grant of £6,500. This remained the site of Scotch College for seventy years, until a transfer to its present grounds in Hawthorn.

Alexander Morrison, 28-year-old son of Scottish farmers, replaced Robert Lawson as principal in 1857. Under Morrison's brisk management, enrolment rose fivefold by 1860 to nearly 300 pupils. Fees were 20 guineas a year for day boys, 40 guineas for day boarders, and 100

Gerald Griffin lithographed this fine view of St Patrick's College in Victoria Parade, which opened in 1855. The section at lower left shows how architect T. A. Kelly connected Bishop Goold's residence (extreme left) to the college through a small chapel.

Inset at left: All that remains today is this eastern tower.

Inset at right: Franciscan monk L. B. Sheil, first president of the college.

guineas for resident boarders. Teachers were paid £115 a year, more than they could get elsewhere.

Morrison appointed the first qualified French and German teachers, and campaigned until languages were accepted as matriculation subjects. He also introduced the first systematic lessons in English grammar and literature, besides appointing Dr John Macadam to teach chemistry and natural science. This educational revolution, interspersed with several hours weekly of compulsory religious instruction, had its reward. Scotch College became Australia's biggest church school, and remained so for many years.

Roman Catholics moved nearly as fast as Presbyterians to take advantage of the generous supply of government money. With a large land grant in Victoria Parade, East Melbourne, and an initial cash grant of £2,500, they engaged architect T. A. Kelly to design St Patrick's College, a large two-storey bluestone building with twin towers, joined to Bishop Goold's residence by a small chapel.

A 40-year-old Irish-born Franciscan monk, Laurence Bonaventure Sheil, was appointed first president, and the school opened on 6 August 1855 with six seminarians and fifty-three lay scholars. Sheil, who was often ill, was apparently not much of a businessman. Rev. Dr John Barry of St Francis Seminary claimed that when Sheil left St Patrick's College on 1 July 1859, the number of pupils had fallen to twenty-five, and income had dropped to £1,600 a year, just enough to pay salaries. 'The public had gradually lost confidence in the institution', wrote Barry. He took over the college, and partly at his own expense installed new classrooms, lavatory, dormitory and library. By 1860 he had increased the number of students to eighty.

Expenses still outran income. Barry began falsifying the books, spent money on a mistress and, wrote Bishop Goold, 'swindled servants, laborers and widows of their all'. On Christmas Day Barry secretly sailed for Ceylon, leaving a bankrupt institution behind him. It closed down for a time, and was not fully resuscitated until Jesuits moved in five years later. Its functions as a Catholic secondary school were finally taken over by Xavier College.

The last major secondary school built in Melbourne during the gold decade was the Church of England Grammar School which still stands in St Kilda Road. According to Judge F. R. Chapman, who enrolled as a

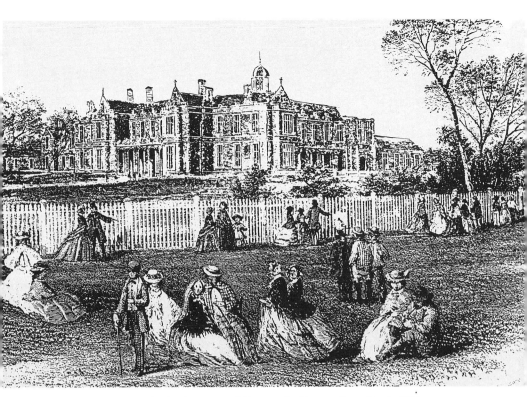

Melbourne Grammar School, whose original bluestone buildings still stand in St Kilda Road, was opened in 1858, fulfilling the dream of the city's first Anglican bishop, Charles Perry.

boy in the first classes, the school's land was 'covered with gum-trees, and blackfellows camped there every year'. Various other locations were considered, but in January 1856 the government approved the 15-acre site bounded by St Kilda and Domain roads, and Domain and Bromby streets. In addition to this gift, the government allotted nearly £14,000 towards building costs.

Bishop Perry engaged partners Charles Webb and Thomas Taylor to design an Elizabethan-style two-storey bluestone school accommodating 400 boys, including fifty boarders, and a dining hall. These were built during 1856-7 by Collingwood contractor George Cornwall at a cost of £16,000.

As first headmaster, Bishop Perry chose 49-year-old Rev. Dr John Bromby, who had been principal of Elizabeth College in Guernsey. Bromby was able to open the school in April 1858 with seventy-seven boys, including twenty-four boarders. Enrolment by 1861 totalled 195 boys, enabling the school to pay its way. One application on behalf of an Aboriginal boy was rejected.

Eastern Hill was confirmed as an educational centre when the government's National Model and Training School opened in 1854 on the odd-shaped block bordered by Lonsdale, Spring, Victoria and Nicholson streets (today occupied by the Royal Australasian College of Surgeons). The school was innovative, and served as a teachers' training ground for the State school system to come. Drawing by S. T. Gill, engraved by J. Tingle, 1857.

Government assistance to these and smaller organisations enabled the number of denominational schools throughout Victoria to increase tenfold from fifty-four in 1850 to 505 ten years later. At the beginning of the decade these schools could accept only 3,870 pupils; by 1860 they were educating 34,700.

Total expenditure on denominational schools increased enormously, and in 1860 was running at £133,000 a year. Of this, two-thirds came from the government, and only one-third from private sources such as school fees. In effect, taxpayers were subsidising a system which tended to keep education in the hands of a privileged, church-going class.

The first National Schools

Church schools did very well out of gold-rush money, but the same could not be said for the newer system of non-denominational schools, at first known as 'National Schools', later as 'Common Schools', and finally as 'State Schools'. In these establishments, religious instruction was not entirely ignored, but only those elements of Christianity common to all creeds were taught for short periods each day.

The non-denominational system was established against great opposition in Sydney in 1848. La Trobe received firm instructions from Governor FitzRoy on 15 April 1850 to divide the available government funds equally between church and national schools in Victoria. This enabled a few small national schools to be set up in rural areas where nothing else existed. The only one in Melbourne before the gold decade was established with J. P. Fawkner's aid at Pascoe Vale, where a £200 school was opened in July 1850 under John Hopkins and his wife.

In the early months of the gold rush, when uneducated children were swarming all over Melbourne and the diggings, the Legislative Council began a fresh attempt to improve school facilities. A storm of religious disputation immediately broke out over the question of national schools. The Roman Catholic Vicar-General, Dr Patrick Geoghegan, said he preferred that 'the child should remain in his simplicity than that he should risk the loss of his faith'. Anglican Bishop Perry was not quite as adamant, believing that 'when people are so divided in opinion as they are in this Colony, the best course is for the State not to inter-meddle with religion at all, but only to take care that facilities for religious instruction are given'.

Powerful spokesmen were also emerging in favour of secular

G. W. Rusden, son of an English parson, fought to establish State education, but also bequeathed £8,000 to St Paul's Cathedral.

Rev. Dr J. E. Bromby, first and most famous headmaster of Melbourne Grammar School from 1858. (VPL).

education. Chief Justice William à Beckett threw his weight behind reformers, saying that 'a child's brain and heart' required 'moral and intellectual furniture', which should be 'supplied to it at the public cost'. G. W. Rusden, who had ridden his horse all over Victoria to inspect schools, asked: 'How shall the people understand the preacher, how shall they respect the laws, how shall they know what senator to support, if they are unable to think and to read?'

The Legislative Council finally approved the establishment of a National Board of Education to operate from the beginning of 1852. Its dominant figure was 25-year-old Hugh Childers, who had been working as Inspector of Denominational Schools. His rules for national education, promulgated in October 1852, began with the 'earnest wish' that 'the Clergy and Laity of the different religious denominations should co-operate with one another in conducting National Schools'.

The government somewhat reluctantly granted £25,000 for this purpose in 1853. About £11,000 was spent on building new national schools at South Melbourne, Port Melbourne, Collingwood, Hawthorn, Heidelberg, Broadmeadows, and on the diggings. By the end of that year, the number of national schools had trebled to twenty-seven, and children enrolled had trebled to 1,750. Despite continued church opposition, the idea of State responsibility for education was becoming more widely accepted.

The £14,000 remaining from the 1853 grant was spent on construction of a National Model and Training School on 2.5 acres of Crown land at the eastern end of Melbourne. Architect Arthur Johnson designed a two-storey building with space for 200 boys, 200 girls and 150 infants, besides offices for the National Board of Education.

Contractor Thomas Mahony laid solid bluestone foundations, but when asked to make savings of £2,000, was forced to erect walls of rubble coated with stucco. This design flaw made it impossible to save the historic building when renovations were suggested in the 20th century. The interior of the 1854 section was completed by builder John Snowball, with two schoolrooms each thirty feet square. When opened on 18 September, the building was acclaimed as by far the best schoolhouse in Melbourne.

The establishment set out to be 'a model school with model teachers and model scholars'. To control it, Arthur and Marie Helene Davitt, distinguished teachers in the Irish National Board system, were brought

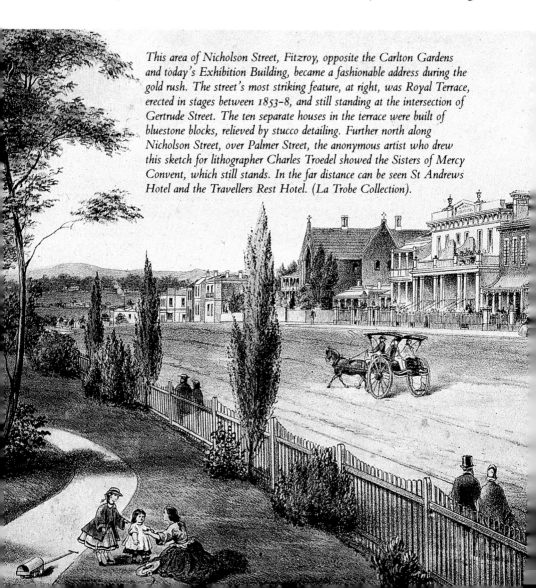

This area of Nicholson Street, Fitzroy, opposite the Carlton Gardens and today's Exhibition Building, became a fashionable address during the gold rush. The street's most striking feature, at right, was Royal Terrace, erected in stages between 1853-8, and still standing at the intersection of Gertrude Street. The ten separate houses in the terrace were built of bluestone blocks, relieved by stucco detailing. Further north along Nicholson Street, over Palmer Street, the anonymous artist who drew this sketch for lithographer Charles Troedel showed the Sisters of Mercy Convent, which still stands. In the far distance can be seen St Andrews Hotel and the Travellers Rest Hotel. (La Trobe Collection).

to Melbourne along with £700 worth of textbooks. Fortunately the pair were childless, for their living quarters at the school consisted of one bedroom, a parlour and a kitchen.

The Davitts introduced a curriculum which was rather radical by the standards of the day. The normal basic subjects of reading, writing and arithmetic were taught, but students could also take Latin, French, art, elocution and dancing. Secular classes lasted four hours each day: scripture was limited to thirty minutes each afternoon. Fees charged ranged from 1s a week for beginners to 2s a week for older children.

Although both boys and girls were accepted, the sexes were rigidly segregated. This was achieved by running a 'bar fence' through the

Victoria Street playgrounds, and by making boys and girls use separate entrances to classrooms.

The Victoria Street frontage of the school was completed by contractor George Cornwall in 1855 at a cost of £14,500. This gave space to accept many more pupils, and to begin training courses for elementary teachers from other schools. In 1857, 'industrial classes' were added so that adults could gain trade qualifications. All teachers were enjoined to 'avoid political meetings of every kind', and to exclude from their classes 'all catechisms and books inculcating peculiar religious opinions'.

Unfortunately the Davitts came into frequent conflict with their own staff and the National Board. Davitt was afflicted with the lung disease phthisis, and was noted for his bad temper; his wife was accused of 'priggishness and overbearing self-esteem'. Savage discipline was permitted: on occasion an entire class of young children would be severely caned. One of the founding teachers, Robert Thynne, resigned in February 1855 as a protest, and later started his own East Melbourne Grammar School. A few weeks after his resignation, another teacher named Alfred Brunton was reprimanded by the board for whipping a pupil so severely that a doctor had to be summoned.

Funds for the school were reduced in 1859, when the board took advantage of the financial stringency to dismiss the Davitts. Arthur Davitt died a year later. He had been replaced as principal by Arthur Orlebar in 1859, and Thomas Smith in 1860. The building was converted into the first Melbourne High School in 1912, and demolished after that institution moved to its present site in South Yarra.

Political battles in the 1850s often reduced the funds available to national schools. By 1854 La Trobe's moderating influence had gone, to be replaced by the autocratic governorship of Sir Charles Hotham. In the Legislative Council, the conservative W. C. Haines and Catholic John O'Shanassy conspired in 1855 to reduce funds granted to the National Board to less than a quarter of the money available to the Denominational Board. The National Board commissioners also suddenly found difficulty in obtaining Crown land grants for new school sites.

A change came in 1857, when the democratic group in the new Legislative Assembly led by Archibald Michie forced an increase in the appropriation for national schools. The results were immediate. The number of national schools increased from twenty-seven in 1853 (1,750 pupils) to ninety-three in 1857 (6,090 pupils).

Hard times returned in 1859 when the Catholic John O'Shanassy again became Premier. His government allotted £92,000 to church schools but only £32,000 to national schools. State teachers' salaries were slashed, and teacher training abandoned at the Model School.

At the end of the gold decade, church schools still greatly outnumbered national schools. Registrar-General W. H. Archer compiled these statistics of schools and pupils for 1860 (pupil statistics rounded):

	No. of schools	No. of pupils
Denominational	505	35,000
National	160	12,000
Private	221	5,000
	886	52,000

Since there were 87,000 European children aged between five and fifteen in the colony, this meant that 60% were now receiving some sort of education. Of the total population under twenty years of age, only about 17% could neither read nor write. This represented a vast change over the decade.

By 1860, a network of national schools had been established in and around Melbourne, including three in the city area; eleven in Collingwood; two in Richmond, North Melbourne, Carlton, South Melbourne, Hawthorn and Coburg; and one in other populated areas. The cost per child per year varied between £2 and £5, including teachers' salaries. Most children receiving instruction were between four and eleven years of age. Twenty schools now ran evening classes for a few hundred older students. Parents of nearly 800 children were classed as destitute, being unable to pay any fees.

The stage was set for a fresh democratic reformer, Richard Heales, to introduce his Common Schools Act in 1862, and force it through Parliament against the dogged opposition of O'Shanassy and Haines. Under this Act, both denominational and national boards were abolished. In their place was established a unified Board of Education with five members, each of whom had to profess a different religion. Any school which desired government aid had to place itself under the new board's general control. The board made considerable progress by amalgamating many schools which had fewer than forty pupils. However, the reformists' ultimate ideal of State education which would be 'secular, compulsory and free' had to wait for another decade.

19

The growth
of science

The Victorian gold rush happened to coincide with a period in human history when men (and a few women) were beginning to question religious dogma and try to substitute scientific observation of the earth and the universe. Clerics generally accepted the bible-based calculations of 17th-century Irish Archbishop James Ussher that the earth was created in the year 4004 BC, but geological discoveries in the nineteenth century showed that this could not possibly be true. If the chronology of the bible was demonstrably at fault, could any of its statements be upheld? Was it not better to rely on the provable findings of science, and the slow accretion of experimental knowledge?

The naturalist Charles Darwin visited the Pacific region, including Australia, in the year Melbourne was founded. At the time of the first gold rush, he was still ruminating at his home in Britain over the possible processes of evolution. Not wanting to offend the religious convictions of his beloved wife Emma, Darwin kept his notes and manuscript of *Origin of Species* locked in a drawer. But the time was nearly ripe for his theories of natural selection to explode over the civilised world and change its thinking forever.

Superstition and fake science of all kinds abounded in Melbourne during the gold decade. An example was the theory called phrenology: the 'science' of analysing a person's mental faculties by the shape of the skull. Philemon Sohier established a 'Phrenological Museum' in Elizabeth Street in 1854, soon moving to Bourke Street, where he offered advice on the 'mental and moral qualities' of business and domestic partners. After examining Aboriginal heads, he told an 1858 parliamentary committee that the native race suffered 'utter want of the power of learning from experience'. Their heads showed them to be 'deceitful, suspicious, slippery, and time-servers, or dissemblers'. Unless native

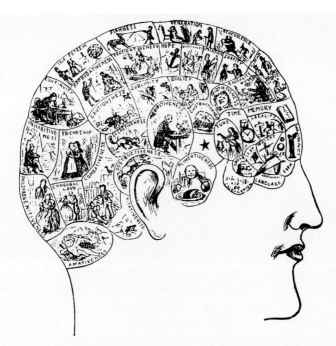

"Phrenology is the Guide to Philosophy and the Handmaid to Christianity."

SOHIER'S PHRENOLOGICAL MUSEUM,

82, ELIZABETH STREET,

(Three Doors South of the Colonial Bank of Australasia).

OPEN FROM TEN A.M. TILL FIVE, P.M.

MR. SOHIER Practical and Consulting Phrenologist (established four years in Melbourne), continues to receive from all individuals of every rank, most flattering testimonials of his success in describing the CHARACTER of persons from the conformation of their Heads, pointing out their mental and moral qualities, whether good or bad, with advice for self-improvement, if desired. Also, directions as to the most suitable occupations, and the selection of partners in business and congenial companions for life—as well as for the proper training of children.

Fee for Phrenological Examination, with a Chart
and a written Sketch of Character   -   -   -   £0   5   0
A Full Written Opinion, with Advice, if desired -   0   10   0
A Complete Study   -   -   -   -   -   -   -   1   0   0
    N.B.—In cases of difficulties, future prospects, matrimonial or family disagreements, and all matters affecting the intimate happiness of the individual, Mr. SOHIER'S advice, founded on systematized wisdom, will be found invaluable.

☞ *In Consultations by Correspondence, the FIRST Letter must*
enclose a remittance of One Pound.

A chart from Philemon Sohier's Phrenological Museum in Melbourne. In 1856 Madam Sohier opened a waxworks next door, exhibiting 'speaking likenesses' of explorers, famous fat girls and boys, generals, royalty, criminals and their victims. The exhibition was said to attract 100,000 visitors a year at 1s each.

children could be separated from their parents' influence, 'the great inferiority of the race, combined with the small brain, will cause the whole race to be extinct'.

The scientific revolution arrived in Melbourne in 1854 with formation of a Philosophical Institute and a Victorian Institute for the Advancement of Science. Both bodies were largely composed of educated and cultured men (no women) who had been attracted to Victoria by the gold rush, and wanted to help gather objective knowledge.

The VIAS was first to be formed, at the instigation of William Gibbons, a Collins Street analytical chemist. Justice Redmond Barry gave his support as president, stating at the inaugural meeting held at the Mechanics' Institute in September 1854 that 'We assemble in the vestibule of the Temple of Science . . . to engage in a course of mutual improvement, and to assist in the cause of general instruction'. Membership grew to about eighty, and five sections were established to concentrate on sanitation, engineering, chemistry, microscopy, and political economy.

The Philosophical Society, which began its meetings soon afterwards, concentrated on botany and other natural sciences, largely under the direction of Dr Ferdinand Mueller. It attracted about 130 members. Surveyor-General Andrew Clarke was elected first president, assuring the society of continued use of a small natural history museum which had been established in the former Assay Office of the Crown Lands building on the north-west corner of Queen and La Trobe streets.

The two societies decided to amalgamate in mid-1855, the new body being known as the Philosophical Institute of Victoria. Initially the secretary was a 30-year-old Hungarian radical named Sigismund Wekey, who had emigrated to the diggings the previous year but gave up the search for gold. Wekey resigned in 1856 when the Institute refused to reimburse him for printing its *Transactions*. He was replaced by science teacher Dr John Macadam, soon to become Government Analytical Chemist.

In 1858 the Institute had progressed to the point of planning its own headquarters. The government granted a triangular piece of land, slightly more than half an acre, bounded by La Trobe, Victoria and Rathdowne streets. Architect Joseph Reed won a competition to design a classical building containing a lecture hall seating 300, and other facilities. Contractor Matthew Taylor built the ground floor in 1859 for

Melbourne Punch *satirised the Royal Society with this cartoon 'Squaring Ye Circle' in 1860. Dr David Wilkie is giving the lecture. Around the table from left are John O'Shanassy, Rev. John Bleasdale, John Macadam, Sir Henry Barkly, Sir William Stawell, Dr Richard Eades, and Professor Frederick McCoy at lower right.*

£2,750, most of the money being provided by the government. The upper storey was added ten years later, and the exterior brickwork stuccoed in 1880, to complete the substantial La Trobe Street frontage which remains today.

Royal approval was granted late in 1859 for the Institute to change its name to the Royal Society of Victoria—a colonial echo of the original Royal Society in London which had been responsible for much scientific progress since 1660. The Melbourne president, Dr Mueller, summoned a special meeting, and on 23 January 1860 enthused to members that

> Our imagination may carry us onward to a distant time, when all assembled with us now shall long have ceased to exist on earth; when other generations have extended this building to one of the more noble of the grandest southern city.

This section of George Rowe's Panorama of Melbourne, painted in 1858, shows part of Professor Georg Neumayer's scientific complex on Flagstaff Hill. In the left foreground is the observatory tent, while closer to the centre is his magnetic observatory with slotted roof. On the right, the tall structure is the meteorological stand; and beside it, a rain gauge. Buildings in the background can be identified from left as: Treasury, Scots Church, Exhibition Building, St James Church, and at extreme right, the gas works. (Melbourne City Council).

Perhaps, added Mueller, 'the memory of this day and our early struggles may not have fully sunk into oblivion, and future generations . . . will gently judge the labors of this epoch'. He could see 'gigantic progress' ahead, in exploration, commerce, communications, agriculture, industry, and the arts. Humanity would be 'elevated more and more by science', and illuminated by 'rays of the dawning civilisation'.

A rough awakening lay ahead for any who thought that such ideals would be easily achieved. In 1857 the Institute had begun to plan a transcontinental expedition aimed at solving some of the puzzles of Australia's unknown interior. Exactly why Victorians felt they had to do this remains a mystery: they seemed to be more impelled by an

emotional desire to beat South Australia to a south–north crossing than by any nobler motive.

The saga began when Melbourne merchant Ambrose Kyte anonymously gave £1,000 towards an expedition, on condition that the public subscribed another £2,000. This was achieved by 1860. But the Institute's exploration committee blundered by passing over as leader the experienced Major Peter Warburton, in favour of Castlemaine police superintendent Robert O'Hara Burke. Burke and his assistant William Wills struggled across the continent, but achieved little towards the advance of human knowledge. Instead, they rejected most assistance from desert Aborigines, and starved to death. The total cost of the expedition, including search parties, came in at £57,000, which would have been far better spent on research projects in Melbourne.

The effect on the Royal Society was serious. When Burke and Wills set out in 1860, the Society had 300 members, including practically every learned man in Melbourne. After the tragedy, most withdrew their support. In 1864, only thirty-nine members voluntarily paid their subscriptions, and the organisation faced a long period of restoring its credibility.

The sciences of meteorology and astronomy in Melbourne owed their development to two gold-rush immigrants, R. L. J. Ellery and Georg Neumayer. Dr Ellery emigrated from London in 1852 and established the first observatory at Williamstown; Bavarian-born Professor Neumayer worked as a digger at Bendigo before establishing a magnetic observatory on Flagstaff Hill in 1857.

The main purpose of Ellery's Williamstown observatory was to calculate highly accurate time signals so that shipmasters could check their chronometers, enabling them to estimate their longitude while sailing. In the days before radio and satellite signals, this was a vital element of safety at sea. Yet the way in which Ellery was dealt with by politicians makes one despair of the democratic process. He was given a broken-down two-roomed timber cottage on Gellibrand Point, and allowed enough money for a few small instruments, with which he commenced hoisting daily time signals in August 1853. The following March, a time-ball apparatus was erected on the bluestone lighthouse (which still stands), replacing the outdated flag system.

Government quarrying operations in the area seriously affected the delicate instruments. In May 1855 the foundations of the old cottage collapsed, and Ellery was forced to suspend operations. After protests from shipowners, the government provided 'a small canvas tent' in which Ellery tried to continue work, but 'the instruments', he reported, 'suffered much from long continued exposure to the excessive dampness'. The government reluctantly erected a timber building adjoining the electric telegraph office, and here Ellery was able to continue operations until the early 1860s.

Meanwhile, in 1858, the government decided to resume the long-neglected task of surveying Victoria, but now by means of geodetic survey which would take into account the earth's curvature. For this, a known starting point based on accurate astronomical observations was essential. Ellery's little timber building at Williamstown thus became the foundation of accurate survey mapping in Victoria.

Melbourne's second observatory, high on Flagstaff Hill at the Dudley Street end (near today's City Bowling Club), was established in 1840 as a flag signalling station to send messages between the city and Williamstown.

Georg Neumayer, a young Bavarian scientist, had searched for riches at Bendigo, but was forced to return home in 1854. King Maximilian II commissioned Neumayer to carry out a magnetic survey

This unusual octagonal building on Flagstaff Hill was first erected as a semaphore station to communicate with the Harbour Master's office at Williamstown. Introduction of the electric telegraph in the 1850s superseded this purpose, enabling Professor Neumayer to convert the building into Melbourne's magnetic survey and meteorological headquarters in 1857. Drawing by George Gilbert; lithograph by Thomas Ham. (La Trobe Collection).

Dr R. L. J. Ellery established Melbourne's first observatory at Williamstown in 1852.

Professor Georg Neumayer set up a magnetic and meteorological observatory on Flagstaff Hill in 1857.

of Bavaria, then sent him back to Melbourne in 1857 with a magnificent gift of £2,000 worth of instruments, in order to conduct magnetic experiments in Victoria. German immigrants in Melbourne added a donation of £500.

The Victorian government, scarcely understanding what was at stake, refused Neumayer his preferred site on the isolated hill above the Botanic Gardens. Instead, it offered him use of the Flagstaff signal station buildings, on condition that he also report on meteorological matters. Neumayer reluctantly accepted, setting up his valuable instruments in a series of small structures shown in George Rowe's painting on pages 376-377. The government also paid small salaries to three assistants: Jacob Bauer; Charles Pickering; and the explorer W. J. Wills, succeeded by C. Moerlin. The meteorological investigations of these poorly-paid scientists helped to lay the foundations of the modern science of weather forecasting, with all its implications for travellers, farmers, and the general population.

As soon as his assistants were trained, Neumayer left in 1858 on an incredible series of journeys throughout Victoria, walking 11,000 miles beside his pack-horse. He set up a series of 230 magnetic stations at all altitudes, intended to show the connection between geological formations and magnetic variations. Neumayer's instruments readily detected an earthquake which took place in South Australia on 21 August 1858; and measured such things as static electricity, and the effect of the earth's atmosphere on the sun's rays.

By 1860 it was universally recognised that both Melbourne observatories had to be moved from their unsatisfactory sites. A 'Board of Visitors' consisting of five government and three Royal Navy officers reported that at Williamstown the railway had been allowed to pass within 180 yards of the observatory, while the Williamstown Artillery detachment was permitted to fire its heavy guns less than 300 yards away. Around Flagstaff Hill, corrugated iron sheds, ironworks and sawmills had sprung up, seriously affecting that observatory's instruments. The best solution, thought the board, would be to adopt Neumayer's earlier suggestion of a combined site above the Botanic Gardens, provided it did not interfere with plans for a future Government House.

Since the Governor, Sir Henry Barkly, played a personal role as chairman of the Board of Visitors, the government found it hard to refuse. A large site was granted in Birdwood Avenue, south-west of the future Government House site, and £7,000 provided in the first year to enable construction to begin.

Ellery was appointed Government Astronomer; and E. J. White, a former gold miner, assistant astronomer. By 1861 a brick astronomical transit room had been built, along with two timber buildings for

Most of the old observatory buildings survive in 'Astronomy Park' in Melbourne's Domain, although now useless for scientific purposes. This is the Astrograph Dome, with offices and laboratories at left.

magnetic measurements. The following year a ten-foot circular observatory was built, with a cupola revolving on cannon balls set in
channels on top of the wall plates. This of course had to be pushed
around by hand, for no mains electricity or electric motors existed.

A Troughton & Simms transit telescope of six feet focal length was
imported, enabling astronomical observations to begin. Gas lighting
was not yet available to the Domain, so the mysteries of the universe at
first had to be recorded and analysed by flickering candle light. Craters
on the moon could be seen with extreme clarity, but to imagine that
human beings might one day travel there was sheer fantasy.

An old Evans clock brought over from Williamstown was found to
keep better time than a new battery electric clock. It was connected by
electric telegraph to the time-ball tower at Williamstown, and to other
time-keepers being installed at telegraph offices throughout Victoria.
By 1863 the telegraph network was also being used to give warnings to
coastal shipping of the approach of foul weather.

The observatory's studies of planets and comets in southern skies
aroused such interest in Melbourne and overseas that funds were readily
raised in the mid-1860s to purchase the world's largest telescope. A
48-inch reflector constructed by Thomas Grubb of Dublin was installed
in 1868 at a cost of £10,000. Called the 'Great Melbourne Telescope', it
remained unchallenged in size if not efficiency for forty years, and was
finally modified for use in the clearer air of Mount Stromlo.

Establishment of a natural history museum was vital to an understanding
of the world's evolution. Dr Ferdinand Mueller was no friend to
Darwinian theory, but even he said in his presidential address to the
Royal Society in 1860 that

> From fossil vestiges, buried in almost unknown rocks, from remnants
> of organic structure concealed in our coal, are to be reconstructed
> yet the forms of vegetation of ages anterior to human life — from
> these also are to be re-established in their outlines the animals of
> now long gone-by times — there are to be re-organised by anatomi-
> cal comparison, triumphantly perhaps from a single bone, the
> colossal creatures of a former world.

In 1853 Mark Nicholson, MLC, an educated 35-year-old squatter from
'Falls of Hopkins' station near Allansford, moved in the Legislative
Council for establishment of a National Museum. He was opposed by

Melbourne's first purpose-built National Museum, erected in university grounds in 1862, attracted tens of thousands of visitors each year.

J. P. Fawkner and a few other members, but in 1854 £2,000 was voted. The project was directed by Surveyor-General Andrew Clarke, who established the first collections in two rooms above his office in the Crown Lands building in La Trobe Street.

A 32-year-old German-born naturalist, William Blandowski, a successful gold-miner at Castlemaine, was appointed as the museum's first zoologist. Enthusiastically, Blandowski trekked to many remote areas of Victoria to collect specimens, and to compile the first professional checklist of the colony's birds and mammals.

During a period of government cutbacks in 1855, Governor Hotham decided that the museum should no longer be financed directly from public funds, but should be offered to the new university. The Philosophical Institute organised protest meetings, believing that the museum should be kept in a location more accessible to the public. But

*Professor Frederick McCoy set up a
'National Museum' at Melbourne
University in 1856.*

*Dr John Macadam, chemistry teacher
at Scotch College, was secretary of
the Philosophical Institute from 1857-9.*

Frederick McCoy, the 'spruce and dapper' 39-year-old Irish-born
Professor of Natural Science, claimed the existence of an agreement
with Hotham. On the very night of the Institute's second public
meeting in August 1856, McCoy lined up a series of horse drays in La
Trobe Street and spirited away the whole collection of bones and
stuffed animals to the partly-built university.

Blandowski was furious, claiming that McCoy had for some time
shown 'animosity' towards him. To get Blandowski out of Melbourne,
the government appointed him leader of an expedition to the Darling-
Murray region, where he collected more than 16,000 specimens,
including many birds and animals now extinct.

On his return to Melbourne in 1857, Blandowski prepared his
findings for publication. Among his discoveries were nineteen different
forms of Murray fish. In an excess of bitterness, Blandowski named two
of them after his enemies in Melbourne. One he described as being
'easily recognised by its low forehead, big belly and sharp spine'. The
second was a 'slimy, slippery fish: lives in the mud'. In the furore which
followed, the Philosophical Institute removed those pages from its
Transactions. After further clashes with McCoy and the government,
Blandowski stole away to Germany with many of his photographs and
4,000 detailed sketches, some of which he later published.

Frederick McCoy meanwhile was organising his museum in four
empty rooms at the university. He took no extra salary for himself, but
with government funds was able to employ four men: the renowned
John Leadbeater as taxidermist, Frederick Scherell as model maker,
Bernhard Shaubel as mechanical draftsman, and William Geoghegan as
caretaker.

When W. H. Archer visited the museum in 1858, he was impressed by the displays of native animals, reptiles, birds, fossils, sponges, meteorites, and models of mining machinery. By 1860, working models of agricultural machinery had been added. These models were frequently studied and measured by inventors attempting to make improvements for local manufacture.

The museum opened from 10 a.m. to 6 p.m., six days a week. It attracted 35,000 visitors in 1860 and 37,500 in 1861, including several thousand Chinese immigrants intent on studying the mineral samples and mining machines.

In 1862 the government granted funds for a complete National Museum to be built in university grounds beside the ornamental lake which then existed. Based on John Ruskin's recent design for the

The National Museum remained under Frederick McCoy's control at Melbourne University for most of the 19th century. This sketch by Sam Calvert shows the Zoology Room—Victorian specimens on left, NSW and African on right. Through the door was the Model Room, mainly mining machinery. (Temperance League Almanac, 1860).

Oxford Museum, the Melbourne Museum had a tall central tower, and a great hall 60 ft by 150 ft, opening on to display rooms lit through Gothic windows.

After McCoy's death in 1899, the government planned a much larger museum in Russell Street, adjoining the Public Library. McCoy's collections were transferred to this building in 1906, where they continued to entrance generations of visitors. Over the years the collections outgrew even this space. During the 1980s most of the natural history groups were transferred to disused suburban warehouses, to await rehousing in a lavish new museum planned for the south bank of the Yarra. After governmental financial disasters of the early 1990s, construction of the new museum was delayed, and at the time of writing much of these historic collections are still shut away from the public.

The University of Melbourne, founded in 1852-3, was an extraordinary creation for a colony just out of its swaddling-clothes. Sydney had opened Australia's first university in 1852, and Melbourne was determined not to be left behind.

Spurred on by Hugh Childers inside the Legislative Council and Redmond Barry outside, the government passed the appropriate Act (16 Vic. No. 34) on 22 January 1853. This was a remarkably well-rounded piece of legislation for the times, specifying that the university should be 'open to all classes and denominations of Her Majesty's subjects', and that 'no religious test shall be administered to any person' before he (not she) became a student or office-holder. An initial appropriation of £9,000 a year was allowed, and entire control given to a Council of twenty nominees, 'of whom sixteen at least shall be laymen'—that is, not ministers of religion.

Anglican Bishop Charles Perry, one of the first members of Council, was not concerned by the university's secular nature, believing that 'religious education is not so necessary [for undergraduates] as for scholars of an earlier age'. Not only that, of the 100 acres granted for university grounds in Carlton, forty acres was reserved for boarding colleges to be built by Protestant and Catholic denominations. These institutions, it was felt, ensured that young men would not lose track of the religious foundations of society.

The land given over to university purposes, bordered by Grattan and Swanston streets, Royal Parade, and College Crescent, was in 1852

Justice Redmond Barry, mainly responsible for foundation of Melbourne University and Public Library in the 1850s. (LTC).

M. H. Irving, first full-time Classics Professor at Melbourne University. (VPL).

largely a rubbish dump divided by a gully running from north to south. As in similar cases, the task of beautifying the area was given to Edward La Trobe Bateman, just returned from a sketching trip to the diggings. Bateman's labourers dammed the gully to form an ornamental lake, filled in areas which had been quarried, spread thousands of loads of good soil, and planted grass, trees and shrubs.

Redmond Barry, automatically elected Chancellor, organised a competition to design the first buildings. A 35-year-old London-born architect, Francis White, won the contest with a design for a stone

EMPLOYMENT

OF

CONVICT LABOR.

Chief Secretary's Office,
Melbourne, 9th September, 1856.

THE following Regulations as to the employment of prisoners for other than convict purposes (in lieu of the Regulations of 15th August, 1856),* have been approved by the Officer administering the Government, with the advice of the Executive Council.

By His Excellency's Command,
WILLIAM C. HAINES.

1. All work performed by prisoners for other than convict purposes is to be paid for by the department or party receiving the benefit thereof, unless special directions to the contrary are given by the Chief Secretary in reference to any particular work.

2. Articles required for the Store branch of the public service are, as far as may be found advantageous, to be manufactured by prison labor.

3. Articles (not coming under clause 2) may also be manufactured, and work performed, for other departments of the public service, upon authorised application from the Head of the Department.

4. Such clothing and accoutrements for the Police and Penal Departments as are paid for by the men may be made, and the payment provided for in such manner as the internal arrangements of those departments may from time to time provide.

5. Prisoners may also be employed for the performance of such private work for the officers and wardens of the Penal Department as they may require, strictly for their own personal or household necessities, on payment of seven shillings and sixpence per man, per diem, for mechanics, and five shillings for laborers, which is to be paid into the Treasury in the manner provided by the Regulations as to revenue; all materials to be found by the party for whom the work is performed.

6. The Inspector General is at liberty to sell by public auction, or otherwise, for the best price that can be obtained for the same, any stone, broken metal, or other raw material, solely the produce of prison labor, to any person or persons, paying the proceeds thereof into the Treasury, as provided by the Regulations as to revenue.

7. A return of all work undertaken by the Inspector General under the preceding clauses is to be forwarded monthly to the Honorable the Chief Secretary.

8. No benefit is to accrue to any department in consequence of receiving supplies of convict manufactures. Each department will be charged the full value of the article: the saving effected by the Government being the difference between the cost of the raw material used, and the price charged, which will be carried to the credit of the general revenue as the proceeds of the labor of prisoners.

9. The Colonial Storekeeper is not to procure in any other manner articles which can be with advantage manufactured by prison labor, provided the Inspector General is in a position to make the supply within such period as may be named.

10. Expenditure in the purchase of materials for manufacturing purposes is, as a rule, to be conducted under the same regulations as govern the entire service. Inasmuch, however, as it is difficult to estimate in sufficient time for the quarterly requisition how much material will be required, requisitions for such "raw material" may be sent in from time to time by

the Inspector General to the Colonial Storekeeper, and they are to be executed by that officer without submitting them for the approval of the Governor, since the material will be required only for works authorised, and will be accounted for both in quantity and value by the Inspector General.

11. The accounts for such supplies being headed according to the requisitions, namely, "Manufacturing purposes of Penal Establishments," after certification by the Inspector General, will be forwarded by the Colonial Storekeeper, in the manner customary, with all accounts, to the Treasury.

12. The whole of the supplies thus furnished are to be charged in the Treasury to an account for "Manufacturing purposes of Penal Establishments."

13. Such supplies as it may be desirable under clause 2 to have manufactured at Pentridge are to be ordered by the Colonial Storekeeper upon the Inspector General, and the articles required are to be manufactured at the earliest possible date.

14. The Inspector General is not to furnish manufactured articles for the public service which are comprised under clause 2 to any other department than the Colonial Stores.

15. No work except in household service is to be performed by the prisoners for the private benefit of the officers and men of the penal establishments, except as is provided under clauses 4 and 5.

16. Accounts are to be made out by the Inspector General against the departments receiving manufactured articles, or for which work is performed, as soon as possible after the execution of the order, and (as to those supplied under clause 2) are to be certified as to the price by the Colonial Storekeeper; and as to the supply by the Head of the Department; and as to the work done or articles supplied, under clause 3, by the Head of the Department only.

17. In these accounts it will be necessary for each description of article or work to be set down by the Inspector General at its value, a distinction being drawn between the cost of *materials* and the value of the *labor*.

18. On receipt of these vouchers, they will be charged by the Treasurer to the several departments, and paid in the usual manner to the Inspector General of Penal Establishments. That officer, upon receiving the monies, will repay the amount into the Treasury, accompanying each payment with a proper voucher, and the total amount will then be brought to account at the Treasury under two heads, viz.:—"Repayment for materials," (which will be credited to the account "Manufacturing purposes of Penal Establishments,") and "Proceeds of the Labor of Convicts," in the General Revenue.

19. At the termination of each half-year the Inspector General will draw up and transmit to the Chief Secretary a statement in the form of a debtor and creditor account, shewing on the one side the quantity and cost of materials, together with the balance from the previous half-year, and on the other the articles issued to the departments receiving same, specifying the date, department for which supplied, and value according to the accounts. The stock and value of manufactured articles on hand are likewise to be shewn; and also the stock and value—at the cost price—of raw material on hand, both of which must be ascertained from actual tally and inspection. The balance in value will, of course, shew the profit upon the transactions for the half-year.

20. These regulations are to come into operation on the 1st of October, 1856.

As in Melbourne's early days, convicts were used as a cheap labour force to build public facilities—even laying out the grounds and gardens at Melbourne University. This 1856 instruction, one of the first under responsible government, laid down conditions on which convicts should be employed.

quadrangle with cloisters and ornamental front 'in the Tudor style of architecture'. By this time the Legislative Council had become miserly: only the east and west sides of the quadrangle could be erected in 1854-5. Contractor John Sinclair laid bluestone foundations for £8,000. John and Alfred Craven built the east and west sides of local bluestone faced with Hobart freestone, and brick internal walls, for £39,000. The north side was enclosed by contractor Abraham Linacre in 1856-7 for £17,000. The south side was never built.

While all this was happening, Redmond Barry was searching Britain for accomplished academics willing to emigrate to Melbourne, at the high salary of £1,000 a year plus accommodation. The first choice was Henry Rowe, Fellow of Trinity College, Cambridge, who was appointed Professor of Classics. Although only twenty-eight years old, Rowe was in poor health, and died in February 1855, five weeks after landing in Melbourne. The next appointee was 29-year-old Irish-born William Hearn, Professor of History and Political Economy. After Rowe's death, Hearn offered also to teach Classics at no extra salary, enabling these classes to begin.

Frederick McCoy, already discussed in connection with the National Museum, possessed no university degree, but was appointed Professor of Natural Science because of his prolific contribution to palaeontology (the study of fossils). William Wilson, 29-year-old founding mathematics professor at Queen's College, Belfast, was named Professor of Mathematics at Melbourne in 1855. The final appointee, 25-year-old Londoner Martin Irving, arrived in Melbourne in 1856 as the new Professor of Classics.

Since the university was still being built, lectures began in the original Exhibition Building in William Street in April 1855. Only sixteen students enrolled, for few young men in Melbourne at the time were interested in non-commercial activities, or had the qualifications necessary to begin university studies. There were no working-class applicants: most such youths could barely read and write, and none could afford the £12 a year fees. Swallowing his disappointment, Redmond Barry addressed the opening ceremony, hoping that the university would become 'the nursing mother and generous instructress of a race of distinguished scholars'. The *Age* editorial writer next morning criticised the large expenditure and 'the humiliating insignificance of the result', pointing out sardonically that 'For one half the money the boy could be sent to Oxford or Cambridge, and maintained there in a sumptuous style', besides being treated to a continental tour.

But that was an unusually shortsighted view. After a two-year law course began in 1857, the total number of students increased to forty-five in 1858, and reached 110 by 1861. That year, architecture, civil engineering and surveying were added to courses offered.

Part of the problem with student numbers was the unsatisfactory state of secondary education in Melbourne. Many undergraduates found they could not handle the mathematical and other skills needed. In a comment eerily reminiscent of today's complaints, the University Council in its 1859-60 report criticised the 'inaccuracy of the training of all the young men who have hitherto come up'. First-year students, said the report, 'have so much to learn at the University, which should have been done at school'.

At Redmond Barry's urging, the government attempted to separate academics from political controversy in 1859, when the university statutes were altered to read 'The Professors shall not sit in Parliament, nor become members of any political association'. Some of today's academics might take note of that ancient wisdom.

By the end of the gold decade, the four professors were delivering nearly 1,300 lectures a year on a vast range of subjects including Greek, Latin, English, advanced mathematics, history, politics, chemistry, botany, and natural science. The university's long-term success was further assured in 1863 when Professor George Halford inaugurated a stringent five-year medical course which later made Melbourne world-famous. Redmond Barry's hopes for the institution at last seemed to be fulfilled.

Redmond Barry's vision for Melbourne ranged far beyond an inevitably elite university. From 1852 he began lobbying for the establishment of what was then unknown in the Australian colonies: a well-organised and well-stocked free library open to general readers without let or hindrance.

The Legislative Council of 1853 agreed with Barry, and granted a two-acre site bounded by Swanston, La Trobe, Russell and Little Lonsdale streets. It allowed £20,000 over two years towards building costs, and £3,000 a year, soon increased to £6,000, for purchase of books. Barry became chairman of a board of five trustees.

The usual design contest was conducted in 1854. It was won by young English architect Joseph Reed, who produced an ambitious plan for a huge institution to cover most of the two acres. Construction of

S. T. Gill's sketch of Melbourne University in 1857 shows the western wing with its Tudor tower; and at left, the northern fill-in which joined it to the eastern wing. The southern side of the quadrangle was never built.

the first central section facing Swanston Street, measuring fifty feet square by thirty-two feet high, was carried out by contractor James Metcalfe.

Meanwhile a well-educated and adventurous 44-year-old Surrey merchant named Augustus Tulk had bought a schooner named *Guyon* and sailed it to Melbourne in 1854 with his wife and six children. Tulk's shipload of mining machinery failed to sell, so he applied for the advertised position of librarian. He was appointed just in time to help Redmond Barry unpack crates of nearly 4,000 volumes arriving from England.

The embryonic library was opened by the Administrator of Victoria, Major-General Sir Edward Macarthur, on 11 February 1856. It was fulsomely praised by the *Age*, which reflected that 'Our wealth is worthless indeed if it cannot purchase us the means of the highest

Melbourne Public Library (now the State Library of Victoria) as it appeared in Swanston Street in this De Gruchy & Leigh lithograph of the 1860s. Inset is Philip Lindo's portrait of Augustus Tulk, a multilingual Londoner, who sailed his own schooner to Melbourne in 1854. Tulk was appointed first Chief Librarian in 1856. (La Trobe Collection).

culture and the purest enjoyment'. The paper liked the 'quiet and studious reading room' (now the entrance hall), but forecast wrongly that it would provide ample space 'for a long time to come'.

Nearly 24,000 visitors used the library during 1856, when it opened between 10 a.m. and 4 p.m. Gas lighting was then installed, enabling the library to open every day of the week until 9 p.m. This increased the number of users to nearly 50,000 in 1857; 78,000 in 1858; and 128,000 in 1859: more than the numbers who frequented the British Museum in London!

Rapid extension of the Melbourne library was essential. The government provided £20,000 for erection of a beautifully-decorated Queen's Hall above the entrance lobby. For many years this remained the main reading room. When opened in May 1859, it provided 5,000 square feet of extra space. This was much needed, for not only visitors but the number of books were still multiplying each year. In 1859 there were more than 10,000 volumes on the shelves, including 'worthy fiction' but excluding 'light novels of no serious purpose'.

The whole institution was managed, day and night, by Augustus Tulk, assisted by one sub-librarian, Henry Sheffield; a clerk; and three attendants; with a total annual salary bill of £1,600. This small staff was sufficient partly because they all worked long hours, and partly because in 1858 the trustees removed 'all needless and arbitrary restrictions on free access to the building and the books', which they said 'only operate as vexatious obstructions to the student'. Each visitor was allowed to find the book he wanted, and replace it after use. A few thefts were dealt with by the police, but in general 'the confidence reposed in the honor of the visitors has not been misplaced', the trustees reported optimistically.

By the end of 1860 the library held 23,000 volumes. Redmond Barry noted 'an increasing demand for accommodation for ladies . . . who, from a disinclination to pursue studies in the chamber now over-crowded with gentlemen, are virtually excluded'. He obtained a further £11,000 from the government to pay for completion of the south wing, which was used as a Ladies' Reading Room, besides providing accommodation for Tulk and his family.

The ever-active Barry organised the beginnings of an art collection in 1859, intending it for 'the instructive illustration of the historical development of art'. Only £2,000 could be spent at first, but a small collection of paintings and casts went on show within a year. When a north wing was added in 1864 at a cost of £15,000, completing the Swanston Street frontage, the works of art were moved there to form the nucleus of a National Gallery of Victoria (now located in St Kilda Road).

Today the State Library of Victoria holds nearly a million volumes, and has built up great collections in many fields, besides offering resources based on electronic technology. As this is written, extra space is being occupied in and around the former museum areas, in an attempt to cater for the vast number of people who wish to use the library's facilities.

As soon as it became obvious that Victoria could gain great wealth from minerals hidden beneath the ground, moves began for a professional geological survey of the colony. Most small-scale maps already produced by the Survey Department were useless for this purpose, as they described only surface features.

La Trobe wrote to the Colonial Office in London in October 1851 asking for a mineralogical surveyor to be sent out. The man selected was Alfred Selwyn, a 28-year-old Somerset-born geologist whose brother had already emigrated to Australia.

Selwyn arrived in Melbourne in 1852, toured the diggings, and in 1853 began detailed mapping of the geology and mineralogy of the Mount Alexander gold region. In 1854 he mapped the whole Western Port and Mornington Peninsula districts, looking particularly for viable coal deposits urgently needed for steam engines and domestic fireplaces. His chief assistant was an unsuccessful 22-year-old digger named Richard Daintree, later to become famous as a field photographer.

Early in 1856 the Legislative Council voted sufficient funds to set up a Mining Commission, charged with 'developing the mineral wealth of the colony'. Selwyn was named Government Geologist. His four surveyors, assisted by twelve labourers, began preparing detailed geological maps to the north-west and south-west of Melbourne, on the large scale of two inches to a mile. As they proceeded, they collected specimens of all interesting rock formations and fossils. These were sent to the National Museum for the attention of Professor McCoy, who had been appointed Government Palaeontologist in addition to his other duties.

With information pouring in, Selwyn now faced the problem of getting it out to the public. His first maps were printed on a hand press at the Crown Lands Office, and hand-coloured by chief draftsman Joseph Pittman. In 1858 Pittman suggested that experiments in colour lithographic printing should be made to speed up the painfully slow process.

After several failures, the renowned 38-year-old lithographer Thomas Ham was appointed to the staff, assisted by artists Edward Gilks and Richard Shepherd. Ham knew the secrets of keeping each colour in perfect register, even when printing from lithographic stones on a hand press. The first colour maps of the Melbourne and Kyneton areas successfully produced for sale in 1859 consisted of base plates engraved on copper by John Ross, with up to seven colours added by lithography. The process was again speeded up in 1860 when a steam-powered lithographic press was installed in the basement of the Government Printing Office, enabling the price of maps to be reduced from 5s to 3s each. This was probably the world's first use of steam power to print colour maps.

By the end of 1860, nearly 10,000 square miles had been surveyed geologically at a cost of less than 2d an acre, and 122 quarter-sheet maps published. These were lauded by the Geological Society in London as being among the best in the world. After examining many quartz reefs, Selwyn reported in 1861 his opinion that Victorian gold mines were 'practically inexhaustible'. But he could not persuade the government of the day to equip a proper metallurgical laboratory in which specimens could be 'correctly tested and their value determined'.

A large part of the problem was that in 1858 the government had

FACING PAGE:

Geological survey map brilliantly printed by a combination of copper engraving and colour lithography in Melbourne in 1860. The area shown is the north-west section of Melbourne and suburbs. Major features are (from top): Pascoe Vale, Wheat Sheaf Inn, Young Queen Inn, Sydney Road toll bar, Moonee Ponds Creek, several stone quarries, Mount Alexander Road, Essendon Hotel, fossil beds, Edinburgh Castle Hotel, Maribyrnong River, Melbourne & Essendon Railway, Brunswick Post Office, Philipstown Hotel, Cornish Arms Hotel, Sarah Sands Hotel, Raleigh's Punt, Braybrook, Royal Park and Model Farm (Experimental Farm), Flemington and bridge, Racecourse and punts, Newmarket Hotel and cattle yards, abattoirs, North Melbourne, hay and corn market, Benevolent Asylum, railway bridge and Footscray junction, Maidstone. (Museum of Victoria).

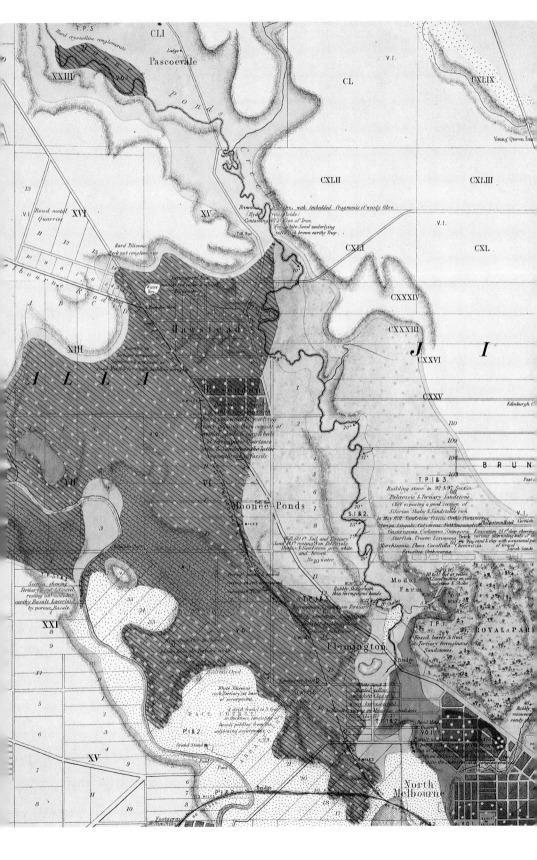

*Alfred Selwyn, brilliant geologist
sabotaged by Victorian bureaucrats.*

*Robert Brough Smyth, ambitious
draftsman who upset many talented
scientists working in Melbourne.*

appointed an ambitious meteorologist and survey draftsman, 28-year-old Englishman Robert Brough Smyth, as secretary of a new Board of Science. This was supposed to be merely an advisory body 'dealing with such scientific or technical matters as may arise in the course of public business'. Smyth however used it as a tool for his own advancement, appointing mining surveyors and preparing his own maps of the diggings. Strongly supported by politicians Heales and Hummfray, who apparently did not understand the need for systematic scientific surveys, Smyth was appointed head of a new Mines Department in 1860. Selwyn's geological survey came almost to a halt, a development described by the *Herald* as 'nothing less than barbarous'.

Smyth simultaneously became secretary of the Board for Protection of Aborigines, where his impatient and unscientific interference similarly did great harm to people who had devoted their lives to the Aboriginal cause.

Selwyn never quite recovered from the underhand attack on his work. He kept on trying to produce maps of 'lasting and permanent value', but bedevilled by Smyth and harassed by politicians, losing the services of a disgusted Richard Daintree, with newspapers finally turning against him because he failed to find large deposits of coal, Selwyn saw his geological survey abolished at the end of 1868. A few weeks later he was snapped up by a more discerning Canadian Government, to which he gave an invaluable quarter-century of service. His expert staff was scattered to the winds, and the survey not resumed until the 1870s. As for Smyth, a public inquiry in 1876 found him guilty

John Osborne, an Irish immigrant, invented the world's first practical method of photo-lithography in Melbourne in 1859. (Georg von Nuemayer Polararchiv).

of 'tyrannical and overbearing conduct' in the Mines Department, and he was forced out in disgrace — too late.

A 31-year-old Irish immigrant named John Osborne, employed as a photographer in the Crown Lands Department, achieved a world first by inventing a practical means of transferring photographic images to lithographic stones.

One day in August 1859 the Victorian Surveyor-General, Charles Ligar, asked Osborne why his glass-plate negatives could not be printed directly on stone instead of having to be drawn on by an artist. Osborne replied that the idea had failed in Europe, because perfect contact could not be achieved between the rigid glass plate and the stone. He promised to experiment.

Within four weeks, Osborne discovered that by coating a sheet of albumen photographic paper with a solution of gelatine and bichromate of potash, exposing it to a negative, then coating the paper with lithographic transfer ink, the greasy ink would adhere faithfully to the image. He then coagulated the albumen image by floating the paper face down on boiling water, and gently removing superfluous ink with a sponge. This left a greasy image of the original, which could be transferred to the lithographic stone in the usual way on a transfer press.

Osborne emphasised that his process was 'chiefly applicable to the reproduction of drawings formed of hard defined lines, such as maps, pen and ink sketches, and important documents'. Its enormous advantage over earlier methods was that suitable originals could be photographically scaled up or down to any desired size before the process began. With care, fine detail almost equivalent to copper engravings could be obtained.

Osborne's process was immediately adopted by the Survey Department for printing subdivisional plans for land sales. Parliament made a personal grant of £1,000, on condition that the process was 'ceded in perpetuity to the Government of Victoria'. In 1862 Osborne went to Europe to exploit his invention, but found that others had copied him (possibly from his full description in the Royal Society's *Transactions* in 1860), and had taken out patents. Osborne then went to the USA, where he introduced the process for the American Photolithographic Company. Today, photolithography is by far the world's most common reproduction process, and was used for printing this book.

When Charles Darwin's *Origin of Species* was published in London in 1859, the furore it caused echoed through the civilised world. Darwin was excoriated from every pulpit; newspapers and scientific journals angrily attacked the idea that God had not created every living species exactly as they stood, instead of through the amazing though cruel process which Darwin called 'natural selection'.

At Oxford, the Master of Trinity College refused to allow a copy of Darwin's book to be placed in the library. In a famous debate at the British Association for the Advancement of Science, Anglican Archbishop Samuel Wilberforce cuttingly asked biologist Thomas Huxley whether he claimed descent from a monkey through his grandfather or his grandmother? Huxley jumped to his feet and gave his famous reply that he would rather have an ape for a grandfather than a bishop who used his high faculties to obscure 'scientific questions with which he has no real acquaintance'.

The controversy was not long in reaching Melbourne. It shook leading scientists to the core, but most of them opted for safety and supported the comfortable old ideas.

Even Ferdinand Mueller, who as a botanist should have been able to see the improvement possible with successive generations of plants and flowers, broke off his earlier correspondence with Darwin. Mueller went so far as to give a monkey belonging to the Botanic Gardens to George Halford, newly-appointed university Professor of Medicine. In July 1863, Halford killed and dissected the monkey, preserved the parts, laid them out beside the dissected parts of a human being, and invited the public to his coach-house in Carlton to see that people could not possibly have evolved from apes. Dr William Thomson of South Yarra accepted the invitation, but when he attempted to discuss Darwin's

Punch's application of science to everyday life (1856).

theories, Professor Halford called him 'a damned villain' and threatened to kick him out of the room.

The opposition of Professor Frederick McCoy to Darwinism was perhaps most surprising of all. As a leading authority on fossils—one of the most convincing proofs of evolution—McCoy should have been the first to admit that the new theories were worthy of examination. Instead, he dug in his heels, to the extraordinary length of ranting for nearly three hours at the Princess Theatre to prove to his audience that there was 'no authority either in scripture or science for the belief in the gradual transmutation from one species into another'.

Most Melbourne churchmen opposed the new theories, holding that 'Man came perfect from the hands of his Creator'. But that remarkably open-minded man, Dr John Bromby, headmaster of Melbourne Grammar School, could see no necessary conflict between the spirit of biblical teaching and the practical discoveries of science. Possibly he had some influence on Anglican Bishop Charles Perry, who seemed to modify his earlier outright opposition to Darwinism by saying that 'the discoveries of astronomy have long since ceased to trouble the reader of the bible, and we doubt not that the discoveries of geology will, ere long, trouble him as little'. In fact it was possible to believe—as many came to do—in a Creator who had set in train forces more complex and wonderful than people of earlier generations could comprehend.

20

Appalling state of
public health

Over the proud new city of Melbourne hung a miasmic curse of neglected sanitation and human suffering, especially among young children who died in agony and in great numbers. The scandal was preventable: several English towns had already installed efficient water and sewerage works. But Melbourne, wealthy Melbourne, simply would not face up to the problem. It almost seemed that its citizens preferred to live among filth and watch unconcernedly as their weaker brethren were carried off by so-called 'zymotic' diseases.

In matters of civic progress, water supply was regarded differently. Everyone knew that people and stock in a warm climate had to have plenty of water, for drinking if not necessarily for bathing. The needs of Melbourne's population for water early in the gold decade grew far beyond the capacity of the few hand-pumps along the Yarra River. Action quickly followed.

In 1853 the Legislative Council established a 'Board of Commissioners of Sewerage and Water Supply' to take over these functions from the City Council (Act 16 Vic. No. 39, 8 February 1853). Under its president, magistrate James Simpson, and chief engineer Matthew Jackson, the board's first move was to install a powerful steam pump at the lower end of the Treasury Gardens, on the east side of Spring Street, to increase supplies from the Yarra.

There were not enough large pipes in Melbourne to connect the pump to the river: contractor Farquhar McDonald was engaged to construct a 1,200-ft timbered culvert to take the water underneath Wellington Parade. The steam pump lifted this water to a large square iron tank which had been built on a high bluestone base at Eastern Hill, on the site of today's Eye and Ear Hospital. When the scheme opened in

1855, water flowed by gravity through the first mains to stand-pipes erected in city and Collingwood streets.

This was only a stopgap solution, for Yarra water was increasingly polluted by effluent flowing downstream from several tanneries in Richmond. Matthew Jackson was given the task of completing James Blackburn's original scheme of diverting water from the Plenty River at Yan Yean, about twenty miles north-east of Melbourne, and piping it to the city. Jackson declared that he was competent for the task, telling one parliamentary inquiry that in England he had been 'more or less upon public works since I was twelve or thirteen years of age', was apprenticed to locomotive builders George and Robert Stephenson, and was recommended for management of Birkenhead Docks before emigrating to Australia.

Jackson employed 400 labourers for the huge Yan Yean project. They were allowed to take wives and children to live in tents in the area, establishing what became the town of Whittlesea. By 1855, under resident engineer Charles Taylor, the men had constructed a stone embankment across a nearby valley, more than 3,000 feet wide and thirty feet high, into which the Plenty River could be diverted at will. When filled, the reservoir occupied an area ten miles in circumference.

At the same time, private contractors were building a horse tramway of timber from Yan Yean to Melbourne to help transport large pipes needed for the mains. The tramline itself cost £56,000, but also needed a bluestone bridge costing £13,000 to cross the Plenty, and a tubular girder bridge across Merri Creek costing nearly £8,000. All told, the Yan Yean scheme cost £750,000, exactly double Jackson's estimate of 1853.

By the end of 1857, the large mains were complete, and a further thirty miles of smaller mains had been laid in the city, Collingwood and Richmond. On 27 December, thousands of people gathered to cheer as Sir Edward Macarthur turned on the main valve in Carlton Gardens, then marched to the intersection of Elizabeth and Flinders streets. While bands played on, an official opened a hydrant to demonstrate the water pressure, and managed to drench part of the crowd from head to foot.

The provision of a copious water supply should have helped to cleanse Melbourne. Unfortunately it had the opposite effect. So much had been spent on the Yan Yean scheme that no money remained to install a

Charles Norton's painting of lower Spring Street in 1862 shows the Yarra in flood and the government pumping station at right. (La Trobe Collection).

sewerage system. Residents began using more water in bathrooms, kitchens and water closets, and to hose out stables, but there was nowhere for the polluted fluids to go except into the city's gutters, and ultimately into the Yarra.

The condition of Melbourne streets had been bad enough even before the Yan Yean scheme. Solicitor J. M. Smith observed to an 1853 Legislative Council inquiry that 'Twelve months ago, a person could walk the streets in comfort, but now that is out of the question, what with the dust and filth that everywhere meets one. It would appear as if all the filth of the town were accumulated in the streets'. In most leading thoroughfares, added Smith, 'the stench will be found to be perfectly frightful'.

Town Hall surveyor James Blackburn reported the same year that although most alleyways had been macadamised or pitchered, some had filled up again with 'accumulations of filth to a depth of three or four feet'. Government surveyor Clement Hodgkinson, making a contour map of the city, observed that many blocks were covered with 'a foetid putrescent mass of tenacious mud'. Behind shop fronts in Bourke Street, today occupied by the Myer Emporium, the land was covered with 'a green putrid semi-liquid mass, partly formed by the outpourings of surrounding privies'.

The 1853 committee emphasised the 'necessary conjunction and mutual dependence of sewerage and water supply', adding that 'neither of these measures could be effectually carried out independently of the other'. Unfortunately for future generations, its advice was disregarded.

The official Commissioners estimated in 1855 that Melbourne could be sewered with 170,000 yards of brick and stoneware underground pipes for less than £100,000. Several English towns had already been sewered and supplied with mains water at similar cost, adding only about five shillings to the rates for each house per year.

But the Victorian economy was already reeling from Governor Hotham's cessation of public works: the Legislative Council would agree to nothing beyond continuation of the Yan Yean scheme. The result by the end of the decade was truly appalling. Irish-born chemist John Hood, MLC, described to the Philosophical Institute in June 1859 the 'dark-coloured and foul out-pourings from house-drains', piles of 'the most offensive material' overflowing from cesspools along Collins Street, and sodden earth under floorboards which became 'saturated with filth'.

After installation of water mains, a much-admired Victoria Fountain was erected in 1859 at the intersection of Swanston and Collins streets. (Samuel Calvert engraving in Temperance League Almanac, *1860).*

Melbourne's magnificent new public buildings and private houses became permeated with malign odours. Town Clerk Edmund FitzGibbon complained that cellars and foundations were 'loaded with faeces', filling the air with 'the foulest stench'. Clara Aspinall wrote that she stayed in 'a handsome house where the atmosphere of the sitting-rooms was, at certain times, so obnoxious that we could not remain in them'.

A 40-year-old Irish-born naval surgeon, Dr William McCrea, had been appointed chairman of a Central Board of Health established in 1854 (Act 18 Vic. No. 13, 19 December 1854). The board's annual reports showed steadily deteriorating sanitation and increasing infectious disease throughout the late 1850s. McCrea's inspectors visited one city lane, to find that 'in eleven instances privies were leaking out' into the street. One privy had been built against the sitting-room window. The yard was covered with twelve inches of 'green stagnant water'. Inside the dwelling, all five children were lying ill, some dying.

In his report for 1860, Dr McCrea noted a huge increase in often-fatal cases of scarlet fever, typhoid, measles, diphtheria, typhus, and respiratory diseases. That year nearly 1,600 deaths, mostly of young children, occurred from so-called 'filth diseases' in Melbourne. There were no proper statistics of total cases of disease, but by comparing the death rates to English experience, McCrea estimated that 120,000 of Melbourne's 125,000 population had suffered to a greater or lesser degree from the infections.

One might have expected this extraordinary incidence of illness to lead immediately to the cure. But no, Melburnians preferred to suffer rather than spend money on efficient sewerage works. For another thirty years, thousands of children continued to die from typhoid, until a very aged Edmund FitzGibbon succeeded at last in the 1890s in sewering Melbourne and removing the deadly tag of 'Smell-boom'.

Gold-rush Melbourne had no infectious diseases hospital or children's hospital. Victims of disease were mostly treated at home by visiting doctors, or left to die. Paupers could sometimes get into Melbourne Hospital, the only public institution, built in 1846-8 on the north side of Lonsdale Street between Swanston and Russell streets. But during the early 1850s, demands for medical services totally overwhelmed the hospital's facilities. Overworked nurses dumped patients' infected excreta into cesspits, which sometimes overflowed into Lonsdale Street. Stenches percolated into every ward and operating theatre. No bath was installed until 1853, and even then it had to be filled with buckets. The death rate of patients often rose to one in four: in 1855 the hospital proudly announced that of 1,600 in-patients that year, only 276 had died.

Instead of spending the money on sewering Melbourne, the government began extending the hospital in 1856. Over the following five years, £80,000 was granted for building and maintenance, outstripping £30,000 in private subscriptions received during the same period. The buildings now covered almost the entire block between Swanston and Russell streets. Accommodation increased from eighty beds in 1851 to 330 beds in 1861. There were also rooms for Superintendent John Williams, four resident surgeons, a matron, and a dispenser. The superintendent was paid £400 a year; the matron £100. Twenty female nurses and trainees worked long shifts, averaging £35 a year each in wages. They were assisted by forty male orderlies who averaged £50 each.

One of the hospital's main problems was the huge number of outpatients, who increased to nearly 12,000 during the epidemics of 1861. An honorary surgeon, a former gold-digger named William

Substantial enlargement of Melbourne Hospital on the block bounded by Lonsdale, Swanston, Little Lonsdale and Russell streets is shown above.

Gillbee, told a Legislative Assembly inquiry that these thousands included 'many cases of trifling ailments, where they could well afford to pay a medical man, but they come here as outpatients and receive drugs and the assistance of the medical men at the expense of the hospital'. Six year later, Dr Gillbee braved the scorn of his unwashed fellow doctors to introduce Joseph Lister's principles of antisepsis to Melbourne, greatly reducing the death rate among surgical patients.

Doctors in Melbourne in the 1850s were a mixed lot, ranging from drunken ships' surgeons to highly-educated men (no women at that stage) earnestly trying to understand medical problems of the day. Their work was dirty, often dangerous, sometimes well-paid. John Chandler, living in Richmond, recalled how his whole family went down with typhoid: the doctor who was called charged five guineas a visit, but also contracted the disease and died. Philanthropist Dr John Singleton then helped the family, but charged nothing.

In South Melbourne, William Kelly related how his doctor died in delirium tremens. Although Kelly had no medical training, the local druggist seriously suggested that he should take over the practice, for 'a tolerably smart man, of good address and general knowledge, with a smattering of Latin, would make a fair average colonial doctor'.

Many among the better class of doctors could be found among the sixteen honorary physicians and surgeons who donated their services to Melbourne Hospital. Perhaps the outstanding physician was (Sir) Anthony Brownless, who emigrated to Melbourne in 1852 at the age of thirty-five. As well as attending the hospital, Dr Brownless helped hundreds of aged paupers at Melbourne Benevolent Asylum, and helped to establish a world-class medical course at Melbourne University.

Melbourne's leading surgeon of the early gold-rush years was probably Scottish-born Dr David Wilkie, who began using chloroform for painless operations in 1848. Four years later Wilkie was elected first president of the Victoria Medical Association, formed in an attempt to rid the profession of quacks. The Association succeeded in getting an Act through the Legislative Council to control the practice of medicine. But what was a quack? According to the *Age* of the day, medicine was merely 'a pretence to a science', and a medical diploma 'merely a certificate to kill according to law'.

Certainly the Medical Act left the way open for some hair-raising practices. Dr James Beaney, 29-year-old veteran of the Crimean War—during which an interfering woman named Florence Nightingale tried to clean up foul hospital conditions ignored by doctors—emigrated to Melbourne in 1857 and bought Dr John Maund's practice in Lonsdale Street. Beaney was brilliant in his way, being a fast and efficient operator with or without anaesthetics. But for many years he did not appreciate the need for cleanliness, and operated in bare hands with diamonds flashing from his fingers and necktie, earning him the name 'Diamond Jim'. If hundreds of patients died later from infection, he felt this could scarcely be the doctor's fault.

Drugs, most of them loaded with opium or mercury, were the anodyne which either helped to kill patients, or enabled them to survive until nature's genuine healing powers took over. Chemists and druggists thrived in Melbourne, nearly 100 being listed for 1860 in city and inner suburbs. Many did not demand doctors' prescriptions, simply issuing powerful potions and powders to customers on their vague description of symptoms.

One of the best-known and most trustworthy chemists in Melbourne was the Irishman John Hood, who pioneered the local manufacture of chloroform. In 1853 he erected a two-storey prefabricated iron pharmacy on the south-west corner of Russell and Little Bourke streets, later rebuilt as today's Wellington Lee pharmacy. Hood was elected to the Legislative Council in 1856, and supported every move to improve the city.

In 1857, when Hood was president of the Legislative Council, he was able to initiate an inquiry into the 'Sale and Keeping of Poisons', which in the hands of unskilled pharmacists had led to many tragedies. City Coroner Dr W. B. Wilmot described deaths resulting from incompetent prescription of medicines containing dangerous elements. In one case, 'essential oil of almonds was given for simple almond oil, and caused death'. Dr Wilmot thought that all poisons, including commonly-used strychnine, oxalic acid, arsenic and opium, should be stored separately under lock and key, and clearly labelled as dangerous.

Acting Coroner Dr Richard Youl told the inquiry of cases where oxalic acid had been given to patients in mistake for Epsom salts. In another case, bags which had contained arsenic were used to store flour, and a whole family was poisoned.

Dr Youl said he had investigated conditions in low lodging-houses and brothels, where 'a great many deaths' occurred. He found that most of the deceased had drunk porter, which had been 'hocussed' by the addition of belladonna (a poisonous alkaloid made from deadly night-shade), so that the victims could be easily robbed. Dr Youl added that many prostitutes and other women who poisoned themselves were able to buy small quantities of laudanum (an alcoholic tincture of opium) at several different pharmacies, until they accumulated enough for a fatal dose.

In an attempt to improve the standard of druggists, John Hood, Joseph Bosisto and a few others formed the Pharmaceutical Society of Victoria. They began publishing a quarterly journal in 1858, when the Society had enlisted about thirty members in the city and several in the suburbs. They attempted to police the new Poisons Act and keep

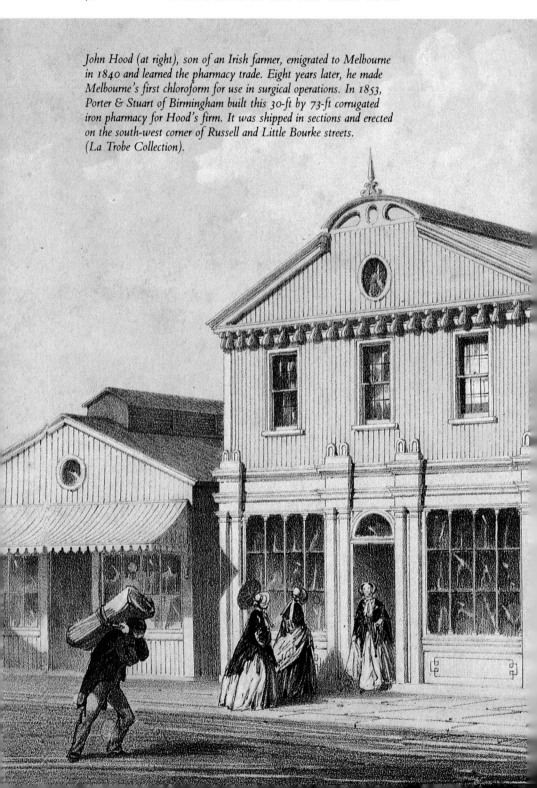

John Hood (at right), son of an Irish farmer, emigrated to Melbourne in 1840 and learned the pharmacy trade. Eight years later, he made Melbourne's first chloroform for use in surgical operations. In 1853, Porter & Stuart of Birmingham built this 30-ft by 73-ft corrugated iron pharmacy for Hood's firm. It was shipped in sections and erected on the south-west corner of Russell and Little Bourke streets. (La Trobe Collection).

dangerous drugs away from a public desperately in need of safe pain-killers.

Perhaps the medical profession's greatest achievement during the gold decade was the establishment in 1856 of the Melbourne Lying-in Hospital. Before that time, working-class women bore all their children at home, often attended by a dirty and drunken midwife. Puerperal infection and painful death was common.

Two doctors who emigrated to Melbourne during the early gold rushes thought that something should be done. They were John Maund, a 33-year-old Englishman, and Richard Tracy, a 30-year-old Irishman. With the help of Frances Perry, wife of the Anglican Bishop of Melbourne, the two doctors formed a committee and rented a house in August 1856 in Albert Street, East Melbourne. Here they established the first maternity hospital for poor women, with Mrs Sarah Gilbee, mother of Melbourne surgeon William Gillbee, as matron.

In 1857 the government granted the committee a two-acre site near the new university in Carlton for construction of a proper Lying-in Hospital. The area, bounded by Madeline (now Swanston), Faraday, Cardigan and Grattan streets, is today the site of the Royal Women's Hospital. The government also made a cash grant of £4,000. Together with private donations of £2,000, this enabled the first wards to be opened in October 1858. Irish-born Dr Gerald Fetherston was appointed resident surgeon, and his wife Sarah acted as matron. To assist them were five nurses and four domestic staff.

During the hospital's first two years, 250 women were accouched without a single fatality, and another 990 treated or advised as out-patients. But Dr Fetherston and his wife left to begin private practice in Prahran. In 1860 something began to go horribly wrong: six mothers and one baby died in the hospital that year, and mortality climbed steadily. By the 1870s the hospital was notorious for its filthy state, with a continuous death rate leading it to be called 'a house of slaughter'. Dr William Thomson claimed that some staff threw placentas under the beds 'to rot and thereby breed bacilli that breed fever'. Many doctors and nurses still could not accept the idea that invisible streptococci could enter mothers' wounds to cause fatal septicaemia.

After a particularly bad year in 1884, when sixteen women died despite the best efforts of resident medical officer Dr Felix Meyer, the hospital was closed for a thorough cleanout and improvement of ventilation. The name was changed to the Women's Hospital, and each section was slowly rebuilt during the 20th century.

Large amounts of public money were spent during the 1850s in attempts to cope with increasing numbers of mentally-ill people in the population. A lunatic asylum had been established in 1846 on the north bank of the Yarra River, on a 640-acre site called Yarra Bend. The building was far too small for the extra population. It was also wracked by scandals, until the arrival of Dr Robert Bowie, an experienced English lunacy reformer, appointed Medical Superintendent at Yarra Bend in October 1852.

Dr Bowie reorganised the mismanaged asylum, and by March 1853 won high praise from Richard Horne in the *Argus* for the institution's 'perfect cleanliness, quietude and order'. Even patients in the refractory ward were now kept 'very clean': whenever they smeared ordure over a wall, 'it is whitewashed the next morning'.

Bowie faced other unusual problems. Melbourne Hospital sometimes tried to transfer hopeless cases to the asylum, so that the obloquy of their deaths would fall upon Yarra Bend. In March 1854 Dr Bowie complained that two such incurable cases had been transferred on a Saturday afternoon. One man had staring eyes, bloodless lips, 'his hands and hip ulcerated and sloughing, his legs and ankles black'. The patient's 'head and body were dirty and swarming with *pediculi* [lice]', and when his clothes were gently cut away from his ulcers, maggots dropped out. He was not insane, merely at death's door.

Dr Bowie also protested against the state in which insane prisoners were received from Melbourne Gaol. 'I can bear testimony to their being brought here disgustingly dirty, swarming with vermin, and either very scantily supplied with clothing or covered with rags smelling most offensively', he reported. One of his female gaol patients was 'covered with contusions from head to foot, which she described as the result of violent blows given by a female attendant'.

By 1856 the government had spent £13,000 on extra accommodation at Yarra Bend, increasing the number of inmates from seventy to 300. The 200 male patients were kept busy where possible in beautifying the grounds, carpentering, and supplying firewood and water. Their gardens produced more than 30,000 lbs of vegetables a year. Some of the 100 female patients helped to clean and whitewash the wards, repaired clothing, and worked in the laundry. Violent patients, 'unless very

Melbourne's original 'Lying-In Hospital' was built in 1857 on the north-east corner of Grattan and Madeline (Swanston) streets, Carlton. (La Trobe Collection).

furious', were wrapped in straitjackets and allowed to walk the grounds under supervision. A return of the sixty-four deaths which occurred at the asylum during 1858 showed that most were due to 'softening of the brain', a euphemism for tertiary syphilis.

Daily care was carried out by a matron, Mrs Rebecca Challicombe (née Faulkner), thirty male attendants, and twenty female attendants, whose wages ranged from £36 to £110 a year. At these rates, there was often difficulty in finding experienced people for the many unpleasant tasks involved.

From 1856 Dr Bowie was assisted by Dr John Callan, who had spent two years as a government surgeon at Geelong. Dr Callan made heated protests against the way lunatics were treated in Geelong and at the Western Gaol in Collins Street, Melbourne. He told one inquiry that it was wrong to mix criminals with lunatics: 'Thieves, madmen, and plunderers, robbers, and murderers, with the helpless insane, all under one roof: it was fearful'. Most of these lunatics were sent to Yarra Bend 'in a very wretched state of health': many of them died 'very soon after coming from the gaols'.

After an 1857 parliamentary inquiry into Yarra Bend found the original stone buildings 'low, close and gloomy', and 'disgustingly foetid', a further £10,000 was spent on building ten small cottages around a common garden centre. The units were separated by shrubs and flowers, presenting 'a cheerful appearance in strong contrast to the remainder of the Asylum'. In 1860 another large stone dormitory to hold sixty violent patients, and a small hospital, were added to bring the total asylum population to nearly 700.

Complaints against Dr Bowie were investigated by parliamentary committees in 1859 and 1861. He was exonerated on all counts, but asked to retire along with Dr Callan in August 1862, apparently because of their long-standing personal feud with Chief Medical Officer Dr McCrea over their allegedly 'soft' treatment of lunatics. The ensuing uproar led to yet another government inquiry, establishment of asylums in the main goldfields cities, and abolition of the practice of committing lunatics to gaol.

Among the flotsam and jetsam left by tides of the gold rush were numbers of 'aged and incurable paupers'. They were not criminals who could be gaoled; not lunatics who could be committed to the asylum; not temporarily ill people who could be treated in Melbourne Hospital.

The only place they could go was the Benevolent Asylum, built in 1850-1 at the Curzon Street end of Victoria Street, North Melbourne, to hold 100 paupers.

The government originally matched private donors £1 for £1 to build and operate the institution, but after the gold rush it became largely a governmental responsibility. In the late 1850s, the government granted £9,000 a year but private donors only one-third of this amount.

The Benevolent Asylum's first honorary surgeon in 1851 was a well-known 35-year-old Mornington Peninsula squatter, Dr Edward Barker, who later became the first lecturer in surgery at Melbourne University. He was replaced at the Asylum by Dr Samuel Cooper. Day-to-day running of the institution was left to the superintendent, James McCutcheon, and his wife Margaret, who acted as matron. They were assisted by six nurses paid £40 a year, six laundress-servants paid £30 a year, and four male assistants paid only £7 a year plus keep.

With the large demand for places after the early gold rushes, the government decided to extend the building. More than £12,000 was spent between 1857-9 to accommodate 250 men and sixty women. As might be expected with aged or incurable inmates, the death rate was high—usually about seventy a year. But there were no overt scandals like those which wracked other government institutions.

James McCutcheon told a parliamentary inquiry in 1863 that the inmates were well fed with a daily ration of a pint of soup, eight ounces of meat, twelve ounces of potatoes, and two ounces of bread. No butter was allowed except on doctor's orders. Only about sixty inmates were fit to work: they were employed on 'picking oakum, some stone breaking, others tailoring and shoe making, others laboring in the garden'.

Dr Cooper told the same inquiry that about 180 of the inmates required constant medical treatment. Their main diseases were paralysis and phthisis. About twenty harmless lunatics were held who should be moved to Yarra Bend, but that institution could not accept them because of overcrowding.

Several private charities were established to assist poor people who thronged Melbourne. One of the most active was the Melbourne Ladies' Benevolent Society, formed in 1846 to visit the poor in their own dwellings and assess their needs. The gold rush greatly expanded the society's work. One of its supporters, Rev. Alexander Campbell, said

Human flotsam left in Melbourne after the gold rush included this blind beggar and his wife or daughter. S. T. Gill ironically described the man as 'A City of Melbourne Solicitor'. Behind him, the wealthy dash past in their carriage. (Mitchell Library).

that 'the distress arises chiefly in families where the father has gone to some of the goldfields, and the onus of supporting a large family falls on the mother'.

The society began holding annual bazaars and other fund-raising activities during the 1850s, earning enough to buy a small building in Melbourne to house urgent cases of destitution. The president, Mrs Jessie Cairns (née Ballingall), wife of Rev. Adam Cairns, told an 1863 inquiry that city magistrates were sending many needy families to the house. 'There are some very sad cases of distress', she said: 300 people including many starving children were receiving food and shelter each week. In winter a soup kitchen provided temporary relief to street dwellers. Branches of the society were formed in North Melbourne, Prahran, South Yarra, Port Melbourne, St Kilda and Williamstown to help local paupers.

Another charity, the Melbourne City Mission, was founded in August 1856 by a meeting of clergymen of the main Protestant denominations at St Peter's Church. It appointed a full-time missioner, Joseph Greathead, to seek out 'deserving poor' in the notorious areas of Little Bourke and Little Lonsdale streets. Greathead was soon joined by the mission's president, 70-year-old Jamaican-born Mrs Hester Hornbrook, who had already done much to provide food and clothing to deserted wives in Collingwood.

By 1857 the City Mission was able to establish a 'Refuge for Fallen Women' near the Lying-in Hospital in Carlton. Here unmarried mothers, many of them domestic servants who had been seduced, were able to care for their babies in peace. Others were apparently prostitutes who had become pregnant. In 1865 the Ladies Committee claimed 'good grounds for hoping that no less than 30 per cent of those who were inmates have been rescued from a life of infamy'.

Mrs Hornbrook meanwhile was attempting to lift gutter children towards a better life by giving them the rudiments of secular and religious education. Her first 'Ragged School' was established in Smith Street, Collingwood, in 1859. By the time of her death in 1862, three more schools had been established in the city's worst areas and one in Prahran. The Hornbrook Ragged Schools Association continued her work, but finally faded out some years after primary education became compulsory.

Many children of the poor matured early, and attempted to live off their wits. Joseph Walker, a National School teacher at Richmond, told an 1860 parliamentary inquiry that 'many boys have recourse to the hotels, and gather about the doors outside, and light their cigars and so on, and entice one another to go in'. Some boys gambled away money they had been given to pay school fees. Walker considered that 'children of the drunkard can easily be distinguished from other children, inasmuch as their habits generally are more vicious'.

For small boys trying to earn an honest living, a Juvenile Traders' Association was formed in Melbourne in September 1856. The honorary secretary, merchant Charles Watt, gave the boys use of a building on the south-east corner of Flinders Lane and Russell Street. The Association's superintendent, Walter Dowding, told the 1860 inquiry that 'As a general rule the boys can scarcely remember their parents, and they have been on the streets nearly all their lives'. Many had been sleeping in 'low lodging-houses' for sixpence a night. During the day they earned money by holding horses, polishing boots, selling newspapers, and collecting rags. At night, said Dowding, the boys were expected to be washed and in their places at evening classes starting at 7.30; but some who had night jobs received no education at all.

The gold-rush years left many other orphans and deserted children in Melbourne. Some were sheltered in the Collins Street Female Reformatory; some in the Benevolent Asylum; and some in the Immigrants' Home. Sheriff Claud Farie protested to the government in May 1856 against allowing small children to remain in gaol:

> These children, if cared for and educated by the country, would probably become able-bodied useful colonists, whereas educated in crime and misery . . . they must necessarily become a disgrace and curse to society.

However, most politicians preferred that charitable people with strong religious convictions should save the children, preferably at low cost. One of the first organisations to attempt this was the Dorcas Society, formed by the congregation of St James Church, and run mainly by Mrs Eleanor Nicholson, wife of city grocer Germain Nicholson.

In 1851 the Society built a weatherboard refuge for orphans on the north-west corner of Bourke and King streets, and employed a matron to care for the thirty inmates. In December 1854 an epidemic ran

Young inmates outside the Protestant Orphans' Asylum, opened in 1856 on a ten-acre site bounded by Cecil, Dorcas, Clarendon and Bank streets, South Melbourne.

through the establishment: the children were removed to tents on a paddock in Kew adjoining the house of magistrate James Simpson and his wife Catherine.

Urgent appeals for assistance went to the government, which in November 1854 granted a ten-acre site for an orphanage in Bank Street, South Melbourne (today occupied by that suburb's town hall). The government also granted £4,500 towards building costs, on two conditions: that the committee raise half as much again, and that the institution be opened to all denominations. The name was changed to the Melbourne Orphan Asylum, extensive designs prepared by architect Charles Webb, and the foundation stone laid by Governor Hotham on 6 September 1855. The buildings were complete enough by March 1856 to move the children in from Kew.

The committee had difficulty in finding a suitable superintendent and matron for the institution. Mr and Mrs Joseph Peart, appointed in 1857, were criticised for appointing a drunken cook, and for sending out very young children to be apprenticed to work long hours. The Pearts resigned in 1858. Their successor, Robert Thompson, was taken to court for failing to have the orphanage's overflowing cesspits pumped out, and was also forced to resign. In 1859, however, a young couple, Edwin Exon and his wife Frances (née Chapple) took over. They were assisted by an honorary secretary, John Browning, two honorary doctors, and twelve paid staff earning an average of £35 a year each.

During 1858-9 the government granted a further £3,500 towards building costs, enabling the west wing to be completed and a hospital and schoolroom added. This gave space to increase the number of children to more than 200. Infants as young as twelve months were now accepted.

In the early summer of 1860, epidemics of measles and scarlet fever swept the institution, infecting more than half the children, and killing the Exons' two small daughters, Jane and Elizabeth. They had no further children, becoming substitute parents to 4,000 motherless and fatherless of all creeds over the following fifty years.

Roman Catholics, demanding equal rights but fearful that their children might be contaminated by Protestantism, insisted on setting up their own orphanage. In 1854 Father Gerald Ward of the St Vincent de Paul Brotherhood managed to set up a small Catholic orphanage in a Prahran cottage. The following year, Bishop Goold was granted a two-acre site for a new orphanage in Napier Street, South Melbourne.

St Vincent de Paul's Children's Home, built for Roman Catholic orphans in 1855-8 and enlarged in 1863-6, still stands in Napier Street, South Melbourne, but is now derelict.

Architects James George and Joseph Schneider designed a 72 ft by 98 ft bluestone building with two wings. This was erected by South Melbourne contractor John Asplund at a cost of £3,000. When opened in 1857, it accommodated about thirty boys and thirty girls aged between three and fifteen years. They were cared for by a matron and five servants, all paid small wages.

The Very Rev. Matthew Downing was named president, but was unable to give the institution much of his time. In 1860, when the number of inmates had increased to ninety, Bishop Goold discovered that the orphanage was overcrowded, insanitary, deeply in debt, and in parts falling down. He asked several newly-arrived Sisters of Mercy to take over. Most of the staff was dismissed, and Mother Joseph Sherlock, Sister Xavier Butler and Sister Austin Collins moved in to work night and day for no payment. Within a year the three nuns, assisted only by a schoolmaster and gardener, had paid off the debts and increased the number of children to 150. The old building where these heroic deeds were performed still stands in South Melbourne, but is now derelict.

21

Alert for an

unknown invader

At the time of the first gold rushes, Victoria had been taken over from the native population by the dominant British race for a period of only about fifteen years. Why should not an even stronger force now attack or even seize the golden land? The question haunted Melburnians, who saw ships laden with gold lying in the bay ripe for plundering, and a wealthy city lying ready for sacking, its banks bursting with bullion—while only primitive means of defence lay at hand.

Skimpy military forces had been kept in Melbourne ever since its first official settlement in 1836, but these were intended more as a reserve police force than protection against external threat. Only the Royal Navy, whose warships were occasionally seen in Port Phillip Bay, stood between the settlers and any invader.

As soon as the magnitude of the gold discoveries became known, La Trobe wrote to the Colonial Office in London in December 1851 demanding that 'one regiment at least' and 'one or two men-of-war should be despatched for the protection of our port'. Said La Trobe, 'There is nothing to prevent a well-armed privateer from anchoring in Hobson's Bay and laying it under contribution to any amount'.

Britain's response was not overwhelming. HMS *Calliope* and several other naval units came to have a look, then sailed away again. A frail sloop-of-war, HMS *Electra*, was detached from the East India Squadron and stationed in Port Phillip Bay from April 1853, but only because Victoria agreed to pay for its maintenance. A few British regular troops and pensioned soldiers were brought from Tasmania and lodged with elements of the 40th Regiment in Melbourne. Major-General Sir Robert Nickle, 68-year-old veteran of the Napoleonic Wars, transferred his military headquarters from Sydney to Melbourne in 1854, but died at Jolimont soon after the clash at Eureka.

The outbreak of the Crimean War in March 1854 terrified Melburnians anew. Rumours swept the city that a Russian fleet was on the rampage in the Pacific. The military was called out one night when explosions and rockets were reported in the bay. It was only the s.s. *Great Britain* celebrating release from quarantine at Portsea, and the soldiers crept back cursing to their bunks.

But what if it had been a Russian warship? Some ancient guns had been taken out of store and installed by Captain A. Ross of the Royal Engineers near Port Melbourne and Williamstown piers. These however were reported to be 'in a very unsatisfactory condition, the carriages and timbers being very old and unfit for further service'. Lieutenant-Colonel Thomas Valiant of the 40th Regiment checked the powder magazine on Batman's Hill on 27 October 1854, and found the ammunition so jumbled that he had to return next day and sort it out. That led him to discover there were only 480 round shot for the 6-pounder guns. For the antique 12-pounder howitzers, he found 476 shells—and these were all empty. Any raider could have come and gone without fatal interference from these weapons.

Victorian politicians were appalled by this state of affairs. During 1854 they hastened to place an order for an armed ship to patrol the bay. Governor Hotham, himself a naval if not a political expert, altered the specifications to those of a blue water vessel capable of guarding the coastline. The ship as finally built on the Thames was named Her Majesty's Colonial Steam Sloop *Victoria*. She was a shallow-draught 580-ton oak-hulled craft equipped with sails and steam engines yielding 150 h.p. Although not fully armed until the following decade, the *Victoria* was fitted for six medium 32-pounder guns to run on tracks, one long 32-pounder pivot gun, and two 12-pounder howitzers. Her total cost to the colony was £38,000, plus wages and upkeep.

Commander W. H. Norman, RN, who had brought Sir Charles Hotham to Melbourne on the *Queen of the South* in 1854, took charge of HMCSS *Victoria* in August 1855, and sailed her to Melbourne with 100 officers and seamen, arriving in May 1856. Melburnians were proud to have purchased Australia's first fighting ship, and no doubt she could have coped with most privateers. But she would have found difficulty in combating a marauding frigate's heavy guns. Captain Norman admitted to a later inquiry that the maximum effective range of the *Victoria's* guns was less than 2,000 yards. Yet if a heavy 68-pounder were placed on board, 'it would very soon tear her all to pieces'. Commander Joseph

The pride of Melbourne's early defences: the 150-h.p. 580-ton armed steam sloop
Victoria, *in a contemporary painting by J. Taylor. (La Trobe Collection).*
Inset: Commander W. H. Norman, senior officer aboard HMCSS Victoria.

Kay, RN, thought the *Victoria* was better than nothing at all, 'but I do not think she is worth much as a protector', he told the inquiry.

The *Victoria* was in fact mostly used as an armed police and customs vessel. During the last half of 1856, for instance, she recovered lost buoys, fetched ships' mails, towed off vessels which ran aground, helped to quell a riot on the *Lysander* convict hulk, and took the Governor on a visit to Geelong. During 1857 she trans-shipped immigrants to Warrnambool, landed stores at Cape Otway lighthouse, laid buoys in several dangerous areas, towed the smallpox-ridden *Commodore Perry* to Portsea, and surveyed the submarine cable route to Tasmania.

In 1858 the *Victoria* chased and arrested two ships whose captains had left Melbourne without paying their debts. The end of that year was spent taking 30,000 rations to Victorian gold-miners said to be starving at Port Curtis in Queensland. The year 1859 was spent on routine duties, but most of 1860 and early 1861 saw the *Victoria* involved in transporting troops to put down the Taranaki rebellion in New Zealand. A small naval brigade which fought on shore was the first Australian unit ever to come under enemy fire. When the *Victoria* returned to Melbourne, she was sent on a mission to the Gulf of Carpentaria in the vain hope of rescuing the lost explorers Burke and Wills.

Most of these activities, reported Commander Norman, 'could only be carried out by a disciplined and armed vessel kept always ready to enforce orders received'. He admitted that the ship cost £13,000 a year to operate, but claimed she performed duties which would have cost the government much more if charged at commercial rates, besides being normally ready for defence emergencies.

Melburnians were still troubled by the fear of invasion by heavily-armed frigates, particularly the fast new propellor-driven types with iron-plated hulls invulnerable to the port's puny firepower. Even one of these frigates would have cost Victoria more than £100,000 to build and £50,000 a year to operate.

Was there another solution? An almost endless series of commissions and committees probed the question between 1858 and 1862. After much confusion, and wasted time and money, decisions were made to construct an outer ring of defences based on powerful forts at the Heads, and an inner ring based on gun emplacements around bayside suburbs. Floating batteries which could move to any other bayside point threatened, such as Geelong, were also proposed.

Before the establishment of Victoria Barracks at the end of the 1850s, officers of the 40th Regiment were quartered in these cottages south of the Yarra, on the east side of St Kilda Road, originally built by the Immigrants' Aid Society. Today the area is part of Queen Victoria Gardens. Pencil and wash sketch by William Strutt (Dixson Library).

The Defence Commission of 1858, presided over by Sir Edward Macarthur, at first rejected the opinion of the British Inspector-General of Fortifications, Sir John Burgoyne, that marauders could be kept out of Port Phillip Bay by heavy guns mounted at Queenscliff and Point Lonsdale to cover the 4,000 yards between the two points.

Macarthur's local experts felt that an invader could sail in under false colours at dawn, and be through the Heads before shore gunners could open fire at extreme range. Floating batteries inside the bay seemed a better idea, supported by shore batteries from Williamstown around to Point Ormond. The guns should be heavy 68-pounders, with a few long 32-pounders capable of firing heated shot to set invading vessels on fire.

Within a year, the defence picture changed entirely. In Newcastle-on-Tyne, a 50-year-old solicitor named William Armstrong, who loved tinkering with machinery of all kinds, invented a remarkable new breech-loading cannon with a spirally-grooved bore, which could fire

Major-General Sir Edward Macarthur (left), eldest son of pastoral pioneers John and Elizabeth Macarthur, was the leading figure in Victoria's defence planning after 1855. (VPL). Below, William Strutt also drew these annotated sketches of the British 11th Infantry Regiment firing a salute at the opening of Princes Bridge across the Yarra River—then misdated his work as 1851 instead of 1850. Several other British regiments also helped to guard Melbourne. (Dixson Library).

Nearly 170 acres of land on the west side of St Kilda Road were reserved for military purposes in 1859. The bluestone A Block of Victoria Barracks, still standing as seen here, was ready for occupation by 1861.

pointed exploding shells more than twice the distance of the old solid cannon balls.

The introduction of this fearful new weapon immediately made it possible to cover the distance between Port Phillip Heads with over-lapping arcs of fire. The Defence Commission pressed the government in 1859 to order twenty-four of the new guns, and install them in 'Martello towers' (small circular forts with massive stone walls) at all vulnerable points. One or two if possible should also go on board the *Victoria*.

A 25-year-old fortifications expert, Captain Peter Scratchley, who had served with the Royal Engineers in the Crimean War, was brought to Melbourne in 1860 to design the defence works. His report that year confirmed and extended the Defence Commission's ideas. By that time, however, Parliament was under the control of radicals like Richard Heales. Scratchley's complete plan would have cost £150,000 for capital

Sam Calvert turned a sardonic eye on military bands spending much of their time serenading visitors at the Botanic Gardens in 1857.

works over several years, but the ruling party decided that the money would be better spent on such things as hospitals. Even when Governor Barkly remonstrated that rifled cannon now brought Melbourne and Geelong 'within easy range of shot or shell' from enemy vessels, Premier Heales stood firm, and nothing was done.

When the American civil war broke out in 1861, and Northern abolitionists threatened to blockade supplies of slave-grown cotton from reaching Britain, the Duke of Newcastle wrote from the Colonial Office in London to Governor Barkly in Melbourne, advising him that 'this country may shortly be involved in war with the United States'. The Duke warned that 'an active enemy' might be able to inflict 'occasional injury on exposed parts of the Empire'. Victoria should lose no time in preparing for the worst.

By this time the conservative W. C. Haines was back in power. His government pressed ahead with completion of heavy batteries at Williamstown, where eighteen old-style 68-pounders were mounted on naval pivot slides. A magazine and shell-room were built nearby. At Port Melbourne, two batteries, each armed with two 32-pounders, were installed along the foreshore. A detachment of Royal Artillery, consisting of 120 trained gunners under Captain P. Dickson, arrived at the end of 1861 to operate the batteries.

However, radicals such as Heales and Lalor still dominated the Legislative Assembly's select committee on defence. In the early months of 1862 they listened to a variety of expert evidence, and discovered that some of the heavier Armstrong guns had blown their vents during trials in Britain. The committee recommended cancellation of Victoria's order for the guns, and a halt on construction of fortifications already begun. Melbourne, they thought, should rely for its seaward defence on 'a fully equipped floating steam battery' to be obtained from Britain.

The Haines government was forced to agree. In vain did the 65-year-old Major-General Sir Thomas Pratt, new commandant of all British forces in Australia, warn that 'At present you are most defence-less . . . what existing means of defence have you against an armed force, if they landed in Western Port for instance?'

Port Phillip's vulnerability was demonstrated on several occasions in the early 1860s. In January 1862 the propellor-driven Russian 40-gun frigate *Svetlana* suddenly appeared in the bay, and inquired politely by signals whether it should fire a salute to the shore batteries. The answer was no, on the ground that if such a salute were given, no reply could be made because there was no ammunition in the batteries. Thomas Loader told Parliament that this was 'a most humiliating position' and 'proof of the inability of our military authorities to take proper care of the honour of the country'.

Even more alarmingly, the *Svetlana* was followed in 1863 by another powerful Russian vessel, the *Bogatyr*. Significantly, one of the Russian navy's leading admirals was on board. The *Bogatyr* spent several weeks making detailed surveys of the deep channels in Port Phillip and Western Port bays, no doubt preparing for the possible removal of guide buoys and lightships should war occur. Sir Charles Darling, who took over the same year as Governor of Victoria, reported anxiously to London on 6 July 1863 that 'we are absolutely without the means of preventing a hostile naval force from occupying Port Phillip and shelling the City of Melbourne'.

Then on the afternoon of 25 January 1865, the heavily-armed American Confederate raider *Shenandoah* sailed into Hobson's Bay. Its captain, J. J. Waddell, had no evil intent: he told Governor Darling that he merely wanted to raise the vessel on the Williamstown slip for

From nature, by

William Strutt captured the scene when Governor Sir Henry Barkly (left of flag in ground on right) reviewed more than 2,000 Victorian Volunteers in 1861 on Werribee Plains, with the You Yangs in the background. (Victorian Parliamentary Library).

Left: George Verdon, officer of Williamstown Rifles, arranged purchase of HMVS Cerberus.
Above: Solicitor J. H. Ross, head of mounted volunteers.

repairs, and restock with food and water. But the authorities also turned a blind eye to Waddell's recruitment of about seventy extra crew members, a distinct breach of Victoria's neutrality, for which an international tribunal later awarded more than £800,000 in damages against Britain.

The year after *Shenandoah* continued on her piratical adventures, the Victorian government sent its treasurer, (Sir) George Verdon, to Britain with £100,000 towards the cost of the impregnable blockship which experts had been demanding for so long. The ugly vessel, named HMVS *Cerberus*, steamed with great difficulty to Melbourne, nearly being swamped by high seas on several occasions. She arrived in Port Phillip in 1871 to show off her four 10-inch muzzle-loading rifle guns, which could accurately hurl a massive 400-pound explosive shell several miles. In 1926 the old ship was scuttled at Half Moon Bay, Black Rock, where its remains may still be seen. Other relics from the ship are in the Museum of Victoria.

The number of British troops stationed in Victoria as a professional fighting and training force varied between 100 and 400, according to demands for their services elsewhere. Major-General Pratt told one Legislative Assembly committee that 'I am bound by my Commission, not to protect Victoria alone, but all the colonies to the extent of my ability'. He agreed there was 'a feeling growing in England that the colonies should maintain their own defences', while the Royal Navy continued to dominate the high seas.

In 1861, British troops stationed in Melbourne numbered fifteen headquarters staff, twenty-four Royal Engineers, 123 Royal Artillery, and 210 soldiers of the 40th Foot Regiment. Victoria contributed about £30,000 a year to their upkeep.

To concentrate this force, 168 waterlogged acres bordered by St Kilda and City roads, and Moray and Park streets, South Melbourne, were granted in May 1859. Here the first three-storey bluestone section of Victoria Barracks (now A Block) was designed by architect Charles Barrett, and erected under Clerk of Works T. A. Eaton at a cost to Victoria of £86,000. A military powder magazine, hospital, stables, water well, cells, parade ground, and quarters for various ranks (now G Block) were gradually added during the 1860s.

The site, and delays in completion, attracted much criticism. Captain Scratchley complained in 1861 that the site was 'totally inadequate for the most necessary buildings', while nothing had been done to connect water and gas. Major-General Pratt told the 1862 inquiry that 'it was a great mistake placing them where they are; I think they are not in a proper position; but when I came here I found enormous sums of money had been spent, and it was useless to attempt to get another place'.

So the barracks went ahead. To give them some defence capability, the western side facing the bay was reinforced with castellated bluestone forts. Here, if the worst came to the worst, the British proposed to make a last-ditch stand against the invader.

By the end of the nineteenth century, South Melbourne's development could no longer be held back by the large open area reserved for military purposes. Victoria Barracks was reduced to the present eight acres held within its high stone walls. Much of the remaining 160 acres was sold for factories and housing, only to be resumed again in modern times for freeways and other governmental purposes.

While all these preparations were being made, Victoria was also raising a corps of armed volunteers for defence against any successful landing. La Trobe earlier had resisted the formation of militia forces, preferring to rely on trained British troops. Governor Hotham had no such doubts, and in November 1854 readily approved a Legislative Council Act to establish a Volunteer Corps of up to 2,000 men, with officers to be appointed by the Governor.* The *Age* warmly recommended the militia: 'Every member of a free community should have arms, and know how to use them'.

---

* Act 18 Vic. No. 7, 30 November 1854; amended by Act No. CXIII, 18 September 1860, to allow up to 10,000 men.

The Melbourne Volunteer Rifle Regiment was formed almost immediately. First man to be sworn in was its Lieutenant-Colonel, 25-year-old William Anderson, who had sold his captaincy in the British Army to return to Victoria as an assistant gold commissioner. He was the only son of wealthy South Yarra landowners Joseph and Mary Anderson. Other prominent men who became officers in the Melbourne Volunteer Rifles were Major John Hodgson, mayor; Captain Alexander Smith, gasworks manager; and Lieutenant William Arthur à Beckett, barrister.

The Richmond Rifles, under elderly merchant Lieutenant Daniel Campbell, drilled in the paddocks around Campbell's house from six o'clock in the mornings and evenings. In South Melbourne, the Emerald Hill Rifles established a firing range near today's Albert Park railway station, originally known as the 'Butts' station. Much practice was needed with the old rifles given by the government, for each powder cartridge had to be bitten firmly between the teeth, the end twisted off so the gunpowder could be shaken into the barrel, then a cloth wad and ball placed in the barrel and rammed firmly home with two strokes of the rod. Men with poor teeth were not welcomed in the volunteers.

Other companies were rapidly formed in populous suburbs, to help meet the feared Russian threat, or what the *Age* described as 'Malay desperadoes or Chinese pirates' who could 'burn our outports, and carry off the shipping'. Former squatter Francis Murphy, MLC, led the East Collingwood Rifles; while Justice Redmond Barry commanded the Fitzroy Rifles.

The renewed defence uproar of 1858 had considerable effects on the voluntary movement. The Defence Commission recommended in December 1858 that a 4,000-strong militia should be trained, to consist mostly of infantry in the Melbourne, Geelong and Portland districts. The foot soldiers would be supplemented by six companies of artillery, three regiments of cavalry, and three companies of naval militia, concentrated around Melbourne. Every effort should be made to raise voluntary forces, but if that fell short, a compulsory ballot for service should be held among men aged eighteen to fifty years. In all schools receiving government grants, military training should be compulsory for all boys over ten.

But compulsion was unnecessary. By the end of 1860, more than 4,000 men had eagerly volunteered to join the militia. Rifle companies with about 100 recruits each were active in fifteen Melbourne suburbs and eight provincial centres. Six cavalry troops with about sixty men each had been formed, including one in South Melbourne.

Colonel W. A. D. Anderson never saw active service, but was appointed officer in charge of all Victorian volunteer forces.

These Customs Department officials, under Captain H. M. Guthrie, formed the backbone of the West Melbourne Rifle Regiment in 1860. Most suburbs had such forces.

Some of the original Volunteer Rifles were converted into artillery companies averaging seventy men each, and allowed to practice with the Royal Artillery's field guns. These companies, all commanded by Colonel Anderson, protected the city, St Kilda, Collingwood-Richmond, Williamstown, South Melbourne, Prahran-South Yarra, and Queenscliff. Two volunteer naval brigades under Commander Kay, RN, were based at Williamstown and Port Melbourne. All these forces, including payments to professional instructors, cost Victoria £15,000 a year.

In order to equip the greatly increased number of foot militia, the government imported 300 muzzle-loading Enfield rifles of .577-inch calibre and 1,200 muskets from the British Army's stocks in Hobart. Another 2,000 Enfield rifles were ordered from England: in the meantime, Melbourne police handed over 300 old rifles for which they had no further use. For officers, cavalry swords and Deane & Adams pistols with 7.5-inch-long barrels were ordered. For the cavalry, Colt's American short repeating rifles were thought the most useful. One million rounds of ball cartridge to fit these various weapons completed the most urgent needs.

Yet after all this trouble and expenditure, it remains uncertain just what would have happened if a determined enemy had attacked Melbourne. In the early 1860s, when most local British forces were engaged in the New Zealand war, the Victorian commandant of volunteers, Colonel Anderson, admitted to a parliamentary inquiry that he had never been on active service. He believed that most of his Melbourne artillerymen ('mechanics, watchmakers and shopkeepers') would acquit themselves well, but admitted he had made no arrangements for 'flying artillery' to be drawn by horses from one firing point to another. Could not the cavalry pull the guns, asked one politician. Anderson replied that was theoretically possible, using a 'lasso-harness', but pointed out that 'The horses in the cavalry are the private property of those gentlemen'. On receiving news of an enemy landing, the only solution Anderson could see was to 'get horses from the police or hire them'.

Lieutenant-Colonel J. H. Ross, an elderly solicitor appointed in 1861 to command the mounted volunteers, thought his horsemen were 'the finest body of men ever known to exist, all ready to learn', but they were 'so scattered that you could not easily bring them together in an emergency'. At that time Ross commanded 600 men, organised into the Royal Victoria Volunteer Cavalry under Major James Stewart; the Melbourne Mounted Rifles under Captain Joseph Wilkie; the Melbourne Volunteer Light Dragoons under Captain Matthew Hervey; and smaller units at Heidelberg, Dandenong, Mornington, Geelong, Bacchus Marsh, Kyneton, and several goldfields centres. Colonel Ross thought that instead of these far-flung groups, 'three hundred men well disciplined, and concentrated near the metropolis, would be worth the whole lot'.

A British officer in Melbourne, Lieutenant-Colonel R. Carey, was horrified by lack of discipline among the volunteer forces, and especially by the fact that they now elected their own officers. Instead of obeying orders without question, they usually gave their own opinion first, making the force 'more a debating society than a military body'. In fact, said Carey, the volunteers were little more than 'a gigantic rifle association'. He was supported by Commander Kay, who told the 1862 inquiry that 'When it comes to real blows, I think the volunteer naval brigade, like a great many of the other volunteers, will be found to volunteer to stop at home and take care of their own families'.

Despite these rather arrogant British comments, the volunteers continued to drill keenly in their new grey and green uniforms. More than 2,000 attended mass reviews before the Governor at Werribee and Sunbury, while their wives and daughters proudly sewed banners to lead them into battle. The tradition continued: the grandsons of these men would form a hard-riding Bush Cavalry which startled even the Boers in South Africa, and another generation after that would form the famed volunteer Light Horse regiments which in World War I made history's last successful mass cavalry charges. Perhaps the amateur soldiers of the long-vanished gold-rush years would not have done so badly after all.

Anyone who wants a shorthand description of the 1850s could say that the first half of the decade was a ferment of gold discovery and political uproar, while the second half was a time for the rebuilding and revitalisation of Melbourne. As we have seen, the reality was rather more complex than that. But the hopeful spirit of the gold seekers remained constant. Theirs was an era of great beginnings: 'always morning', as Richard Horne wrote, aglow with 'power that shapes new life'. In his poem 'Ancient Idols', Horne even addressed us today:

Then, Spirit of the Future, turn thy eyes
Backward an instant with a kindly glance
Upon these efforts, in a purblind time,
Of those who gave their souls up to a task
Which for completion needed higher gifts,
And periods fitted to receive such truths.

This sense of the continuity of human effort, suffering setbacks but constantly rising again, joins the gold generation to our own times, and links today to the unknowable years ahead.

APPENDIX A

Main imports into Melbourne in 1860

(figures rounded)

Alcoholic drinks

Beer and cider (2,800,000 gallons)	£614,000
Spirits (1,020,000 gallons, mostly brandy and gin)	£510,000
Wine (118,000 gallons)	£215,000
Ice (860 tons)	£5,000

Non-alcoholic drinks

Tea (530,000 lbs)	£520,000
Coffee (83,000 lbs)	£74,000
Chicory (500,000 lbs)	£11,000

Building materials

Building iron (28,000 tons)	£370,000
Timber	£345,000
Window and other glass	£74,000
Wallpaper	£28,000
Slates (2.27 million)	£26,000
Lead sheet and pipe (965 tons)	£24,000
Paint	£24,000
Tin sheet	£10,500
Zinc (306 tons)	£7,500

Domestic goods

Ironmongery	£380,000
Candles	£277,000
Stationery	£203,000

MAIN IMPORTS IN 1860: CONTINUED

Furniture	£96,000
Earthenware	£53,000
Matches	£44,000
Fancy goods	£42,000
Plateware	£18,000
Soap (440 tons)	£16,000
Seeds	£13,000
Indiarubber goods	£12,500
Chinaware	£12,000
Starch	£11,000

Entertainment

Books	£97,000
Musical instruments	£36,000
Photographic goods	£7,000

Food

Grain	£845,000
Flour	£504,000
Butter	£394,000
Fruit	£260,000
Sugar (18,000 tons)	£110,000
Cheese	£86,000
Preserved fish	£67,000
Potatoes (5,000 tons)	£49,000
Salt (9,500 tons)	£47,000
Preserves	£26,000
Spices	£15,000
Vinegar (140,000 gallons)	£14,000

Industry and science

Industrial machinery	£270,000
Agricultural machinery	£33,000
Coal (74,000 tons, mainly for gas)	£156,000
Tools	£44,000
Steel (620 tons)	£33,000
Scientific instruments	£11,000
Printing materials	£11,000

Medical

 Drugs   £110,000

 Opium (30,000 lbs)   £28,000

 Mercury   £24,000

Tobacco

 Processed tobacco (1,270,000 lbs)   £242,000

 Cigars (153,000 lbs)   £62,000

 Snuff (800 lbs)   £300

Transport

 Rail equipment   £326,000

 Saddlery   £68,000

 Carriages   £53,000

 Horses (933 for breeding)   £47,000

Wearing apparel and linen

 Drapery and haberdashery   £1,600,000

 Boots and shoes   £727,000

 Apparel, general   £587,000

 Woollen goods   £195,000

 Hats and millinery   £116,000

 Jewellery   £71,000

 Silks   £70,000

 Hosiery   £66,000

 Watches and clocks   £33,000

Appendix B

Churches, chapels, schoolhouses and private dwellings used for public worship as at 31 December 1860

	No. of buildings	No. of persons they could contain
Wesleyan Church	217	34,763
Church of England	190	30,619
Roman Catholic Church	119	27,486
Presbyterian Church of Victoria	113	11,300
Primitive Methodist Church	71	7,214
Congregational Church	42	11,205
Baptist Church	36	8,450
United Methodist Free Church	16	3,090
Bible Christian Church	16	1,723
Free Presbyterian Church	13	4,200
Disciples of Christ	11	670
Lutheran Church	10	2,200
United Presbyterian Church	5	2,050
Jewish synagogues	5	2,150
Israelites' Church	3	500
Unitarian Church	2	320
Free Church of England	1	400
Society of Friends	1	250
Welsh Calvinistic Methodist	1	140
Reformed Presbyterian Church	1	500
Moravian Church	1	150

Source: V&P, LA, 1861-2, vol. 3.

Bibliography

Users should also refer to the bibliography in Cannon: *Old Melbourne Town before the gold rush*, Loch Haven Books, Main Ridge, Vic., 1991.

Aldous, Grant, *The stopover that stayed: a history of Essendon*, City of Essendon, 1979.

Aldwell, J. A., *Prize essay of the Melbourne Labor League, on the eight hours and early closing question*, Melbourne, 1856.

Allan, J. A., *The old model school . . .*, Melbourne University Press, 1934.

Allen, Maree, *The labourers' friends. Sisters of Mercy in Victoria and Tasmania*, Hargreen, Melbourne, 1989.

Anderson, Hugh (ed.), *The Goldfields Commission Report*, Red Rooster Press, Melbourne, 1978.

Anderson, Joseph, *Recollections of a Peninsular veteran*, Edward Arnold, London, 1913.

Archer, W. H., *Facts and figures . . .*, Fairfax, Melbourne, 1858; Queensberry Hill Press, Melbourne, 1977.

——, *Statistical notes on the progress of Victoria, 1835-1860*, Government Printer, Melbourne, c1861.

——, *The statistical register of Victoria . . .*, Government Printer, Melbourne, 1854.

Architecture, building, *see Australian builder* (1855-61); Casey (1975); De Jong (1983); *Historic houses* (1974); Lewis (1977); *Melbourne historic buildings* (1976-7); *Register of . . .* (1991); Robertson (1977); Saunders (1966); Shaw (1972); Tanner (1981); Turnbull (1945); Wilson & Sands (1981).

Armour, James, *The diggings, the bush, and Melbourne . . .*, Mackellar, Glasgow, 1864.

Aron, Joseph, and Arndt, Judy, *The enduring remnant: the first 150 years of the Melbourne Hebrew congregation 1841-1991*, Melbourne University Press, 1992.

Aspinall, Clara, *Three years in Melbourne*, Booth, London, 1862.

Austin, A. G., and Selleck, R. J. W., *The Australian government school, 1830-1914 . . .*, Pitman, Melbourne, 1975.

Austin, A. G., *George William Rusden and national education . . .*, Melbourne University Press, 1958.

Australian builder and land advertiser, Melbourne, 1855-6.

Australian builder, Melbourne, 1859-61.

Australian dictionary of biography, vols 3-6, Melbourne University Press, 1969-76.

Australian magazine (ed. J. J. Hain), C. H. Compton, Melbourne, 1859.
Australian medical journal, Melbourne, 1856--.

Bagot, E. D. A., *Coppin the Great: father of the Australian theatre*, Melbourne University Press, 1965.
Balfe, Harold, *The story of the century 1851-1951*, Government of Victoria, Melbourne, 1951.
Ballingall, James, *Retrospect of shipwrecks* . . ., Melbourne, 1858.
———, *Shipwrecks, their causes and the means of prevention*, Melbourne, 1857.
Banking, *see* Blainey (1958); Butlin (1951, 1961); Cooch (1934); Craddock & Cavanough (1967); *Melbourne's first bank* (1938); Murray & White (1992); Nunn (1988).
Barrett, Bernard, *The civic frontier* . . ., Melbourne University Press, 1979.
———, The *inner suburbs: the evolution of an industrial area*, Melbourne University Press, 1971.
Barry, Rev. Dr John, *Statement of accounts of St Patrick's College* . . ., Melbourne, 1862.
Barry, J. V., *The life and death of John Price*, Melbourne University Press, 1964.
Barry's 'Great Emporium', State Library of Victoria, Melbourne, 1981.
Bate, Weston, A history of Brighton, Melbourne University Press, 1983.
Beaney, J. G., *Contributions to practical surgery* . . ., Wilson & Mackinnon, Melbourne, 1861.
Becker, Ludwig (trans. T. A. Darragh), *A letter from Australia*, Garravembi Press, Bacchus Marsh, Vic., 1992.
———, *Men of Victoria*, Melbourne, 1856.
Benson, C. I., *A century of Victorian Methodism*, Spectator Publishing, Melbourne, 1935.
Bibbs, T. F., Map of Melbourne, 1858.
Blainey, Geoffrey, *A centenary history of the University of Melbourne*, Melbourne University Press, 1957.
———, *A game of our own: the origins of Australian football*, Information Australia, Melbourne, 1990.
———, *Gold and paper; a history of the National Bank* . . ., Georgian House, Melbourne, 1958; rev. ed. Macmillan, Melbourne, 1983.
———, *The tyranny of distance*, Sun Books, Melbourne, 1966.
Blake, L. J. (ed.), *Vision and realisation; a centenary history of state education in Victoria*, 3 vols, Education Department, Melbourne, 1973.
Bonwick, James, *An octogenarian's reminiscences*, Nichols, London, 1902.
Bonyhady, Tim, *Burke and Wills, from Melbourne to myth*, David Ell Press, Sydney, 1991.
Books, libraries, literature, *see Barry's 'Great Emporium'*; Holroyd (1968); McVilly (1975); Pearl (1960); Rae-Ellis (1979).
Booth, E. C., *Another England; life, living, homes and homemakers in Victoria*, Virtue, London, 1869.
Borchardt, D. H., *Checklist of Royal Commissions* . . ., Part III, Victoria 1856-1960, Wentworth Books, Sydney, 1970.
Bowden, K. M., *Samuel Thomas Gill, artist*, The author, Melbourne, 1971.

Bradshaw's guide to Victoria . . . 1856-60, Bradshaw, Melbourne, 1856-60.

Brighton, *see* Bate (1983).

Brisbane, Katharine (ed.), *Entertaining Australia: an illustrated history*, Currency Press, Sydney, 1991.

Brodzky, Maurice, *Historical sketch of the two Melbourne synagogues*, Melbourne, 1877.

Brothers, C. R. D., *Early Victorian psychiatry 1835-1905*, Government Printer, Melbourne, c1962.

Brown, Henry, *Victoria as I found it* . . ., Newby, London, 1862.

Burchett, W. H., *East Melbourne 1837-1977* . . ., Craftsman Press, Melbourne, 1978.

Burke and Wills, *see* Bonyhady (1991); Moorehead (1963).

Butler, J. C., *The first hundred years: being a brief history of the Melbourne Orphanage from 1851 to 1951, The Orphanage, Melbourne, 1951.*

Butlin, S. J., *Australia and New Zealand Bank*, Longmans, Green, London, 1961.

———, *A century of banking in Victoria*, Bank of New South Wales, Sydney, 1951.

Butterfield, Joseph, *Melbourne commercial, squatters' and official directory for 1854*, J. J. Blundell, Melbourne, 1854.

———, *Melbourne commercial directory for 1855*, J. J. Blundell, Melbourne, 1855.

Cage, R. A., *Poverty abounding, charity aplenty*, Hale & Iremonger, Sydney, 1992.

Calvert's illustrated almanac, Melbourne, 1856-61.

Campbell, Isabella (Mrs A. Prior), *Rough and smooth: or, Ho! for an Australian gold field*, Hunter, Rose & Co., Quebec, 1865.

Campbell, Ruth, *A history of the Melbourne law school* . . ., Faculty of Law, University of Melbourne, 1977.

Cannon, Michael, *Life in the cities*, Nelson, Melbourne, 1975.

———, *Lola Montes*, Heritage Publications, Melbourne, 1973.

———, *Old Melbourne Town before the gold rush*, Loch Haven, Main Ridge, Vic., 1991.

———, *The Victorian gold fields 1852-3. An original album by S. T. Gill*, Currey O'Neil, Melbourne, 1982; State Library of Victoria, Melbourne, 1992.

———, *Who's master, who's man?*, Nelson, Melbourne, 1971.

Carboni, Raffaello, *The Eureka stockade*, Melbourne University Press, 1963.

Carlton, *see* Chambers (n.d.).

Casey, Maie, et al (eds), *Early Melbourne architecture 1840 to 1888*, Oxford University Press, Melbourne, 1975 (rev. ed.).

Catalogue of Messrs. Baume & Kreitmayer's grand anatomical museum, Melbourne, 1861.

Centenary of the Scots Church, Melbourne, 1838-1938, Ramsay Publishing, Melbourne, 1938.

Chambers, Don, *Historical tours of Carlton*, The Carlton Association, Vic., n.d.

Charity, *see* Allen (1989); Butler (1951); Dale (1962); Jaggs (1986, 1990, 1991); Kent Hughes (1950); Mary Ignatius (1954); Singleton (1891).

Chinese, *see* Cannon (1971); Cronin (1982); Loh (1985); 'One who knows' (1857); Price (1974).

Churchill, D. M., et al, 'The published works of Ferdinand J. H. Mueller', in *Muelleria*, July 1978, and supplement, 1983, National Herbarium of Victoria, Melbourne.

Clarke, Michael, *'Big' Clarke*, Queensberry Hill Press, Melbourne, 1980.

Cole, C. E. (ed.), *Melbourne markets, 1841-1979 . . .*, Melbourne Wholesale Fruit & Vegetable Market Trust, Footscray, Vic., 1980.

Collingwood, *see* Barrett (1971).

Commerce, finance, *see* Cooper (1934); Graham (1985); Hall (1968); *House of Were* (1954); *Protection . . .* (1860); Train (1970); *Victoria of today* (1902).

Cooch, Alexander, *The State Savings Bank of Victoria . . .*, Macmillan, Melbourne, 1934.

Cooper, J. B., The *history of Prahran . . .*, Modern Printing Co., Melbourne, 1924.

——, *The history of St Kilda*, vol. 1, Printers Pty Ltd, Melbourne, 1931.

——, *Victorian commerce 1834-1934*, Robertson & Mullens, Melbourne, 1934.

Craddock, T., and Cavanough, M., *One hundred and twenty-five years. The story of the State Savings Bank of Victoria*, The Bank, Melbourne, 1967.

Cricket, *see* Dunstan (1974); Fairfax (1857-9).

Cronin, Kathryn, *Colonial casualties. Chinese in early Victoria*, Melbourne University Press, 1982.

Curnow, Heather, *The life and art of William Strutt*, Alister Taylor, Martinborough, New Zealand, 1980.

Dale, Percival, *Loving service in our community 1855-1962, being the story of the Melbourne City Mission*, The Mission, Melbourne, 1962.

Daley, Charles, *The history of South Melbourne . . .*, Robertson & Mullens, Melbourne, 1940.

Darragh, T A., 'Frederick Proeschel, colonial map maker', in *Bibliographical Society Bulletin*, March 1992.

Darwin, Charles, *On the origin of species by means of natural selection . . .*, Murray, London, 1859.

Davitt, Arthur, *Origin and progress of the National System of education . . .*, Wilson, Mackinnon & Fairfax, Melbourne, 1856.

Day, David, *Smugglers and sailors . . .*, AGPS, Canberra, 1992.

Defence, *see* 'Non-official' (1862); Price (1973); Puttman (1855); Vazenry (1985); Ward (1989).

De John, Ursula, *William Wilkinson Wardell. His life and work: 1823-1899*, Department of Visual Arts, Monash University, Melbourne, 1983.

De Serville, Paul, *Pounds and pedigrees. The upper class in Victoria 1850-80*, Oxford University Press, Melbourne, 1991.

Directories, *see* Bradshaw's (1856--); Butterfield (1854, 1855); Fairfax (1859); Needham (1856); *New quarterly . . .* (1853); Pierce (1853); Sands & Kenny (1857--).

Dunstan, David, *Governing the metropolis . . .*, Melbourne University Press, 1984.

Dunstan, Keith, *The paddock that grew; the story of the Melbourne Cricket Club*, Cassell, Melbourne, 1974.

Dutton, Geoffrey, *S. T. Gill's Australia*, Macmillan, Melbourne, 1981.

East Melbourne, *see* Burchett (1978).

Education, *see* Allan (1934); Austin (1958, 1975); Barry (1862); Blake (1973); Davitt (1856); Gregory (1958-9); Kiddle (1937); Nicholson (1952); Rankin (1939).

Elsum, W. H., *The history of Williamstown . . .*, Craftsman Press, Melbourne, 1985.

Essendon, *see* Aldous (1979).

Eureka stockade, *see* Carboni (1963); O'Brien (1992); O'Grady (1985).

Fauchery, Antoine (trans. A. R. Chisholm), *Letters from a miner in Australia*, Georgian House, Melbourne, 1966.

Finlay, Alexander, *Goldrush. The journal of Alexander Finlay while at the Victorian gold diggings, May 1852*, St Mark's Press, Sydney, 1992.

Fitzroy, Melbourne's first suburb, Hyland House, Melbourne, 1989; Melbourne University Press, 1991.

Football, *see* Blainey (1990); Harrison (1924).

Footscray, *see* Lack (1991).

Fowler, Frank, *Southern lights and shadows . . .*, Sampson Low, London, 1859; Sydney University Press, 1975.

Freedman, H., and Lemon, A., *The history of Australian thoroughbred racing*, vol. 1, Classic Reproductions, Strathmore, Vic., 1987.

Frost, Lucy, *A face in the glass. The journal and life of Annie Baxter Dawbin*, Heinemann, Melbourne, 1992.

Game, Peter, *The music sellers*, Hawthorn Press, Melbourne, 1976.

Gas, *see* Keating (1974); Proudley (1987).

Gill, S. T., *Sketches in Victoria*, J. J. Blundell, Melbourne, 1855; *see also* Bowden (1971); Cannon (1992); Dutton (1981).

Gold, *see* Anderson (1978); Armour (1864); Campbell (1865); Cannon (1971); Fauchery (1966); Finlay (1992); Howitt (1855); Korzelinski (1979); McCulloch (1977); Quaife (1975); Serle (1963); Wathen (1855).

Goodman, George, *The church in Victoria during the episcopate of the Rt Rev. Charles Perry*, Melville, Mullen & Slade, Melbourne, 1892.

Graham, H. B., 'Happenings of the now long dead past: the centenary of the Medical Society of Victoria', in *Medical Journal of Australia*, vol. 2, 1952.

Graham, Sally, *Pioneer merchant. The letters of James Graham 1839-54*, Hyland House, Melbourne, 1985.

Grant, J., and Serle, G., *The Melbourne scene 1803-1956*, Melbourne University Press, 1957.

Gregory, J. S., 'Church and state, and education in Victoria to 1872', in *Melbourne Studies in Education*, 1958-9.

Griffith, C. J., *Observations on the water supply of Melbourne*, Melbourne, 1855.

Griffiths, T. (ed.), *The life and adventures of Edward Snell*, Angus & Robertson, Sydney, 1988.

Haldane, R., *The people's force*, Melbourne University Press, 1986.

Hall, A. R., *The Stock Exchange of Melbourne . . .*, ANU Press, Canberra, 1968.

Hamilton, Robert, *A jubilee history of the Presbyterian Church of Victoria*, Hutchinson, Melbourne, 1888.

Harrison, H. C., *The story of an athlete*, Alexander McCubbin, Melbourne, 1924.

Historic houses of Australia, Australian Council of National Trusts, 1974.

Hoare, M. E., '"The half-mad bureaucrat": Robert Brough Smyth', in Australian Academy of Science *Records*, May 1974.

——, 'Learned societies in Australia . . .', in Australian Academy of Science *Records*, December 1967.

Horne, R. H., *Australian facts and prospects*, Smith, Elder, London, 1859.

Hotham, Sir Charles, *see* Roberts (1985).

House of Were 1839-1954 . . ., J. B. Were & Son, Melbourne, 1954.

Howitt, William, *Land, labour and gold*, Longman, London, 1855; Lowden, Kilmore, Vic., 1972; Sydney University Press, 1972.

Hughes, Helen, 'The eight hour day and the development of the labour movement in Victoria in the 1850s', in *Historical Studies*, vol. 9, 1961.

Illustrated Journal of Australasia (ed. Sydney Gibbons), George Slater and W. H. Williams, Melbourne, 1856-8.

Immigration, *see* Cannon (1971); Lemon & Morgan (1990); Serle (1963).

Inglis, K. S., *Hospital and community: a history of the Royal Melbourne Hospital*, Melbourne University Press, 1958.

Jaggs, Donella, *Asylum to action: family action 1851-1991 . . .*, Family Action, Oakleigh, Vic., 1991.

——, *Neglected and criminal: foundations of child welfare legislation in Victoria*, Phillip Institute of Technology, Melbourne, 1986.

——, *Victoria: institutions for children and young people, 1850-1980*, Phillip Institute of Technology, Melbourne, 1990.

Jenkins, G. H., *A short history and description of the Parliament House*, Melbourne, Government Printer, Melbourne, 1886.

Jones, M. A., *Nature's Plenty. A history of the City of Whittlesea*, Allen & Unwin, Sydney, 1992.

Just, Patrick, *Australia . . . 1851 to 1857 . . .*, Durham & Thomson, Dundee, 1859.

Keating, J. D., *The lambent flame*, Melbourne University Press, 1974.

Kelly, William, *Life in Victoria*, Chapman & Hall, London, 1859; Lowden, Kilmore, Vic., 1977.

Kenyon, A. S., *The story of Melbourne*, Lothian, Melbourne, 1934.

Kerr, Joan (ed.), *Dictionary of Australian artists . . . to 1870*, Oxford University Press, Melbourne, 1992.

Kiddle, J. B., *Liber Melburniensis, 1848-1936 . . .*, Roberton & Mullens, Melbourne, 1937.

Korzelinski, Seweryn (trans. S. Robe), *Memoirs of gold-digging in Australia*, University of Queensland Press, Brisbane, 1979.

Kynaston, Edward, *A man on edge* [Ferdinand Mueller], Alan Lane, Penguin Books, Melbourne, 1981.

Lack, John, *A history of Footscray*, Hargreen, Melbourne, 1991.

Leavitt, T. W. H., and Lilburn, W. D. (eds), *The jubilee history of Victoria and Melbourne*, 2 vols, Duffus, Melbourne, 1888.

Lemon, A., and Morgan, M., *Buried by the sea. A history of Williamstown cemetery*, Rivka Frank & Associates, Melbourne, 1990.

Lewis, Miles, *An industrial seed bed* [south bank of the Yarra], Department of Planning, Melbourne, 1983.

——, *Victorian churches*, National Trust (Victoria), Melbourne, 1991.

Loh, Morag, *Sojourners and settlers. Chinese in Victoria 1848-1985, Victorian Government China Advisory Committee, Melbourne, 1985.*

Love, Harold, *James Edward Neild, Victorian virtuoso*, Melbourne University Press, 1989.

Lutheran Trinity Church Restoration Appeal, The Church, Melbourne, 1973.

Lynch, Caroline (née Caroline Harper), *Ladies almanack 1858*, Calvert, Melbourne, 1858.

McCombie, Thomas, *Australian sketches, second series*, Sampson Low, London, 1861.

——, The *history of the Colony of Victoria*, Sands & Kenny, Melbourne, 1858.

McCoy, Frederick, *The order and plan of Creation . . .*, Fergusson & Moore, Melbourne, 1870.

McCulloch, Alan, *Artists of the Australian gold rush*, Lansdowne, Melbourne, 1977.

Mackaness, G. (ed.), *The Australian journal of William Strutt, A.R.A.*, 2 vols, The Editor, Sydney, 1958; Review Publications, Dubbo, NSW, 1979.

Mackenna, J. W., *Mortality of children in Victoria*, Fairfax, Melbourne, 1858.

McKinlay, Brian, *A documentary history of the Australian Labor movement 1850-1975*, Drummond, Melbourne, 1979.

McNicoll, Ronald, *The early years of the Melbourne Club*, Hawthorn Press, Melbourne, 1976.

McVilly, David, 'History of the State Library of Victoria, 1853-1974', MA thesis, Monash University, 1975.

Mackle, Francis, *The footprints of our Catholic pioneers . . .*, Advocate Press, Melbourne, 1924.

Malone, Betty, *Early Prahran 1850-1863*, Prahran Historical Society, 1982.

Manufacturing, *see* Willes (1954).

Markets, *see* Cole (1980).

Martin, R. M., *Australia . . .*, John Tallis, London, 1853.

Mary Ignatius, Sister, *The wheel of time (a brief survey of the ninety-six years' work of the Sisters of Mercy in Victoria, 1857-1953)*, Sisters of Mercy, Melbourne, 1955.

Mason, Cyrus, *Book of reference to Mason's map of Melbourne*, Mason, Melbourne, 1854.

Melbourne 1840-1900, 'The phenomenal city', State Library of Victoria, Melbourne, 1984.

Melbourne Church of England Messenger, 1850-4.

Melbourne Club, *see* McNicoll (1976).

Melbourne. *Historic buildings study.* CBD areas 1, 2, 3, 4, 5, 6, 7, 8 (10 vols), Historic Buildings Preservation Council, Melbourne, 1976-7.

Melbourne-South Yarra. A case for conservation in an historic inner suburb, James Coleman, St Leonards, NSW, 1972.

Melbourne Young Men's Mutual Improvement Association. Annual reports, Melbourne, 1856--.

Melbourne's first bank. The Bank of Australasia, The Bank, Melbourne, 1938.

Melbourne's parks and gardens . . ., Melbourne City Council, 1984.

Meredith, Louisa Anne, *Over the straits; a visit to Victoria,* Chapman & Hall, London, 1861.

Michie, Archibald, *Victoria suffering a recovery* . . . , George Robertson, Melbourne, 1860.

Moorehead, Alan, *Cooper's Creek,* Hamish Hamilton, London, 1963.

Municipal government, *see* Barrett (1971, 1979); Dunstan (1984); Verdon (1858).

Murphy, W. E., *History of the eight hours' movement,* vol. 1, Spectator, Melbourne, 1896.

Murray, R., and White, K., *A bank for the people. A history of the State Bank of Victoria,* Hargreen, Melbourne, 1992.

My note book (ed. James Neild), Melbourne 1857-9.

Nayler, B. S., *The battle of science* . . ., Melbourne, 1869.

Neale, R. S., 'H. S. Chapman and the "Victorian ballot"', in *Historical Studies,* vol. 12, 1967.

Needham, John, *Melbourne commercial, professional, and legal directory for 1856,* J. J. Blundell, Melbourne, 1856.

New quarterly Melbourne directory, n.p., Melbourne, 1853.

Newnham, W. H., *Melbourne, the biography of a city,* Cheshire, Melbourne, 1956.

Newsletter of Australasia . . ., Melbourne, 1856-62.

Nicholson, G. H. (ed.), *First hundred years. Scotch College Melbourne 1851-1951,* The College, Melbourne, 1952.

'Non-official, a', *Considerations on the defences of the colony,* Melbourne, 1862.

Nunn, H. W. (ed.), *Select documents of the nineteenth century,* vol. 1, National Australia Bank, Melbourne, 1988.

O'Brien, Bob, *Massacre at Eureka,* Australian Scholarly Publishing, Melbourne, 1992.

O'Grady, Desmond, *Raffaello! Raffaello! A biography of Raffaello Carboni,* Hale & Iremonger, Sydney, 1985.

O'Kane, Frances, *A path is set: the Catholic Church in the Port Phillip District . . . 1839-62,* Melbourne University Press, 1976.

Oldham, T., and Rawlinson, T. E., *Treatise on railway and harbour accommodation for Victoria . . .,* J. J. Blundell, Melbourne, 1855.

'One who knows them', *The Chinese question analyzed . . .,* Fairfax, Melbourne, 1857.

Opinions of the press on Messrs Spiers & Pond's . . ., Herald, Melbourne, 1861.

Packer, D. R. G., 'Victorian population data 1851-1861 . . .', in *Historical Studies*, vol. 5, 1953.

Parks and gardens, *see* Churchill (1978); Kynaston (1981); *Melbourne's* . . . (1984); Pescott (1982); Rogers (1989); Swanson (1984); Watts (1983); Willis (1949).

Paynting, H. H., and Grant, M. (eds), *Victoria illustrated 1834-1984*, James Flood Charity Trust, Melbourne, 1985.

Pearl, Cyril, *Always morning. The life of Richard Henry 'Orion' Horne*, Cheshire, Melbourne, 1960.

———, *The three lives of Gavan Duffy*, NSW University Press, Sydney, 1979.

Perry, Charles, *Science and the bible*, Samuel Mullen, Melbourne, 1869.

Pescott, R. T. M., *Collections of a century. The history of the first hundred years of the National Museum of Victoria*, The Museum, Melbourne, 1954.

———, *The Royal Botanic Gardens Melbourne* . . ., Oxford University Press, Melbourne, 1982.

———, 'The Royal Society of Victoria from then, 1854, to now, 1959', in *Royal Society of Victoria Proceedings*, new series, vol. 73, February 1961.

Pharmaceutical Society of Victoria, Quarterly journal . . ., Melbourne, 1858-61.

Pierce, P. W., *Melbourne commercial directory* . . . *1853*, Shanley, Melbourne, 1853.

Police, *see* Haldane (1986).

Politics, *see* Jenkins (1886); Neale (1967); Sayers (1957); Sweetman (1920); Thomson & Serle (1972); *Victoria Felix* (1985); Worthington (1909); Wright (1992).

Port Melbourne, *see* U'Ren & Turnbull (1983).

Prahran, *see* Cooper (1924); Malone (1982).

Pratt, Ambrose, *The centenary history of Victoria*, Robertson & Mullens, Melbourne, 1934.

Price, C. A., *The great white walls are built* . . ., ANU Press, Canberra, 1974.

Price, J. E., 'A history of the defence of Port Phillip Bay', in *Sabretache*, vol. 15, No. 3, March 1973, Military Historical Society of Australia, Melbourne.

Prisons, *see* Barry (1964); Prout & Feely (1967); White (1890).

Protection as a national system suited for Victoria . . ., George Robertson, Melbourne, 1860.

Proudley, Ray, *Circle of influence. A history of the gas industry in Victoria*, Hargreen, Melbourne, 1987.

Prout, D., and Feely, F., *Fifty years hard*, Rigby, Adelaide, 1967.

Public health, *see Australian medical journal* (1856--); Beaney (1861); Brothers (1962); Graham (1952); Hobbs (1857); Hood (1859); Inglis (1958); Mackenna (1858); *Pharmaceutical Society* (1858-61); Sayers (1956); Syder (1855); Welch (1969); Willson (1859).

Public works, *see* Trethowan (1975).

Puseley, Daniel ('An Englishman'), *The rise and progress of Australia* . . ., Saunders & Otley, London, 1857.

Puttman, H. W., *The rifleman's manual* . . . *for the Victoria Rifle Regiment*, J. J. Blundell, Melbourne, 1855.

Quaife, G. R. (ed.), *Gold and colonial society 1851-70*, Cassell, Sydney, 1975.

Racing, *see* Freedman & Lemon (1987).

Radford, Joan, *The chemistry department of the University of Melbourne . . .*, Hawthorn Press, Melbourne, 1978.

Rae-Ellis, Vivienne, *Louisa Anne Meredith. A tigress in exile*, Blubber Head Press, Hobart, 1979; St David's Park Publishing, Hobart, 1990.

Railways, *see* Griffiths (1988); Oldham & Rawlinson (1855).

Ramsay-Laye, Elizabeth [Massary, Isabel], *Social life and manners in Australia . . .*, Longmans, Green, London, 1861.

Rankin, D. H., *The history of the development of education in Victoria, 1836-1936 . . .*, Arrow, Melbourne, 1939.

Records of the pioneer women of Victoria 1835-1860, Women's Centenary Council Historical Committee and Osboldstone & Co., Melbourne, 1937.

Register of historic buildings, Historic Buildings Council, Melbourne, 1991.

Reid, Gordon, *From dusk till dawn: a history of Australian lighthouses*, Macmillan, Melbourne, 1988.

Reilly, Dianne, and Carew, Jennifer, *Sun pictures of Victoria*, Currey O'Neil Ross, Melbourne, 1983.

Religion, *see* Aron & Arndt (1992); Benson (1935); Brodzky (1877); *Centenary of Scots Church* (1938); Goodman (1892); Hamilton (1888); Lewis (1991); *Lutheran* (1973); Mackle (1924); O'Farrell (1969); O'Kane (1976); Perry (1869); Robin (1967); Rubinstein (1986).

Robb, E. M., *Early Toorak and district*, Robertson & Mullens, Melbourne, 1934.

Roberts, Shirley, *Charles Hotham, a biography*, Melbourne University Press, 1985.

Robin, A. de Q., *Charles Perry, Bishop of Melbourne*, University of Western Australia Press, 1967.

Rogers, Helene, *Early ballooning in Australia*, Set & Forget Press, Melbourne, 1989.

Rubinstein, H. L., *The Jews in Victoria 1835-1985*, Allen & Unwin, Sydney, 1986.

Ruhen, Olaf, *Port of Melbourne 1835-1976*, Cassell, Melbourne, 1976.

St Kilda, *see* Cooper (1931).

Sands & Kenny's directories, 1857-61.

Saunders, David, *Historic buildings of Victoria*, Jacaranda, Melbourne, 1966.

[Sayers, C. E.], *One hundred years of responsible government in Victoria, 1856-1956*, Government Printer, Melbourne, 1957.

———, *The Women's*, The Hospital, Melbourne, 1956.

Science, *see* Darwin (1859); Hoare (1967, 1974); McCoy (1870); Nayler (1869); Pescott (1954, 1961); Stirling (1970); *Transactions . . .* (1860).

Scott, Ernest, *A history of the University of Melbourne*, Melbourne University Press, 1936.

Selby, Isaac, *The old pioneers' memorial history of Melbourne*, Old Pioneers' Memorial Fund, Melbourne, 1924.

Serle, Geoffrey, *The golden age . . .*, Melbourne University Press, 1963.

Shipping, *see* Ballingall (1857, 1858); Blainey (1966); Cannon (1991); Day (1992); Oldham & Rawlinson (1855); Reid (1988); Ruhen (1976).

Sierp, Allan, *Colonial life in Victoria*, Rigby, Adelaide, 1972.

Singleton, John, *A narrative of incidents in the eventful life of a physician*, Hutchinson, Melbourne, 1891.

Smith, James (ed.), *Cyclopedia of Victoria*, 3 vols, Cyclopedia Co., Melbourne, 1903-5.

——, 'Melbourne in the fifties', in *Centennial Magazine*, ii, Sydney, 1889.

Smyth, R. B., *see* Hoare (1974).

Social classes, *see* Cannon (1971); De Serville (1991); McNicoll (1976); Ramsay-Laye (1861).

South Melbourne, *see* Daley (1940); Lewis (1983).

South Yarra, *see* Cooper (1924); *Melbourne-South Yarra* (1972).

Southern Spectator (ed. Rev. R. Fletcher), W. Fairfax & Co., Melbourne, 1857-9.

State Library of Victoria, *see* Barry's *'Great Emporium'* (1981); McVilly (1975).

Statistics, *see* Archer (1854, 1861, 1977); Packer (1953).

Stawell, Mary, *My recollections*, Richard Clay, London, 1911.

Stirling, Alfred, *Joseph Bosisto*, Hawthorn Press, Melbourne, 1970.

Stoney, H. B., *Victoria: with a description of its principal cities . . .*, Smith, Elder, London, 1856.

Strutt, William, *see* Curnow (1980); Mackaness (1979); Tipping (1980).

Stuart, Lurline, *James Smith. The making of a colonial culture*, Allen & Unwin, Sydney, 1989.

Sutherland, Alexander, *Victoria and its metropolis*, vol. 1, McCarron Bird, Melbourne, 1888; Today's Heritage, Melbourne, 1978.

Swanson, Rex, *Melbourne's historic public gardens*, City of Melbourne, 1984.

Sweetman, Edward, *Constitutional development of Victoria 1851-6*, Whitcombe & Tombs, Melbourne, 1920.

Syder, Dr Mingay, *The voice of truth in defence of nature*, Geelong, 1855.

Tanner, Howard (ed.), *Architects of Australia*, Macmillan, Melbourne, 1981.

Temperance League Almanac, Melbourne, 1860.

Theatre, *see* Bagot (1965); Brisbane (1991); Cannon (1973); Love (1989); Thorne (1971).

Thomas, R. M., The *present state of Melbourne . . .*, W. Kent, London, 1853.

Thomson, K., and Serle, G., *A biographical register of the Victorian legislature, 1851-1900*, ANU Press, Canberra, 1972.

Thorne, Ross, *Theatre buildings in Australia to 1905*, 2 vols, Architectural Research Foundation, University of Sydney, 1971.

Tipping, Marjorie (ed.), *Victoria the golden . . .*, Library Committee, Parliament of Victoria, Melbourne, 1980.

Toorak, *see* Robb (1934).

Train, G. F. (ed. E. D. & A. Potts), *A Yankee merchant in goldrush Australia; the letters of George Francis Train 1853-55*, Heinemann, Melbourne, 1970.

Transactions of the Philosophical Institute, Melbourne, 1860.

Trethowan, Bruce, *The Public Works Department of Victoria 1851-1900 . . .*, 2 vols, Department of Architecture and Building, University of Melbourne, 1975.

Troedel, Charles (ed. Clive Turnbull), *The Melbourne album . . .*, Georgian House, Melbourne, 1961.

Turnbull, Clive, *Bluestone. The story of James Stephens*, Hawthorn Press, Melbourne, 1945.

Turner, H. G., *A history of the colony of Victoria*, vol. 2, Longmans, Green, London, 1904; Heritage, Melbourne, 1973.

Uhl, Jean, *A woman of importance* [Emily Childers], The Author, Blackburn, Vic., 1993.

University of Melbourne, *see* Blainey (1957); Campbell (1977); Radford (1978); Scott (1936).

U'Ren, Nancy, and Turnbull, Noel, *A history of Port Melbourne*, Oxford University Press, Melbourne, 1983.

Vazenry, G. R., *Victoria Barracks Melbourne. Historical notes to 1985*, ms., Victoria Barracks, Melbourne, 1985.

Verdon, G. F., *The present and future of municipal government in Victoria*, Fairfax, Melbourne, 1858.

Victoria. Acts and ordinances in force in Victoria (ed. Travers Anderson), 2 vols, Government Printer, Melbourne, 1855-6.

Victoria Felix. A celebration of the 50th Parliament of Victoria, State Parliament, Melbourne, 1985.

Victoria Illustrated, first series, Sands & Kenny, Melbourne, 1857; Lansdowne, Sydney, 1971.

Victoria Illustrated, second series, Sand & Kenny, Melbourne, 1862; Lansdowne, Sydney, 1971.

Victoria of today: a review of trade and progress . . . 1851-1901, Daily Australasian Shipping News, Melbourne [1902].

Victoria, the first century, Robertson & Mullens, Melbourne, 1934.

Victorian Historical Journal, February 1975 to date.

Victorian Historical Magazine, January 1911 to November 1974.

Victorian monthly magazine, Gordon & Gotch, Melbourne, 1859.

Victorian Parliamentary Papers, 1851-62.

Ward, G. F., *Victorian land forces, 1853-1883*, The Author, Croydon, Vic., 1989.

Ward, J. M., *Earl Grey and the Australian colonies 1846-1857 . . .*, Melbourne University Press, 1958.

Water supply, *see* Griffith (1855); Jones (1992).

Wathen, G. H., *The golden colony: or Victoria in 1854*, Longmans, London, 1855.

Welch, J. H., *Hell to health. The history of quarantine at Port Phillip Heads 1852-1966*, Nepean Historical Society, Sorrento, Vic., 1969.

Westgarth, William, *The colony of Victoria . . . to the end of 1863*, Sampson, Low & Marston, London, 1864.

——, *Personal recollections of early Melbourne & Victoria*, George Robertson, Melbourne, 1888; Rippleside Press, Geelong, Vic., n.d.

White, H. A., *Crime and criminals . . .*, Ballarat, 1890.

Willes, Moira (ed. G. A. Derham), *The first hundred years, 1854-1954; Swallow & Ariell Ltd*, Troedel & Cooper, Melbourne, 1954.

Williamstown, *see* Elsum (1985); Lemon & Morgan (1990).

Willis, Margaret, *By their fruits. A life of Ferdinand von Mueller*, Angus & Robertson, Sydney, 1949.

Willson, Rt Rev. R. W., *A few observations relative to the Yarra Bend Lunatic Asylum*, Melbourne, 1859.

Wilson, G., and Sands, P., *Building a city. 100 years of Melbourne architecture*, Oxford University Press, Melbourne, 1981.

Women, *see Records of* . . . (1937).

Working class, *see* Aldwell (1856); Hughes (1961); McKinlay (1979); Murphy (1896).

Worthington, J. M., *Index to the Parliamentary papers . . . 1851-1909*, Government Printer, Melbourne, 1909.

Wright, Raymond, *A people's counsel. A history of the Parliament of Victoria 1856-1990*, Oxford University Press, Melbourne, 1992.

Acknowledgements

This book could not have been written without the expert assistance of many staff members of the State Library of Victoria, especially in the La Trobe Library collections. The author's debt to the La Trobe Picture Collection and the Victorian Parliamentary Library will be especially obvious. Grateful thanks are also due to the State Library of New South Wales; City of Melbourne; Royal Historical Society of Victoria; Mr Tom Darragh of the Museum of Victoria; and the Pfalz Museum für Naturkunde, which supplied the only known photographs of some individuals. Dr David Branagan of Sydney supplied the only available photographs of Alfred Selwyn. The Historic Buildings Council of Victoria gave ready access to its files on surviving historic buildings.

Conversion of measurements

White settlers of Australia brought with them the imperial system of weights and measures. This system continued until decimal currency was introduced in 1966, followed by the metric system from 1970.

Currency

The standard unit of currency was the pound (£).

£1 consisted of 20 shillings (20s) each of 12 pence (12d). The penny was divided into 2 halfpennies or 4 farthings. A guinea equalled £1 1s; a crown equalled 5 shillings; a half-crown equalled 2s 6d.

When decimal currency was adopted, £1 equalled $2. The value of money in the nineteenth century is not directly comparable with values in later centuries.

Weight

The imperial pound (lb) was the most common unit of mass.

1 lb = 454 grams.

1 lb comprised 16 ounces (oz); 14 lbs = 1 stone; 8 stones = 1 hundredweight (cwt); 20 cwt = 1 ton (1.01 tonnes).

Length

The foot was the standard measure of length.

1 foot (1 ft or 1′) = 30.48 cm.

There were 12 inches (12 in. or 12″) in a foot; 3 ft in 1 yard (1 yd); 1760 yards in 1 mile (= 1.61 km).

1 chain = 100 links = 66 ft = 20.177 metres.

A league was approximately 3 miles.

Area

The acre was the standard measure of land area.

1 rood = 40 perches = 1210 square yards = 0.25 acres = 0.101 hectares.

1 acre = 10 square chains = 0.404686 hectares.

For large areas the square mile was the unit.

1 square mile = 640 acres = 258.9988 hectares.

Capacity

The pint was the basic measure of liquids.

1 pint = 568 mL.

8 pints = 1 gallon = 4.55 litres.

Spirits were often measured by the gill, which was a quarter pint = 0.142 litres.

The bushel was used as a measure of grain.

1 bushel = 8 gallons = 36.4 litres.

Index